POPULAR CULTURE
AND CRITICAL PEDAGOGY

Welcome to college & best wishes

[signature]

PEDAGOGY AND POPULAR CULTURE
VOLUME 2
GARLAND REFERENCE LIBRARY OF SOCIAL SCIENCE
VOLUME 1163

PEDAGOGY AND POPULAR CULTURE

SHIRLEY R. STEINBERG AND JOE L. KINCHELOE, *SERIES EDITORS*

AMERICAN EDUCATION
AND CORPORATIONS
The Free Market Goes to School
by Deron Boyles

POPULAR CULTURE
AND CRITICAL PEDAGOGY
*Reading, Constructing,
Connecting*
edited by Toby Daspit
and John A. Weaver

POPULAR CULTURE AND CRITICAL PEDAGOGY
READING, CONSTRUCTING, CONNECTING

EDITED BY
TOBY DASPIT AND JOHN A. WEAVER

GARLAND PUBLISHING, INC.
A MEMBER OF THE TAYLOR & FRANCIS GROUP
NEW YORK AND LONDON
2000

Published in 2000 by
Garland Publishing Inc.
A Member of the Taylor & Francis Group
29 West 35th Street
New York, NY 10001

10 9 8 7 6 5 4 3 2 1

Library of Congress Cataloging-in-Publication Data

Popular culture and critical pedagogy : reading, constructing, connecting /
    edited by Toby Daspit and John A. Weaver.
        p.   cm. — (Garland reference library of social science ; v. 1163.
    Pedagogy and popular culture ; v. 2)
        Includes bibliographical references and index.
        ISBN 0-8153-3864-3 (alk. paper)
        1. Critical pedagogy.   2. Popular culture.   I. Daspit, Toby .
    II. Weaver, John A. III. Series: Garland reference library of social science ;
    v. 1163.   IV. Series: Garland reference library of social science. Pedagogy
    and popular culture ; v. 2.
    LC196.P67   1999
    370.11'5—dc21   98-8645
                                                                                CIP

Printed on acid-free, 250-year-life paper
Manufactured in the United States of America

John:
For
My Brother Michael
In Gratitude to Scholar, Friend, and Mentor
Mark B. Ginsburg

Toby:
To the Memory of Thomas Wayne Daspit

Contents

Acknowledgments

There are many people we wish to thank and acknowledge, but first and foremost we have to thank Shirley Steinberg and Joe Kincheloe. Their presence and inspiration is felt in the pages of this book and throughout the fields of education, critical pedagogy, and cultural studies. It is their leadership, vision, and persistence that has made a book such as this one possible. Throughout their careers and lives they have exposed and broken down arbitrary barriers that separate academic work from life. We hope this book is a continuation and extension of their work.

We want to thank Roberta Reese of The University of Akron. The authors in this volume wrote the chapters but if it were not for Roberta's expertise and service their work would not have seen the light of day. And while we get the credit for writing these pages, Roberta stands in the background not demanding credit but deserving more than anyone can imagine.

Michele Zyracki at Garland Publishing deserves great credit too. Anyone who meticulously went through this manuscript numerous times looking for discrepancies deserves more than credit. Her copy editing skills are appreciated. We would like to thank Karita France dos Santos, Michael Spurlock, and Seema Shah, also at Garland Publishing.

Normally, in a book there is a section in the acknowledgments where the author(s) thanks all those who read the manuscript while exonerating the readers for any "errors" of interpretation that remain in the text. Well, we certainly want to thank all of those people who have read portions or all of this book including Michele, Joe, Shirley, and others we cannot remember. However, if we are going to accept that there are multiple ways of reading a text then we have to dispense with this notion of "error." In reading popular or canonical texts, there are only distortions. The myth of one True reading is just that, and a dangerous one at that.

Finally, we want to thank all those creators of popular culture texts from Roseanne to Matt Groening ; from Ice Cube to Queen Latifah; from Robin Williams to Michelle Pfeiffer; from Octavia Butler to Alice Walker. Their creations make academic work a lot more adventurous and more real to life than traditional research and research methods permit us to be.

Individually, Toby says: I'd like to acknowledge the lengthy list of people who helped me reach this point in my life and who have played a role in my work in popular culture.

Many people during my undergraduate and Master's work at the University of Southwestern Louisiana (USL) encouraged my initial forays into popular culture and education, notably the late Milton Rickles, Patricia Rickles, the late Hal Petersen, Vincent Marino, Henry Pitchford, Thomas Schoonover, Kathy Lewis, David Hoch, Adele Builliard, Jeanette Parker, Sally Dobyns, Jim Flaitz, and Clark Robenstine. It was at USL that I first met Patrick Slattery, who besides encouraging me to continue my education, has become a treasured colleague and friend.

While pursuing my doctorate in Baton Rouge at Louisiana State University I had the opportunity to work with faculty and colleagues who have provided support for my writings and interests. I am particularly indebted to Bill Pinar whose search for vision in curriculum scholarship has immeasurably impacted my own quest. Additionally, Pamela Dean, Petra Munro, Wendy Kohli, William Doll, Denis Egea-Kuehne, Jon Davies, Vikki Hillis, Elaine Reilly, Tayari kwa Salaam, Denise Taliafero, LaVada Taylor, and many others deserve special thanks. Also special thanks to Marla Morris and Mary Aswell Doll who have supported me unconditionally throughout my stint at Baton Rouge and at the Global Wildlife Center.

Mary Young deserves special thanks as does her husband, Kent, and children, Philip and Stuart.

Conversations with my friends is where many of my ideas emerge and are challenged. Thanks to Neil Vincent, Dennis and Alida Kirtley, Lee and Michelle Papa, Scott Fontenot, Jerrod Breaux, Shala Carlson, Jamie Credle, Pat Kahle, Cathie Schramm, Avery Davidson, Ryan and Lisa Judice, Stephanie Hotard, and Michelle Livermore. And a special acknowledgment to my friends Bill Davis and Mason Ruffner who make a living in the practical world of popular culture. A special thanks for technical and familial support to my cousins Todd, Matt, and Chad LeBlanc.

My students in New Iberia, Delcambre, Baton Rouge, and Kalamazoo have taught me more about popular culture than they will ever know.

I cannot thank my immediate family enough. My parents, James and Anna LeBlanc Daspit have encouraged me and endured years of noise emanating from upstairs. Thanks to Toni and her husband Brent, Terry, and Tracy and his wife Tricia.

Finally, I want to thank my fiancee, Morna McDermott. All I need to say for now and forever is, OCN.

Individually, John wishes to acknowledge the contributions Mark Ginsburg, Noreen Garman, Eugenie Potter, Don Martin, and Roland Paulston made while at the University of Pittsburgh. Also the contributions Ken Yount, James Daddysman and Alderson-Broaddus College made to the development of my distorted mind.

I want to thank my colleagues Rita Saslaw, Ron McClendon, and Gini Doolittle at the University of Akron. Who could forget the department of educational foundations and leadership and the collegial place they have constructed, where diverse ideas and forms of scholarship are accepted unconditionally and without arbitrary boundaries of what knowledge is?

Finally, I want to thank my family, Wendy, Rachel, Ian, and Emma; my parents Connie and Larry Lauchner; my sister Brenda and her husband Jeff; my father Henry Weaver; and my friends Kevin Diehl and Brent Keller. And who could forget Cartman and others who touch our lives in so many ways?

Critical Pedagogy, Popular Culture and the Creation of Meaning

John A. Weaver and Toby Daspit

As treasured and guarded academic boundaries implode from the power of a postmodern shift towards interdisciplinarity and assumptions of what is real blur from a bombardment of images, Henry Giroux (1994) ponders why few have incorporated cultural studies into their critical analysis of education (p. 278). In his recent reflections on the role of cultural studies in critical pedagogy and education, Giroux (1996a) suggests that while a film such as *Kids* by Larry Clark romanticizes youth violence, sexuality, and drug use, there are examples such as *Harlem Diary* in which youth are able to represent themselves on video and provide insights into the ways they read themselves and the world around them. The authors of this edited work attempt to incorporate cultural studies into our understanding of schooling not only to address how students read themselves but how they, along with teachers and administrators, read popular culture texts in general. In fact, the purpose of this book is to suggest some alternative directions critical pedagogy can take in its critique of popular culture and education. Specifically, there are two issues the essays in this book will attempt to address in multiple ways: decentering critical pedagogy by inviting multiple readings of popular culture texts into our analyses of schooling and seeing many forms of popular culture as critical pedagogical texts. In the remainder of this introduction, we will discuss why critical theorists should begin to seek alternative directions in relationship to popular culture, and, in a cursory way, we will touch upon the ways in which the essays that follow offer insights into how we can go about addressing the issues raised below.

DECENTERING CRITICAL PEDAGOGY AND INVITING MULTIPLE READINGS

In discussing the issue of decentering critical pedagogy and multiple readings, we want to establish two significant markers in the construction of our position. First, when we discuss these issues we are referring only to critical pedagogy's recent turn to cultural studies and not to its critiques of vocational education (Kincheloe, 1995), predatory culture and postmodernism (McLaren, 1995), critical literacy (Lankshear & McLaren, 1993), multiculturalism (Sleeter and McLaren, 1995), teacher education (Kincheloe, 1993), or emancipatory politics (McLaren & Lankshear, 1994). It is clear to us that in light of criticism from post-structuralists such as Jennifer Gore (1993), Carmen Luke and Gore (1992), and Elizabeth Ellsworth (1989), and in spite of dated criticism from Gerald Graff and Gregory Jay (1995), critical theorists have decentered its pedagogy and sought out multiple perspectives in regard to these issues. Critical theorists are painfully aware of the contradictory potential of critical pedagogy in the name of liberation to indirectly promote the silencing of oppressed groups. Just as Giroux suggests that the film *Harlem Diary* "refuses to romanticize resistance and the power of critical pedagogy," so do critical theorists. Yet, we contend when it comes to popular culture, this unromantic approach has not manifested itself on the level of practice.

Second, when we discuss the need to decenter critical pedagogy in its critique of popular culture, we refer here only to practice. In theory, critical pedagogy addresses the potential for multiple readings of popular cultural texts, the contradictory and shifting meanings of texts, and the shifting power struggles over control of texts. Giroux, for instance, maps out theoretical space that is mindful of multiple readings and shifting meanings of popular cultural texts. In his latest essays on cultural studies Giroux (1994a; 1996b) calls for a shift away from traditional ahistorical, decontextualized approaches to schooling and culture and towards a decentered, post-structural approach. Teachers, administrators, and parents should treat students not as manageable products quantifiable by standardized and normed tests. Rather, they ought to approach "students as bearers of diverse social memories with a right to speak and represent themselves in the quest for learning and self-determination" (1994a, p. 279). Critical theorists, Giroux continues, should follow Peter Hitchcock's lead and map out a cultural terrain that promotes

> an awareness that the cultural identities at stake in 'other' cultures are in the process-of-becoming in dialogic interaction and are not static as subjects; but . . . the knowledge produced through this activity is always already contestable and by definition is not the knowledge of the other as the other would know himself or herself (1996b, p. 51).

Critique of popular culture in this light is not placed in a subordinate position within a hierarchical knowledge structure based on a false dichotomy of high/low culture. Instead, it is a layering process in which meanings are altered and always already contested by the very fact that popular culture is being interpreted or read. If students, along with teachers and administrators, are being constructed by popular culture texts then their identities are not only shifting but the meaning of these texts constantly shift also as they read them.

For Giroux (1994b) there is a need to develop a critical pedagogy in order to navigate the terrains of popular culture texts. "Defined as an attempt to alter experience in the interest of expanding the possibilities for human agency and social justice," he suggests, "critical pedagogy makes visible the need for social relations that inform a number of considerations that cut across the terrain of cultural studies" (p. 133). Moreover, critical pedagogy should promote the creation of interdisciplinary, border crossing students, teachers, and administrators who are able to negotiate within the terrains of popular culture and to constantly remake their own identities in response to ever changing postmodern worlds in which images construct reality and access to information implies political and economic power. Students, teachers and administrators have to become readers of popular cultural texts in order to construct meaning out of their lives and develop ethical imperatives that serve as (albeit temporary) markers and springboards to promote democratic schools and societies in which all voices are nurtured rather than ignored, erased, or silenced.

Douglas Kellner's (1995) work also creates theoretical space that stresses the important issue of how popular culture texts are read and how meaning is constructed from these readings. In *Media Culture*, Kellner sketches what we see as a modified Frankfurt School approach.

Kellner's approach abandons the deterministic analysis of the Frankfurt school in which popular culture was viewed as an ideological tool used to pacify and alienate the "masses" while commodifying culture in order to legitimate the status quo. Kellner does, however, wish to continue the Frankfurt tradition of reading artifacts of culture through the lens of critical social theories. To do so, Kellner (1995) contends there is a need to focus more analytical attention on "the political economy of the media . . . more empirical and historical research into the construction of media industries and their interaction with other social institutions . . . [and] more studies of audience reception and media effects" (p. 29). In order to accomplish his agenda, Kellner turns to the British cultural studies' work on articulation and audience reception. The British school, Kellner contends, "directed cultural studies toward analyzing cultural artifacts, practices, and institutions within existing networks of power and of showing how culture both provided tools and forces of domination and resources for resistance and struggle" (p. 36). Still Kellner (1995) warns that even though British cultural studies views audiences of popular culture as active participants there is a tendency to overemphasize "reception and textual analysis, [while] under-emphasizing the production of culture and its political economy" (p. 41). Thus an eclectic approach is better equipped to understand the relationship between popular culture texts, the process of constructing meaning from these texts, and the ways power blocs inscribe meaning while localizing blocs re-inscribe their own meaning in resistance to or independent of power blocs.[1]

In both Giroux and Kellner's case their theoretical framework is constructed to address issues of multiple readings, but when they shift from theory to practice the primary focus is placed on the meanings power blocs inscribe upon popular culture texts and how critical theorists read these inscriptions. That is, a decentered approach is abandoned thereby placing critical theorists in a precarious position of privileging their reading while ignoring the ways individuals use their localizing powers to interpret popular culture texts to construct multiple readings. Giroux's (1996b) recent work on youth fugitive cultures serves our point. In "White Panic and the Racial Coding of Violence," we are presented Giroux's readings of such films as *Slackers*, *A River's Edge*, and *My Own Private Idaho* and how these films construct public images of white youth. For example, in his analysis of *Slackers*, Giroux (1996b) reads it as a depressing example of postmodern youth who "reject most of the values of the Reagan/Bush era in which they came of age, but have a difficult time imagining what an alternative might look like . . . [have] little, if any, sense of where they have come from . . . [while] Reality seems too despairing to care about" (p. 37). Only for a brief moment within his narrative on *Slackers* does Giroux (1996b) mention that his students read the film differently. They "did not despair over the film. They interpreted it to mean that 'going slack' was a moment when young people could . . . make some important decisions about their lives" (p. 39). However, this excursion into the world of his students is merely a side-bar rather than an alternative narrative flowing along side of Giroux's own reading. As a result, we are left with some complicated questions about multiple readings. How did Giroux's students resist or adopt his reading and the film's images in order to create their own interpretation and thereby create agency in their lives? How did these students take their community experience of reading film in a seminar in order to think about the course of their own lives? Was critical pedagogy a catalyst for their agency or just another alternative reading that they see as not speaking to but at them? As we explain in more detail below, we believe a decentered critical pedagogy provides better insight into how these processes emerge in the classroom.

If Giroux offers little space to develop alternative narratives within his text, then Kellner presents even less in his practice. Where Giroux focuses on contemporary films, to represent the ways in which images of youth cultures are constructed, Kellner focuses his energy on *Beavis and Butthead*. Kellner (1995) reads the MTV series as "'postmodern' in that it is purely a product of media culture, with its characters, style, and content almost solely derivative from previous TV shows" (p. 145). As a result, they are misogynist, narcissistic, and ahistorical. For Kellner, the popularity of *Beavis and Butthead* can be explained by its utopian appeal to youth cultures in which there is "no parental authority and unlimited freedom to do whatever they want whenever they want to" (p. 146). However, Kellner does not provide any readings of *Beavis and Butthead* beyond his own. We are left to ponder if there are any alternative readings of the MTV series or how young adults read the show. Is it their time to dream of a utopia where parents are outlawed as part of their animated fantasy world, do they read *Beavis and Butthead* in ways that are not seen as utopic, or do they read it at all?

We do not want to give the impression that we disagree with Giroux and Kellner's readings. We merely wish to point out that if critical theorists are to offer critiques of popular culture texts and construct a powerful and persuasive critical pedagogy, then we have to decenter our own readings and develop alternative readings of popular culture alongside our own. Nor do we wish to suggest that the tendency to abandon a decentered approach in practice is only found in Giroux and Kellner's work. To the contrary we believe their efforts to make sense out of our postmodern world of media images are indispensable. Whereas, Giroux and Kellner at least recognize theoretically alternative readings of popular cultural texts, other critical readings do not. For example, in Paul Farber and Gunilla Holm's work on the construction of schooling in popular films, there is no recognition of alternative readings. Like Giroux and Kellner, Farber and Holm (1994), from our perspective, present a persuasive and germane critique of the ways in which teachers and schooling have been constructed in a recent flurry of Hollywood films on life in public schools. Farber and Holm challenge the tendency of recent films on schooling like *Dead Poets Society*, *Lean on Me*, and *Stand and Deliver* to suggest that the solution to the serious problems public schools face today is to submit to the notion of the Superhero teacher or administrator. They point out that this genre not only simplifies the problems of public schooling but also suggests collective action is frivolous, men are almost always the best qualified to lead reform efforts, and authoritarian approaches to reform are the most successful.

However, Farber and Holm provide little space for alternative readings of these films. For instance, how do teachers and administrators interpret these films? Do they agree with Farber and Holm, are they incensed by the overt messages, or do they merely go to films for pleasure unaware of and uninterested in any political message imbued in the text of these films? Farber and Holm offer little insight into these issues. In fact, their readings of these films do not give viewers an opportunity to raise such questions nor do they recognize that viewers read films in spite of the intentions of the director. Co-opting Wayne Booth, they ask if the superhero film genre invites the reader to join the directors "in creating the meaning of events and actions of the story" (1994, p. 169). Rhetorically, they answer their own inquiry. "The framing of the story," they respond, "the use of music, the presentation of characters--all are consistently designed to produce a specific response in us as viewers" (1994, p. 169). We contend that at the very least we do not know how someone responds to the messages of such films until we understand how meaning is constructed from these films and what role this meaning plays in the lives of students, teachers, and administrators.

By decentering we do not mean the abandonment of emancipatory agendas, ethical imperatives, or radical democratic projects. It does mean, however, that critical theory drops any notion that these goals be undergirded by what the radical postmodern feminist Wendy Brown calls political entailments or an epistemological assumption that implies our political agenda guarantees progress or liberation. We do not see the abandonment of political entailments as antagonistic with critical pedagogy. To the contrary we see it as a call to voice political agendas and to construct radical democratic projects. By abandoning any notion of political entailments, we realize that the issues we find imperative for a dynamic participatory democracy must be voiced because if we remain silent our visions, dreams, and voices are stationed on the brink of erasure from the collective memory of society.

Nevertheless, our abandonment of political entailments will dramatically change the way critical theorists read popular culture texts. According to Brown (1995), our readings will focus less on outcomes or potential messages and more on practices that promote a "conversation oriented towards diversity" and "a taste for ... argument" (p.128). We will shun the "preference for ... truth (unchanging and uncontestable) over politics; for certainty and security ... over freedom ... for discoveries (science) over decisions (judgments)" (p. 117). Brown's notion of the postmodern in this sense deconstructs the notion of one reading. The dominance of one reading in a text becomes a form of political action that is shunning conversation and argument; therefore any reading of popular culture texts should reflect multiple readings that often contradict each other or act independently from each other. It means we purposively seek out those voices that do not fit our world view or our readings of popular culture texts.

Penny Smith's contribution to this book demonstrates that such a strategy is possible. In her chapter "Rethinking Joe," Smith presents her reading of the film *Lean on Me* from a critical theory perspective. She questions the film's misogynist undertones and the way it legitimates authoritarian reform efforts, thereby subverting any efforts to democratize schools for students and teachers. However, in the second part of her chapter she decenters her reading and attempts to enter into a conversation with students, teachers, and administrators in order to find out how they read the film. As Smith points out, her reading was not theirs. They did not necessarily find the film sexist or destructive to democratic reforms. Instead they took from the film what best offered them insights into their own experiences and positions within the school system.

Don Guenther and David Dees' piece also attempts to focus on multiple readings. Within the context of a social foundations course, they seek "to encourage [their] students to engage in personal critical reflection on important societal issues without imposing and forcing 'a' truth perspective onto them." As they read a segment of the briefly run sitcom *The Faculty*, the students construct their own readings of the episode based on their experiences and expectations as pre-service teachers. At the same time Guenther and Dees interject their own reading and demonstrate why, from their own critical pedagogical and historical context, they focus their readings on racist, sexist, ablest, and homophobic tendencies in education, society, and popular culture. Following Gadamer, they are able to construct a critical reading of *The Faculty* by repositioning their reading, as well as the readings of their students, as a perspective focused "towards dialogue itself" rather than a direct or assumed emancipatory end.

Mary Reeves' contribution complements the two chapters above as she reveals the multiple readings within a discussion group that meets weekly to read the television animated comedy *The Simpsons*. Similar to Fiske (1993) and Ang's (1985) work, Reeves demonstrates how readers re-inscribe meaning into a popular culture text and relate to the images they absorb. In one telling exchange, the participants in the discussion group struggle over the meaning of Mrs. Krabapple, Bart's teacher, and whether she is a burned-out teacher who is indifferent, someone who cares but whose spirit has been crushed by the educational system, or someone who, along with Principal Skinner, is "so wound up in the way they think things have to be run that they aren't terribly effective." Reeves reminds us that the importance of reading popular culture characters like Mrs. Krabapple is that "for the most part, school is a place of, at best, boredom and trivia, and, at worst, a place of torture and humiliation. The degree to which the writers of *The Simpsons* emphasize the lack of caring . . . highlights their importance to real students in real classrooms. The knowledge that teachers privilege, enjoy, and desire to pass along are inconsequential to a child who does not feel cared for."

Reeves' focus on multiple readings does not begin with the discussion group, however. There are two other narratives running through her chapter. In order to make meaning out of what the Simpson's discussion group is doing, she enters into the debate within scholarly circles over the meaning of popular culture texts. At the same time, she reflects on the ways in which television culture has influenced her life and shaped her attitudes about education as well as her students. Reeves' interweaving of multiple readings demonstrates that there are intricate webs of interpretations (e)merging within each popular culture text that shape the meaning of the text and our lives.

Decentering of critical pedagogy also highlights the need to redefine popular culture beyond traditional notions of high/low culture and domination and subordination. To place popular cultures into binary relationships as in high/low distinctions or in even more flexible notions as domination and subordination limits the meaning of popular culture to its relationship to something else that is usually assumed superior. Decentering implies we see the reading of popular culture texts primarily as counter or independent readings that flow within or alongside of our own narratives. The work of Paul Gilroy and Dick Hebdige offer insights into the importance of counter or independent readings. Gilroy (1993) in *The Black Atlantic* reminds us that counter or independent readings of popular culture texts sometimes exist "under the nose of the overseers" (p. 37). Gilroy points out that these counter or independent readings are not counter-discourses. To label these readings as counter-discourses limits their force to construct meaning to a reaction. Readings that exist under the nose of overseers, Gilroy (1993) submits, are examples of a counterculture "that defiantly reconstructs its own critical, intellectual, and moral genealogy in a partially hidden public sphere of [its] own" (p. 38). As Hebdige (1988) reveals countercultures or subcultures form "up in the space between surveillance and the evasion of surveillance" and "are neither simply affirmation or refusal, neither 'commercial exploitation' nor 'genuine revolt'" (p. 35). Decentering seeks out these counter or subcultures, and to do so we have to look in the interstices between domination and subordination, high and low cultures. Although these cultures exist under the noses of overseers, they constitute their own worlds which implies they offer alternative readings of popular culture based on their own standards. To force these readings into our paradigmatic mappings and theoretical constructs is to strip them of their meaning and to indirectly subordinate these voices in the name of critical theory.

In his chapter, Peter Appelbaum attempts to understand the countercultures of schooling. He looks at the counterculture of Saturday Morning Cyborg cartoons and the ways in which elementary school children read them. From his work Appelbaum attempts to create a curriculum with the teachers of these elementary school children that is not based on any notion of a standardized or state-guided curriculum but one that stems from the children's cyborg counterculture. It is important to note that Appelbaum provides some insights into countercultures without ignoring dominant and subordinate relationships. He reveals that these relationships often enter into the process of reading popular culture texts when he tries to describe to teachers his curriculum projects. As he notes, some teachers wonder why he is coming to them to find out how they can create a curriculum from the children's reading of Saturday Morning Cyborgs and not telling them what they should be doing. When teachers respond in this manner it places Appelbaum and the teachers themselves into a traditional hierarchical relationship that sees the flow of knowledge moving only in one direction: from professor to teacher then to student. By labeling knowledge as a hierarchical act of dissemination these teachers place Appelbaum in a relationship of domination, even though it is not his intention, and thereby reinstitute a high (teacher knowledge)/low (Saturday Morning Cyborg knowledge) notion of culture that Appelbaum is trying to subvert and contest.

Jason Earle's chapter also presents insights into countercultures. Where Appelbaum's focus is on elementary school children, Earle's concern lies with pre- and in-service teachers and their co-optation of popular culture texts as a source of knowledge to define and make sense out of the art of teaching. For these teachers, popular culture texts create inspiring models of the type of teachers they wish to become. Moreover, these texts present more concrete insights into problems and issues teachers face today. As Earle notes these "teachers appropriate popular culture texts because they find them recognizable and empowering." They make visible dimensions of their private and professional lives that the "official knowledge" silences or delegitimates. On the other hand, these teachers find little value in what Earle labels "university based instructional research texts." They do not capture the life they will experience as teachers, nor offer a vision of inspirational teaching beyond the traditional image of the teacher imparting knowledge to the students. If these university based texts have any value, these teachers see it in their ability to explain and map out the dominant culture of schooling. These texts act as a conduit for teachers to acquire the official knowledge needed for credentialing while the popular culture texts offer them a way to overcome the silencing of the official knowledge and to create space in order to envision their own classrooms as dynamic spaces for learning and transformation.

Aimee Howley and Linda Spatig's chapter also offers further insight into the formation of countercultures. Relying on Hebdige's (1988) work on countercultures, Foucault's notion of disciplining, and their own interviews with teachers, Howley and Spatig focus on the popular culture of teaching as a "disqualified discourse about teaching." This disqualified discourse becomes a counterculture which offers teachers the opportunity to validate their own local knowledge within and beyond the dominant high culture of researchers, teacher educators, and staff developers. It is here in the realm of the counterculture with all its relationships of ambiguity, contradiction, rupture, domination, subordination, and transformation that teachers leave their mark on the educational system.

Creating a decentered critical practice of reading popular culture texts also implies the need to reconfigure the epistemological foundations that undergird our notions of knowledge and method. That is, we need to ask how do we, as academics, come to understand the ways in which students, teachers, and administrators read popular culture texts and construct multiple readings of these texts, or how do we construct the reader/viewer of popular culture texts? The main reason why, to this point, most academics outside of cultural studies have not taken up this question is found in the traditional epistemological assumptions about academic and "popular" knowledge. Academic knowledge is often perceived as canonical, the norm by which other sources of knowledge can be evaluated, decoded, re-interpreted, and co-opted. This traditional epistemological foundation often manifests itself in the form of a deep suspicion of popular culture texts that either completely dismisses the role of popular culture in our lives, thereby erasing it as a form of knowledge, or treats popular culture texts as homes for latent, cryptic messages ready to ambush any unsuspecting couch potato who is conveniently constructed as a Nielson rating point unable to interpret, discern, negotiate, reject, or re-invent possible meanings of popular culture texts.

To avoid these two traditions, critical theorists need to begin to see popular culture texts as hypertexts. The power of hypertext, according to George Landow (1994), not only is its ability to be stored digitally so as to "provide countless virtual versions of it to readers, who then can manipulate, copy, and comment upon it without changing the material seen by others" but it also reconfigures the notion of cultural critic as it has been defined by modern notions of texts (p. 11). A hypertext encourages the reader to become also an author, constructing meaning from a text that the original author may not have intended. As a hypertext, popular culture changes and shifts in meaning as the reader/viewer of these texts reads, plays, manipulates, resists, and/or accepts them without monopolizing the meaning. The reader becomes a cultural critic/author and the purpose of the cultural critic/author is no longer to "master" the meaning of a text like modernist literary and other cultural critics assumed. Instead, the purpose becomes to create meaning from a text. Therefore, instead of constructing the reader/viewer of popular culture texts as receiving meaning rather than creating it, critical theorists need to construct the reader also as an author creating multiple meanings as they read a text and act upon the meaning they create.

Methodologically, the epistemological foundations of academic knowledge manifests themselves in at least two ways. First, when academics do raise the issue of understanding how individuals construct different readings from popular culture texts, rather than capturing the contradictions, ambiguities, and fleeting nature of meaning making, the methods utilized often reify and petrify the process of reading popular culture texts. Such approaches turn the act of reading popular culture texts into a stagnant process in which meaning is fixed above time unable to shift and change from moment to moment. That is, the meaning making process is turned into something unnatural as it is forced into a linear, generalizable, cause-effect relationship, rather than seen as an organic process with a life of its own with an unpredictable future. Second, the very notion that multiple interpretations can be captured by using "proper" methodological techniques stunts the ability to understand the ways in which multiple readings of popular culture texts are constructed. The fact that academics give attention to methodological approaches and search for replication in order to verify their "findings" misses the point that understanding the processes of multiple readings of popular culture, or any, texts is not about trying to maneuver our "findings" so that they will correspond to some arbitrarily contrived but craftily disguised notion of objective reality, good taste, political entailment, or transcendent truth. When we try to align our methods with a fictitious notion of reality, our attention shifts to a fixation of getting the method "right" and away from the ways in which multiple readings of popular culture texts are invented and situated within what Kincheloe calls a "web of reality" (1999).

A decentered critical practice means we have to begin by following Ava Preacher Collins' (1993) lead and recognize that canon (knowledge) formation "is basically selective remembrance . . .in which certain cultural texts compete" for and control "cultural authority, establishing their own systems of valuation for what should be remembered and how it should be remembered" (p. 89). And in the modernist dichotomy that arbitrarily separates academic and popular culture knowledge, canon formation is part of a tradition that selectively remembers the value of academic texts while erasing the ways in which popular culture texts are dynamic sites of meaning making and sources of knowledge for students, teachers, and administrators. All the chapters in this book reconfigure the epistemological notion of knowledge and method in relation to the ways in which students, teachers, and administrators enter into a dynamic and forever shifting relationship with popular culture texts in order to construct multiple meanings of the texts, schooling, and society.

We recognize that by taking a postmodern anti-foundational stance against academic knowledge and methods, we are taking intellectual risks by transgressing many sacred boundaries. As Marleen Barr (1993) proclaims, however, in her work *Lost in Space: Probing Feminist Science Fiction and Beyond*, "I am glad I damned the torpedoes," "accepted the risks for choosing the 'wrong' field of study," and "gave myself the right of way before I had obtained a permanent license to teach" (pp. 4, 12). Like Barr we believe that doing work on popular culture texts that does not look upon them suspiciously is worth the risk. Part of the disconnectedness, meaninglessness, and hopelessness that students, teachers, and administrators feel towards schooling are caused by academic discourses that promote the disconnectedness between school knowledge and popular culture knowledge. The academy's suspicion of popular culture and its use of stagnating methodological approaches assists in creating a school culture that devalues the knowledge students, teachers, and administrators bring to the school. Instead, it constructs a hierarchy that values university knowledge that is hailed as the answer to school problems because it has connected itself to the ideology of science and the power of state departments of education. Rather than suspiciously looking down upon popular culture texts, a decentered approach turns the panopticon gaze of suspicion onto academic discourses. As Earle and Howley and Spatig's chapters in particular point out, a decentered gaze sees scientific knowledge as partial rather than as factual; containing not the kernels of re-vitalization and reality but rather the seeds of myths, stories, and legends that privilege academic discourses over other forms of meaning making. It sees all knowledge as ambiguous, facts debatable, reality contestable, and multiple meanings inevitable. As Giroux (1993) states, academics need to recognize "the partiality of their own narratives, so as to address more concretely the ethical and political consequences of the social relations and cultural practices generated by the forms of authority used in the classroom" (p. 253). These essays are attempts to put the act of seeing knowledge partially into action.

POPULAR CULTURE TEXTS AS FORMS OF CRITICAL PEDAGOGY

While the first issue we raised is concerned with how we read popular culture, the second issue deals with how we see popular culture. We believe critical theorists should begin to see popular culture texts as forms of critical pedagogy. When we accept popular culture texts as a form of critical pedagogy, we begin to focus on the ways in which these texts challenge power blocs while creating alternative visions of the world. When critical theorists offer their reading of popular culture texts, they often emphasize the ways in which these texts reinscribe or resist the hegemonic status of power blocs. We contend that while we should continue this tradition of critical reading, we should also recognize how popular culture texts contain their own pedagogical messages that share in our vision as critical theorists. Just as critical pedagogy strives to construct a pedagogy of possibility and what Giroux (1994b) calls a "pedagogy of representation" that illuminates "the various ways . . . representations are constructed as a means . . . to legitimate and secure a particular view of the future," popular culture texts offer their own critique of power blocs (p. 87). There is *Roseanne*, which articulates the plight of working class families in a society that is unable to address the issues they face both in the popular media and society; Madonna and Dennis Rodman, who constantly re-make their identities in order to challenge/uphold hegemonic and dominant power blocs who wish to control and regulate the power to define the limits of taste and the body; Ice Cube, who chronicles the racist roots of urban decay; and TLC, who voice the effects of urban decay and sexist lyrics.

It is important to note that we are not suggesting that popular culture texts are free from contradictions and ambiguities. We view all popular culture texts as inscribed within a history and culture that is shaped by capitalism, consumerism, choice ideologies, white supremacy, sexism, and homophobia. In other words, we recognize that just as Roseanne, Madonna, Rodman, Ice Cube, and TLC challenge power blocs they also are complicit in maintaining them. Roseanne, Madonna and Rodman often promote a narcissistic attitude, glorifying choice ideologies, consumerism, and self-gratification at anyone's expense. Ice Cube, TLC, and other rap groups often promote a ruthless form of capitalism that legitimates the myth of the self-made man and contributes to the escalation of urban decay they condemn in their lyrics. We are positing that each one of these popular culture texts offers a pedagogy of possibility in which societal problems are addressed, silenced voices heard, and alternatives envisioned. We need to study the ways in which popular culture offers alternative possibilities just as much as it articulates or resists the agenda of power blocs. In order to stress this point we wish to focus on two areas within popular culture that we think symbolize its connection with critical pedagogy: rap and feminist science fiction.

Rap is neither oppositional nor a counter-discourse responding to power-blocs; it is a counterculture constructing meaning from societal problems it experiences in the urban, and in some cases in suburban, centers of America. As a counterculture it is simultaneously a movement that "refuses to be treated as a minority culture--disadvantaged and excluded" and seeks to critique and replace power blocs that impede their development (Scott, 1995, p. 170). In this sense, Rap is critical pedagogy. It has focused on the frequent occurrences of police brutality, exposed the conditions of urban decay brought on by rabid capitalism, and tapped into the frustrations of urban populations while providing the lyrical messages for constructing an alternative world--a world filled with contradiction and ambiguity but nevertheless one where rap artists seek "a place within it on its own terms" (Brennan, 1994, p. 679). Rap seeks its own voices in order to draw attention to the historical and cultural conditions that have created it.

Rap and critical pedagogy have merged recently--creating a new hybrid--in their critiques of the schooling process. In particular Joe Kincheloe and Peter McLaren see neo-conservatives taking control in order to erase "dangerous memories" through a sanitized curriculum that re-instates the dominant myths of manifest destiny and rugged individualism through rote memorization and disconnected "facts" (Steinberg, 1995, p. 145). Just as Kincheloe and McLaren speak about the need to transform schools that take our cyber-children of the information age and thrust them into a school setting modeled on 19th-century principles of a fixed universe, linear time, replicable laws of social behavior, and static knowledge bases, rap artists lend their voices to the transformation of schools as well. Leaders of the New School, for instance, in "Teachers Don't Teach us Nonsense" have this to say about the current state of the public school curriculum:

> All I learn was when, where, what, how, and why . . . And then I asked do you think this is true/ Out like a strike that is 3 in a number, public education is making us dumber . . . further and further away, doing it out of sight/ energy of the young, teachers who teach us right . . . screaming for the team who asks where do we go from here . . . curriculum beat'n him down/ ask the teacher to teach me something I can use . . . I try to comply his lies . . . so I reply what about life/ the real uncut, uncensored deal . . . stop the brainwash, hang out to dry/ nonsense I am convinced it's lies . . . teach'n us no justice . . . teach the truth . . . stop teach'n us nonsense (*A Future Without a Past*, 1991).

This theme of curriculum reform emerges in Rage Against the Machine as well when they urge students to "Take the Power Back" and see schooling for what it is. "In the right light, study becomes insight/ But the system that dissed us/ Teaches us to read and write/ So-called facts are fraud . . . The present Curriculums/ I put my fists in'em/ Eurocentric every last one of'em . . . With lecture, I puncture the structure of lies" (Rage Against the Machine, 1992). Leaders of the New School and Rage Against the Machine envision a new curriculum that is not based on the foundation of fraud and nonsense, rote memorization, and disconnectedness but incorporates their personal experiences and fosters the development of a critical lens within students so they may connect their education to "the real" in order to construct a strategy to overcome the lies and begin the search for justice.

Toby Daspit's chapter attempts to make further connections between critical pedagogy and rap. He seeks to blur the hybrid of rap more by turning the students into teachers as they claim their voices in and outside of a school system that continues to ignore or erase them. If we are to construct radical pedagogies, then the terrain of popular culture and, in particular, rap is indispensable. It is not only a hybrid in terms of the mix'n of different forms of music but in terms of who listens to it as well. Rap is a sign with no fixed signifier, noise with no one message, and a commodity with no targeted audience based on income, race, gender, class, or ethnicity. It is an amalgam defined by and defining of these forces. If we reject rap as a form of radical pedagogy, just as we reject other forms of popular culture as merely the re-articulation of the dominant or the pure essence of resistance, then, as Daspit asserts, we miss an opportunity to ask ourselves as critical theorists "how might a 'classroom,' a 'school,' an 'education' infused with popular culture manifest itself?" How might popular culture re-configure the meaning of schooling, the role of the teacher, and the message of the critical theorist?

A second example is feminist science fiction. Science fiction as a genre is often seen as sexist and racist both in terms of who writes it and how women and people of color are constructed. It is also criticized for preserving a conservative social order intellectually with its privileging of scientific facts over other forms of knowledge and politically with its incremental attitudes towards social change. However, as Robin Roberts (1993) points out, feminist science fiction challenges these trends by re-telling the stories male science fiction writers create. She suggests that feminist science fiction writers "create an empowering portrayal of female strength. Women writers appropriate the female alien, utopias, and the woman ruler [often constructed as a threat to human kind in male science fiction] and transform them into feminist models" (p. 3). Moreover, feminist science fiction "with its imaginative possibilities . . . provides women opportunities denied them in the real world," Roberts (1993) contends, as it "call[s] into question the legitimization of patriarchy through conventional science" and "authorizes the experience of women" (p. 6).

Donna Haraway (1989, 1997) in her works shares Roberts' insights and calls for a blurring of the lines that demarcate academic works of fiction and science fiction. She calls for the end of "'the culture of no culture'" in which the (male) scientist is seen as the modest witness who "is objective . . . guarantees the clarity and purity of objects" (1997, p. 24) and represents the reality of nature in an "unadorned, factual, compelling" way that allows "facts to shine through, unclouded by the flourishes of any human author" (1997, p. 26). In place of a "'culture of no culture',," Haraway (1997) wants to "queer the modest witness" in order to expose the ways in which stories have been erased from the story and culture of science, women have "lost their security clearances very early in the stories of leading-edge science," and dichotomies have separated politics from science, objectivity from subjectivity, male from female, and Western academic work from the work of the non-academic and western worlds (p. 29).

Instead of avoiding the world, the new queer modest witness has to "make a difference in the world, to cast our lot for some ways of life and not others. To do that, one must be in the action, be finite and dirty, not transcendent and clean. Knowledge-making . . . must be made relentlessly invisible and open to critical intervention" (Haraway, 1997, p. 36). For Haraway (1989), feminist science fiction with its focus on the stories and myths of science and the blurring of gendered lines of identity offers one form of critical intervention. It provides "ways of understanding the production of origin narratives in a society that privileges science and technology in its constructions of what counts as nature and for regulating the traffic between what it divides as nature and culture" (p. 370). Moreover, it affords an opportunity to critically intervene in the production of all forms of academic knowledge as it deconstructs the arbitrary lines that have been constructed to demarcate and delineate between academic culture and popular cultures and to disguise the power that has been granted academic culture over popular cultures to control the latter's potential to transform the academy and society.

It is in the same vein of feminist science fiction and the pedagogy of possibility it creates that Dianne Smith's contribution can be read. Smith sees the power of (un)popular popular fiction to construct a critical pedagogy that leads "toward a terrain of healing and self-actualization" as readers live within these texts, make connections with their own life stories and thereby re-define themselves within a new terrain yet to be constructed in society but already visualized within themselves and popular culture texts. These texts are places where boundaries are transgressed as pressing societal problems (i.e., racism, incest, homophobia, and rape) are addressed as opposed to academic and societal discourses where they often remain repressed, covered over by layers of denial and silence. For Smith (un)popular popular fiction offers us the opportunity to construct a critical pedagogy that abandons the "'culture of no culture,'" overcomes the complicity of silence and "empowers us to practice dreams."

Finally, Patrick Slattery's essay is an attempt to chart a course for reconceptualizing university and public school curriculum in light of our attempts to read popular culture texts from multiple perspectives and view popular culture texts as forms of critical pedagogy. Slattery points out these acts re-constitute our pedagogy as we envision popular culture and our teaching as a synthetic moment in which multiple voices and identities emerge from the interplay between text and reader. Arbitrary lines between high and popular culture are exposed, stagnating curricula are re-invigorated, and standardized forms of knowledge are eliminated as we move from the complete dismissal or critical suspicion of popular culture and other personal forms of knowledge to the deconstruction and interrogation of our arbitrary boundaries of knowledge formation. This means rather than seek out a specific reading of a popular culture text, we "emphasize the primacy of experience, the merging of form and content, the recursion and convergence of time, the celebration of the self-conscious individual, and the understanding of phenomenological experience. This perspective . . . offers the individual a process for growing and becoming. It also offers schools an opportunity for critical reflection which is open to what has not yet been but what is also absolutely possible." It is through multiple readings and seeing popular culture texts as forms of critical pedagogy that the potential for students and teachers to grow and emerge becomes "absolutely possible."

NOTES

1. We borrow the terms power blocs and localizing powers from John Fiske. In *Power Plays, Power Works*, Fiske describes what is meant by these terms. A power bloc is an ever-shifting group that has the ability to control meaning. It possesses an imperializing power and its aim "is to extend its reach as far as possible" (1993, p. 11). A localizing power does not try to extend its

reach beyond those parameters that directly impinge upon their everyday experiences. It implies that there is not an interest "to dominate other social formations. . . . The function of this power is to produce and hold onto a space that can . . . be controlled" independently of imperializing powers (p. 12).

REFERENCES

Ang, I. (1985). *Watching Dallas*. New York: Methuen.

Barr, M. (1993). *Lost in space: Probing feminist science fiction and beyond* (Chapel Hill, North Carolina).

Brennan, T. (1994). Off the gangsta tip: A rap appreciation, or forgetting about Los Angeles. *Critical Inquiry* , *20*, 663-693.

Brown, W. (1995). Feminist hesitations, postmodern exposures. In Gabriel Brahm Jr. & Mark Driscoll (Eds.), *Prosthetic territories: Politics and hypertechnologies* (pp. 112-150). Boulder, CO: Westview.

Collins, A. (1993). Loose canons: Constructing cultural traditions inside and outside the academy. In J. Collins, H. Radner, & A. P. Collins (Eds.), *Film theory goes to the movies* (pp. 86-102). New York: Routledge.

Ellsworth, E. (1989). Why doesn't this feel empowering? Working through the repressive myths of critical pedagogy. *Harvard Educational Review* , *59*(3), 297-324.

Farber, P., & G. Holm. (1994). A brotherhood of heroes: The charismatic educator in recent American movies. In P. Farber, E. Provenzo, Jr., & G. Holm (Eds.), *Schooling in the light of popular culture* (pp. 153-172). Albany: SUNY.

Fiske, J. (1993). *Power plays, power works*. New York: Verso.

Gilroy, P. (1993). *The black Atlantic: Modernity and double consciousness*. Cambridge, MA: Harvard.

Giroux, H. (1996a). Hollywood, race, and the demonization of youth: The "kids" are not "alright." *Educational Researcher*, *25*(2), 31-35.

Giroux, H. (1996b). *Fugitive cultures: Race, violence & youth*. New York: Routledge.

Giroux, H. (1994a). Doing cultural studies: Youth and the challenge of pedagogy. *Harvard Educational Review* , *64*(3), 278-307.

Giroux, H. (1994b). *Disturbing pleasures*. New York: Routledge.

Gore, J. (1993). *The struggle for pedagogies: Critical and feminist discourses as regimes of truth*. New York: Routledge.

Graff, G., & Jay, G. (1995). A critique of critical pedagogy. In M. Bèrubè & C. Nelson (Eds.), *Higher education under siege: Politics, economics, and the crisis in the humanities* (pp. 201-213). New York: Routledge.

Haraway, D. (1997). *Modest_witness@second_millennium. FemaleMan meets_onco mouse: Feminism and technoscience* New York: Routledge.

Haraway, D. (1989). *Primate visions: Gender, race, and nature in the world of modern science.* New York: Routledge.

Hebdige, D. (1988). *Hiding in the light.* New York: Routledge.

Kellner, D. (1995). *Media culture: Cultural studies, identity, and politics between the modern and the postmodern.* New York: Routledge.

Kincheloe, J. (1999) "Introduction: The Foundations of a Democratic Educational Psychology." In J. Kinchloe(Ed.) *Rethinking Intelligence* (pp.1-26).

Kincheloe, J. (1995). *Toil and trouble: Good work, smart workers, and the integration of academic and vocational education.* New York: Peter Lang.

Kincheloe, J. (1993.) *Toward a critical politics of teacher thinking: Mapping the postmodern.* Westport, CT: Bergin & Garvey.

Landow, G. (Ed.). (1994). *Hyper/text/theory.* Baltimore: Johns Hopkins.

Lankshear, C., & McLaren, P. (Eds.). (1993). *Critical literacy: Politics, praxis, and the postmodern.* Albany: SUNY.

Leaders of the New School. (1991). *A future without a past.* New York: Elektra.

Luke, C., & Gore, J. (Eds.). (1992). *Feminisms and critical pedagogy.* New York: Routledge.

McLaren, P. (1994.) *Critical pedagogy and predatory culture.* New York: Routledge.

McLaren, P., & Lankshear, C. (Eds.). (1994). *Politics of liberation: Paths from Freire.* New York: Routledge.

Rage Against the Machine. (1992). *Rage against the machine.* New York: Sony.

Roberts, R. (1993). *A new species: Gender and science in science fiction..* Chicago: University of Illinois.

Scott, J. (1995). Critical aesthetics on the down low. *The Minnesota Review*, (43 & 44), pp. 164-171.

Sleeter, C., & McLaren, P. (Eds.). (1995). *Multicultural education, critical pedagogy, and the politics of difference.* Albany: SUNY.

Steinberg, S. (1995). Critical multiculturalism and democratic schooling: An interview with Peter McLaren and Joe Kincheloe. In C. Sleeter & P. McLaren (Eds.), *Multicultural education, critical pedagogy, and the politics of difference* (pp. 129-154). Albany: SUNY.

Critical Pedagogy as Multiple Readings

CHAPTER ONE

Rethinking Joe: Exploring the Borders of *Lean on Me*

Penny Smith

OK, I admit it. I hated *Lean on Me*. It seemed to be a classic example of popular culture pushing a dominant ideology in ways that pandered to the very groups it implicitly, albeit without subtlety, criticized. If Antonio Gramsci were correct and what one needed to do to ensure the preservation of ideological hegemony was to "capture the culture," then *Lean on Me* was/is a work of political art and artifice. It dramatically displayed what is wrong with our nation's public schools in ways that reflected the analysis of such individuals as William Bennett and Ronald Reagan, while simultaneously extending their analysis to other dimensions of the public world. For example, *Lean on Me* anticipated the current demonization of the single, welfare mother. It also popularized a direction for reform, one that was consistent with the ideas of competition, appropriate authority, hierarchy, and individual responsibility. The system was not flawed; the folks who operated the system were corrupt. Fix the individuals and the system recovers, success and achievement flourish, and it becomes "morning in America" again.

My views of the film were not isolated, nor particularly unique, ones. It was generally criticized, both by academics and by the popular press. David Denby (1989) of *New York* magazine called it a "fraudulent movie," that found answers to complex problems "in wish fulfillment" (p. 74). "Order is celebrated as an end in itself. Hungry for solutions, neoconservatism, in this demagogic movie anthem, blunders into neo-Fascism" (p. 75). Richard Schickel (1989) concluded that "complexity is sacrificed to fast-food inspirationalism. After the cheers die and the tears dry comes the realization that *Lean on Me* is serving up empty emotional calories. They don't leave you sick, just hungry for an honest meal" (p. 82). Irwin Hyman (1989) characterized Joe Clark, the principal whose efforts to improve Eastside High School in Paterson, New Jersey, provide the story on which the film is based, as a "charismatic authoritarian who offers himself as the answer to social crises" (p. 27). "*Lean on Me* is a box-office smash because it fulfills the fondest dreams of a public that yearns for the good old days of education. Unfortunately, those days never existed, except in the fantasies of those who would like a simpler, safer world" (p. 29). I agreed with Denby, Schickel, and Hyman, concluding that the film was an extension of the romantic political gaze exemplified by Reagan and his followers.

However, I discovered that some of the African American parents whose students attended the middle school in which I worked as principal were not as offended by the movie as was I. Indeed, many of them were not offended at all. Several of my students thought it was compelling story. Later I found that some of my European American colleagues liked the film and thought Joe Clark was an appropriate role model, both for their African American students and for themselves. Last year one African American principal, interviewed by one of my college students for an assignment in an introductory administration course, noted that he prepared for each new school year by renting and viewing a copy of *Lean on Me*. The movie was the top money earner in the week it came out, was in the top fifty films for 1989, and has been a steady earner of rental money since that time. Obviously, there were people enjoying it or at least finding in the film something worth the price of a ticket or an over-night rental.

I started to ask myself what's wrong with this picture? Is someone missing the political boat here? Did we see the same film? Eventually I came to the conclusion that they did not see what I did, that there were several boats afloat in the same viewing sea, and that they took ones other than the ship I boarded. It is the potential for multiple interpretations in *Lean on Me*, a film I once, and to some extent continue to, argued to be a tool of the dominant culture—one decidedly unfriendly to schools, African Americans, women, and poor people, that I will explore in this paper. I will first look at my reading of the film in some detail, partially because it sets the stage for subsequent discussion, then at the potential for alternative readings, and conclude by suggesting possible implications of those alternatives.

READING *LEAN ON ME* WITH ITS CRITICS

The plot or story that *Lean on Me* tells is a commonplace in American popular culture. A solitary man strides into a dismal situation and, against almost insurmountable odds, at personal and professional cost, without consistent help, and in opposition to sinister forces, manages to vanquish the wicked, reclaim the innocent, and convert misery into happiness. Sodom and Gomorrah become an Eden. Since the popularity of Indian captivity narratives, arguably our first indigenous popular literature, we have been enchanted by the efforts of individuals to do battle with savages on their territory and win, thereby restoring the "proper" balance between wilderness and civilization. The latter is called to subdue and hold dominion over the former. From the advent of dime novels and the adventures of mountain men, such tales have been gendered male. It was men who ventured into the maws of danger. Lewis and Clark traversed the country; Davy Crocket killed a bear at three; Andy Jackson slew the Indians at Sand Creek and the Europeans at New Orleans; and Teddy Roosevelt led the Rough Riders up San Juan Hill. While Louisa May Alcott's Jo stayed home and wrote stories or supervised her sisters, Mark Twain's undomesticated Huck sailed on the Mississippi River with a run-away slave. In our celluloid variations of those stories, Shane rides into town and two hours of movie time later disappears, alone, into the sunset. The Marlboro Man captures our image of the prototypical rugged individual: he is a man of the frontier, upright, lank, determined, a worthy opponent of the forces of nature. It is not an accident that John Wayne has become our cinematic national grandfather, Clint Eastwood's "make my day" is a synonym for just retribution, and Ronald Reagan is our most popular President since Franklin Roosevelt. Those men appealed to our suspicion of central authority in the guise of government institutions, all of which are too tame, too domesticated, too feminine, or too weak. They benefit from our bent to root for the rebel and from our inclination to wait for salvation to come riding in on a metaphorically (and all too often literally) white horse to save us from them, whoever "they" might be or whomever we have allowed "them" to become. These men have not been subject to the debilitating effects of serious intellectual endeavor, of complexities, of subtlety. They act and in acting receive our applause. They get things done and we are inclined to question neither their results nor methods. As then Secretary of Education William Bennett once said about educational leaders, "sometimes you need Mr. Chips and sometimes you need Dirty Harry" (Hyman, 1989, p. 27). As a nation we seem more comfortable with Harry.

Lean on Me opens in Joe Clark's classroom. It is the Eastside High of our memories. Students are seated in rows. They are dressed neatly, even formally. They raise their hands, are polite and eager to learn, obey the teacher who is more than a sage on a stage; Clark is a master instructing his disciples. Most of the students are European American, a contrast to Clark whose identification with his African heritage is reinforced both by his dress and his lesson. Called away because of a union controversy, his last words to his class are a definition of "imbrue." He tells them that "the cancer of racism imbrues our national character," an example they are diligently copying into their notebooks as Clark hurries to his meeting. There he discovers that a political deal will exile him from the school. In his confrontation with the union's executive committee, Clark condemns his colleagues for capitulating to the school board, to "them." "If you had any nerve at all you'd be on my side." In response they tell him that in return for salary increments, they have agreed to his involuntary transfer. Sold down the river by white political overseers engaged in a corrupt bargain with weak fellow travelers, he leaves the school. The immediate cinematic transition to Eastside High today implies that their bargain is one reason for the school's subsequent deterioration.

The beginning of the film beguiles us. Life at Eastside was once educationally progressive and challenging. Students had the benefit of dedicated and capable teachers like Clark. Political topics, if not political realities, were part of the curriculum. Yet the film also lets us know from the beginning that teachers like Clark were considered dangerous. They were candidates for removal and that removal was aided by the work of corrupt men—by unions and school boards. Blood was on *their* hands. Imbrue, after all, means, as *Webster's New World Dictionary* (second college edition, 1970) tells us, "to wet, soak, or stain, esp. with blood." One of the reasons that *Lean on Me* works as a piece of propaganda is that it mixes religious and racial tropes effectively. Clark is pictured as the victim of unfair practices. He is removed without consideration of his personal claims to place and position, thereby making those claims tentative and dependent. He is owned by the system's masters who can dispose of him as they wish. He is also the sacrifice the union makes with its employers for the personal profit of its other members. By the film's end Clark as Christ figure is obvious; his entrance into that role begins when the movie starts to roll.

The seriousness of Eastside's decline is evident in the transition from Clark walking out of the school in the 1960s to the montage of school life in the 1980s that leads to the opening credits. During the span of two decades we have left the clean hallways of the good, old days and entered the province of the savage. It is a tale told in black and white, quite literally. The student body has gone from one that conforms to a middle class European American ideal to one that embodies their nightmare fantasies of nature uncontrolled, a loud, violent, and sexually charged space occupied primarily by African Americans. For the thick of head in the audience, the music that backs the montage is "Welcome to the Jungle," itself a testimony to the racial stereotypes that pervade the film.

The catalogue of evils that greet the audience during those minutes will be familiar to anyone who has spent much time viewing high school films. Like such recent examples of the genre as *Stand and Deliver* (1988), *The Principal* (1987), and *Teachers* (1983), *Lean on Me* starts with school yard and hallway chaos. African American girls surround a European American classmate in the bathroom, strip her of her blouse and bra, and drag her into the crowded corridors to be jeered by fellow students. Drug deals go down. Teachers are harassed. Students pass weapons around metal detectors. They show contempt for the adults with whom they share the building. When a teacher attempts to stop a fight, he is assaulted and brutally beaten. Eastside High has all the overt symptoms of school failure: Racial strife, disrespect for authority, ineffective educators, drugs, guns, physical violence, graffiti, dirt, broken equipment, smoke-filled bathrooms, noise, and the palpable sensuality of unmonitored adolescent hormones. In case we missed the message that these are all signifiers of failure, we are told that Eastside is in danger of government take-over as a result of its dismal performance on the state minimum competency exam.

Who can save the school? The mayor wants action now. The Superintendent suggests Clark. The mayor resists, implying that Clark is still considered by the establishment to be dangerous. Yet the situation is sufficiently grave ("I have an election coming up and you hook me with this.") that he agrees that Clark, politically neutralized in an elementary school administrative position, might be the necessary remedy. These are, after all, desperate times. After the Superintendent, himself African American and a supporter of Clark, convinces him to transfer to Eastside, we see Clark's pain as he re-enters the building that was formerly the site of his social studies classroom. He is both saddened and angered by what greets him, by what others have allowed to happen.

Clark's approach to change is direct and swift. "No one talks in my meetings. No one." "Forget about the way it used to be. This is not a damn democracy. We are in a state of emergency. My word is law." "Think you can run this school? If you could I wouldn't be here." "This is an institution of learning. If you can't control it, how can you teach?" Clark has the faculty identify the trouble-makers and, in an auditorium meeting with the entire student body somewhat reminiscent of that earlier confrontation at the OK Corral, he has those young people brought on stage and announces that they are expelled. "I want you to look at the people on stage . . . these people are incorrigible." Turning to them, he pronounces sentence: "You are expurgated. You are dismissed. You are out of here forever. I wish you well." There is no hearing, no survey of evidence, no confrontation with accusers. They are, simply and without appeal, gone.

To the students who remain he declares that the "next time it may be you." If they are to stay, they must begin to work. "My motto is simple. If you do not succeed in life . . . , blame yourself. The responsibility is yours." In establishing the school goal to conquer the competency tests, Clark tells them that "if you don't have these basic skills, you will find yourself locked out." You will "fall into the trap of crime, drugs, death." "Welcome to the new Eastside High."

Lean on Me begins with a basic reform message: get rid of the bad kids and challenge the remaining ones to assume responsibility for their lives. The film does not challenge a system that permits Eastside Highs to exist. It does not question the relationship between basic skills and jobs, nor does it pay attention to the dearth of employment possibilities in inner-city urban New Jersey. Through Clark *Lean on Me* speaks the American Dream language of Benjamin Franklin and Ronald Reagan. Work hard, strive, and you can make it. If you fail, it is not the system that is flawed, but you. All we need as a nation to hold crime and drugs at bay is young people with basic skills. Who benefits from that analysis of school failure? The defenders of the status quo, the authors of *A Nation at Risk* (National Commission on Excellence in Education, 1983), a business community reluctant to put additional resources into public schools, the privileged classes whose children do not attend Eastside High School, politicians who are reluctant to increase taxes or reallocate money. We, the general public, are rescued from the threat of further intrusion into our middle class bank accounts. There will be no new taxes. Who is to blame for the failure? Corrupt political insiders, suspect unionists, ineffective educators, effeminate advocates of due process, savage, underachieving and unredeemable youth.

Lean on Me never obscures the politics of educational disaster at Eastside. The film distills those disparate enemies of truth, justice, and the American way into a central symbol. Almost immediately after throwing the corrupt inhabitants from the temple, Clark encounters the woman who becomes the embodiment of the disloyal opposition. Mrs. Barrett, the mother of one of the expelled students, confronts Clark at a parents' meeting, arguing that "what happened this morning is an outrage." She concludes that "he turned on his own people." To conservatives, Clark's response is sweet music. "It's a war to save other students . . . Get yourself off welfare. Give them some pride. Get your priorities straight." Barrett complains that Clark resorts to preaching, but Clark welcomes the invocation of sacred authority. God told him to "do whatever you have to and he didn't say be polite." "I gave my word to God and that's why I threw those bastards out and that's all I'm going to say." Clark has become an avenging angel, an agent of God, and as such has the right to transgress temporal rules. There is a higher law and it is to that law that he appeals. His actions are a personification of tough love. It hurts him more than it does you, but for the greater good he will do it.

In a transition scene that humanizes Clark and that supplies him with a new type of disciple, he permits one of the expelled students, Thomas Sams, to re-enter school. He is touched by Sams, partially because the child admits that his father no longer lives with his family. Through the relationships he builds with students like Sams, Clark becomes a surrogate father, their missing paternal influence. The implication is that part of what's wrong in the lives of these children is the *right* family, the family with mom at home and dad at work. There is only a diminished, feminine center for these youngsters, a fragmented, fractured and woman-led family, and, consequently, the center cannot hold.

Mrs. Barrett is a single mother as are the mothers of two of the three featured students: Thomas Sams and Kneesha. The parent or parents of the third are simply absent; they do not appear as characters. Although Clark cannot redeem Barrett's son (he was one of the expurgated), he reclaims Thomas by re-admitting him into the fellowship of his school and Kneesha by healing the girl's rift with her mother. When he learns of Kneesha's pregnancy, he comforts her with the assurance that *he* will make sure things work out ("We'll have your mother come to school . . . the three of us will put our heads together."). However, he is spared the details of that assignment by the rapid conclusion of the film, a conclusion that leaves unexamined the consequences of Kneesha's dilemma. But it is not such messy personal issues with which the film is concerned; it is with the larger consequences of absent father figures—disordered schools, disorderly young people, and a chaotic, violent and economically compromised society. Promiscuity issues from the deficits of single mother homes. When Kneesha asserts that she never meant to get pregnant, Clark tells her that "you girls never do." "So many of you are bringing babies into this world to show you can accomplish something." Both arguments reject a need to examine the difficult, confusing and diverse reasons for adolescent pregnancies. The problem can be solved with present or surrogate fathers; it requires only putting heads together. Pregnancies occur because fathers are gone (did their women push them away?), mothers are not vigilant, and girls promote a life style that makes a pregnancy likely. Clark does not consider, for instance, whether "you boys" ever mean to impregnate girls. "You girls never do" places females in passive, yet seductive and complicit roles. If only girls would find a more constructive way to accomplish something, Clark implies, adolescent pregnancies would be a thing of the past. Two are not necessary to do the pregnancy tango at Eastside High School.

Kneesha's pregnancy is a minor and largely unresolved sub-plot, although it does have some implications for the film's on-going repudiation of welfare (to her credit, the film argues, Kneesha's mom, even though she had a child at 15, did not want to nor did she go on welfare) and its suspicion of state agencies (foster home officials try to convince Kneesha's mom to give her up). The real conflict is between the forces of evil (Mrs. Barrett and the politicians) and the forces of good (Joe Clark). They battle for the educational souls of Eastside's students and Clark takes no prisoners in that struggle. Although his initial speech to students indicates that they are responsible for their actions, he quickly shifts blame to the adults. (Consistency is not a necessary ingredient in the story *Lean on Me* tells.) Mr. Darnell, the African American football coach, is demoted for having a losing team, then humiliated in front of students in the cafeteria for picking up a piece of paper, then illegally suspended for questioning Clark. He is later reinstated and the film hints at a budding mentoring relationship between the two. Not so fortunate is the school's chorus teacher, Mrs. Elliott. European American, Elliott has managed to create, in the midst of Eastside chaos, an exemplary chorus that performs annually at Lincoln Center. The music they sing is classical and difficult. Interrupting her class, Clark tells her that he wants the students to learn the school song and that it is her responsibility to ensure that happens. She replies that the school song is "fine," but that she was at that moment doing Mozart. "If you want us to respect your work, you could try to appreciate ours." Clark has no patience with that response. "Who do you think you're talking to?" She asserts that she's speaking to "a man who seems to be threatened when any other adult in this school does something the children like." Clark declares her concert canceled. Elliott retorts that he is "a bully, a despicable man." Clark, who apparently can tolerate no challenge to his authority, fires her. "Get out right now."

The unlikelihood of those autocratic expulsions happening without due process in a real school notwithstanding, they tell us something about the way *Lean on Me* constructs appropriate educational administration in urban schools. In a war for the minds of children, legalities should not stand in our way. Educators must act decisively and soon; they should discount the importance of civil niceties like constitutional rights and contracts, of established, effective educational practices, of success through subordinates, of trust-building. Clark is a Patton surrounded by cowardly soldiers in need of sharp whacks on the sides of their heads. He has little patience with legalistic Eisenhowers and Bradleys. The encounters with Darnell and Elliott also tell us something about the way the film constructs power relationships. It is the man who eventually is retained and the woman (we later learn that she is perhaps the school's best teacher) who is let go. It tells us about the relative importance of individuals and the group. For the sake of question-proof solidarity, Clark sacrifices a superior teacher whose defiance of his authority should have reminded him of himself several years earlier. He teaches us that strength is in his group and that the roles and rights of other individuals must, in a war, be curtailed even if that war is being fought to preserve such ideals as competition among individuals. That exchange also has curricular implications. Mozart is out and the school song is in. High culture is out and patriotism is in. Complexities are out and basics are in. The war, after all, is not really about education or the empowerment of those without voices; it is about minimal skills and preparation for the work force. When Ms. Levias, one of the school's Assistant Principals, tells him that he is creating chaos, that "no one knows what you're doing," Clark replies that "that's the way I like it." Schooling is not a participatory venture pursued by a community of learners; school is a battlefield and there can be only one commander-in-chief.

Once the riffraff (unruly students and insubordinate teacher) are no longer at Eastside, Clark can rebuild his school. The halls begin to look clean. The school song is rewritten; students know and sing it. However, he still faces the specter of the competency test, and the results from a practice exam do not bode well for Eastside's performance. How does Clark motivate his faculty? He has them all assemble in the gymnasium, in the presence of some of the students, and divides them into two groups.

> Everyone in this section raise your hands. Put them up. You reflect the 70% who failed the practice test. The failure is yours. How many hours do you spend preparing your lessons? How often are you here? Keep hands up high. Look at yourselves. Because you are failing to educate them, this is the posture they'll be in, but they'll be staring down the barrel of a gun.

After that pep talk, the faculty now blamed, rather than the students, for educational malaise are professionally reborn. We are treated to a montage of frenetic classroom activities as teachers, stimulated by a Clark-inspired energy infusion, teach. The film moves through frames of joyful youngsters eagerly learning from energetic, enthusiastic, and creative educators. The halls are redecorated, the students dress more carefully, guns and drugs are banished, visitors are impressed, and mayhem exists only outside the doors of Eastside High. Inside is an oasis of tranquillity and purposefulness.

However, outside the sinister forces continue to plot against Joe Clark. Mrs. Barrett strikes a deal with the mayor, the second corrupt bargain of the film. He appoints her to the school board and she promises to deliver the African American vote for him. When he asks her what she wants, Barrett replies "Clark." Because Clark has padlocked the doors at Eastside in an effort to discourage drug sales and to keep non-students out of the building, he is vulnerable on charges of disobeying the city's fire codes. Barrett is aware of that vulnerability. And things become somewhat less than perfect within when Ms. Levias threatens to leave. She confronts Clark about his brutal tactics with teachers. "The same people who are supporting you are the ones you're beating up." Will Clark manage to win back Ms. Levias? Will he be able to defeat Barrett's efforts to catch him in violation of city ordinances? Will his students pass the competency exam? Will good triumph? Unlike Saturday morning serials that left you hanging after ten or fifteen minutes of excitement to be continued later, *Lean on Me* rushes toward its conclusion, situated appropriately in the numbers race of state competency examinations.

In a pre-test assembly, Clark gives his final pep talk. He tells his students that "the people out there" are calling them names, are saying that they are failures, are "niggers, spics, poor white trash." But "you are not inferior." "You can turn that around." Eastside High is "a spirit that will never die." Clark asks Mrs. Powers, Elliott's former piano accompanist and current replacement, to lead the school in a song. Appropriately titled "Lean on Me" and equally appropriately echoing old-time gospel music, it tells us that we have someone who will "help you carry on." "Just call on me, brother . . . we all need somebody to lean on." The entire school sings, Powers and Clark hold hands and lead the students, Levias tears up her resignation letter, and everyone moves with determination into the testing arena.

Almost immediately after the testing is completed, fire marshals descend on the school and Clark is arrested. Led off in handcuffs, he is moved to a cell conveniently located in the very building that houses the school board that, at that very moment, is considering his removal. Simultaneously, the student body marches on the jail, demanding that Clark be freed. Barrett, outside trying to calm the crowd, is derided by the students, until one suggests that they "listen to the old loud-mouthed wench." An exchange about Clark, education, and the law ends with a student asserting that Barrett is "twisting the law to . . . [her] advantage." Clark is not the devil Barrett says he is, but "like a father" to Eastside's young people. The police begin to circle the students, armed with nightsticks. Because of the potential danger to "his people," Clark is persuaded to talk with the crowd. Without apology for timing, in the very next instant a car manages to move slowly through the crowd and stop in front of the city hall/jail steps and Ms. Levias emerges. In her hands are the results of the competency test, which, to no one's surprise, indicate that the requisite number of students have passed the exam. Barrett is defeated and trails the mayor inside. Clark is left with his friend and supervisor, Napier the Superintendent, and Thomas Sams, who rushes from the crowd to embrace him. The camera freezes, holding in its frame the faces of three African American men: the older Napier, the militant Clark, and the young Sams—a trinity promising a bright tomorrow. It unfreezes as Clark descends into the crowd, fading to open on a graduation ceremony backed by the song "Lead on to Victory."

Lean on Me exploits stereotypes and popular fears to construct a story of school reform that is, at least to me, simple-minded, dangerous, and intoxicating. It does so by demonizing some single African American mothers and their progeny, by inferring that most (all?) government officials are interested only in the preservation of their political power, by implying that educators in the absence of a strong authority figure will not work, and by suggesting that one can make dramatic and lasting changes quickly, easily, and without expenditure of additional resources. It sets up, as the salvation of our schools, charismatic individuals, diverting our attention from the system itself. It reinforces a curriculum of basic skills, the idea that inner-city students are only able to master that level of competence, and that such competence will be sufficient to end urban blight, drug addiction, violence, and unemployment. Finally, it affirms stereotypical ideas about race, class, and gender, thereby failing to question positions of privilege embedded in our culture. In the guise of a story about an overbearing, albeit heart of gold rebel, the film really tells us the value of the status quo.

The characters who fail children, at least up close and personally, in *Lean on Me* are women. Mrs. Barrett anticipated the powerful image created during the last congressional session of the economically and spiritually corrupt welfare mother. We are asked to believe that she has the political influence to cut a deal with the mayor and his cronies, to lead the community away from the church and Clark, to challenge the man who wants to end the dominance of drug dealers, weapon pushers, and violent delinquents in the community's school. We never see

Barrett's followers, nor are we shown any evidence that suggests there is a reason to believe that they exist. We know only that she is a failed mother (her son is out of control) and a failed productive citizen (she is on welfare).

The politicians in *Lean on Me* are oafish. They make a bargain with the film's metaphorical devil, fail to lead, and consider themselves above the interests of the community they have been chosen to represent. Given the evidence we have of their duplicity and lack of popular support, one wonders how they managed to get elected and to stay in power. They are representatives of politicians whose political commitments include social action funded at public expense. Consummate insiders, they serve as a contrast to Clark, the principled outsider. Their conduct impugns that of all civil workers and establishes truth, justice, and the American Way outside the hallowed halls of government. One could argue that the film, then, attacks the institutions of the dominant culture. However, it attacks those institutions in their role of supporting the political and economic claims of Mrs. Barrett and, by extension, the Mrs. Barretts of our world, by supporting "non-working, welfare queens." As Michael Weiler and Barnett Pearce (1992) contend, it is the rhetoric of populism that is the discourse of the dominant culture, not the rhetoric of collective action through government. Ronald Reagan, for example, allied "himself with 'the people' against the government" (p. 12), as does Joe Clark. In so doing, Weiler and Pearce contend, Reagan diminished "the discursive terrain for dealing with complex public issues," and, by using what becomes basically a ceremonial discourse, detaches the discussion "from political reality" (p. 13). Clark also seeks allies among "the people," uniting them in opposition to the political insiders of Paterson, New Jersey, who are held accountable in unexplained ways for the decline of Eastside High. Populist outsiders, paradoxically, become the voices of the American people. In such roles, they are prone to assume that those voices are really singular, that those messages are essentially identical, and that they have been chosen to serve as our messenger.

Teachers at Eastside High, reflective of educators in most school genre films, are reluctant workers at best. Their expectations of the intellectual potential of their students, particularly if they are identified as minority, urban youngsters, are low, whereas their toleration of inappropriate and, at times, illegal behaviors appears to be high. Their ability to connect with such young people is absent, as are any efforts to do so. They occupy space, often move through their daily activities either fearfully or desolately, and are culpable for the failures of their students. Fix them and schools are basically fixed. Certainly that is the message that one finds in such films as *Teachers* and *Stand and Deliver*, as well as a recent entry to the school film canon, *Dangerous Minds* (1995). Excellent, dedicated teachers are rare; it takes someone tough, a Joe Clark or the title character in *The Principal* to compel most educators to do their jobs. "You," Clark asserts, "are failing to educate them." The logical extension of that accusation is that if teachers collectively would simply work, young people would all learn, that they would learn the right lessons, and that America would then be populated with educated citizens ready to tackle the rigors of a global business economy. Such an accusation deflects attention from an educational system supported by and supportive of a particular economic, ideological, and cultural perspective, from the contradictory assumptions that undergird the system, and from more troublesome questions about the ready availability of meaningful employment when the school work is finished.

That accusation also implies that there is no need for additional resources to support schools. We do not need more teachers; we need the ones we are already paying to do their jobs. As Rick Latimer, the Clark counterpart in *The Principal*, tells his staff: "Come on, you people, you can't just pick and choose your students. You can't just teach the easy ones and throw the rest in the garbage." Clark revitalizes Eastside in the span of a school year, apparently without additional programs or teaching faculty. He does bring with him security officers, but the public appears to consider such expenditures sound investments. In *Lean on Me* their task apparently becomes less the monitoring of the students within the school than the exclusion of street influences from the school.

That message, combined with the identification of single mothers, politicians, and ineffective teachers as "the problems," provides the foundation for *Lean on Me*'s proposed solution to our educational malaise: Joe Clarks. It's not the system, stupid; it's the leaders and their experts. We simplify the debate, then propose the most cost-effective solution. Mona Harrington (1986) argues that, as a nation, we have embraced a "myth of deliverance," one strand of which reflects our suspicion of big government, professionals, and unions. The people are inherently good, local solutions inevitably best, and cities ultimately corrupt. If the United States is in trouble because of its schools, the

position taken in *A Nation at Risk* (1983), it can be returned to its
rightful international position in ways that are efficient (read
inexpensive), simple, the result of hard, honest labor at the local level,
and direct. Such an analysis of problems and their solutions dismisses,
Harrington asserts, "the significance or even the reality of economic,
social, or technological complication" (p. 268). We only need to find
the folks with the right stuff, the Joe Clarks of this world.

And what salvation will they bring to the students in our inner city
schools? In the case of *Lean on Me* the solution to our problems resides
in the basics, in the numbers games of standardized tests. It resides,
consequently, in disembodied knowledge, external to immediate
experience, fragmented and tied to traditional disciplinary divisions.
Smart kids get the sophisticated curriculum (Elliott's Mozart); urban,
minority children are ready only for minimum skills and cant (the
school song). Granted, one can argue that students need minimum skills
as a foundation upon which to build other knowledge. That discussion
raises the issues of what constitutes the knowledge worth knowing and,
consequently, what basic skills are necessary to acquire that knowledge.
Unlike earlier school films, for example, *To Sir with Love* (1967) and
Conrak (1974), that challenge the prevailing ideas about what's worth
knowing and seek answers from the students themselves, more recent
exemplars of the genre validate the current, standardized course of
study. They tout advanced placement and self-discovery for the
privileged (the 1989 film *Dead Poets Society*) and minimal
competencies for the culturally disenfranchised (for example, *Summer
School* (1987) and *Lean on Me*). In the one recent exception to that
practice, *Stand and Deliver*, calculus becomes a sign for success in a
high tech world, not a way to understand self or society. It does not take
an economist to point out that high school graduates with basic skills
are neither readily employable in jobs that might promise a career nor
likely to be living in areas where such employment might even be
available. Rather than teaching students that knowledge is a tool that
can empower them, we teach students the knowledge we think will help
them find their niche in our economy. By its evident concern for "the
basics," the film promotes the most fundamental of what Mas'ud
Zavarzadeh and Donald Morton (1991) call the "new middle
postindustrial careerism" (p. 2). *Lean on Me* validates the pedagogy of
the oppressor and not that of the oppressed.

However, perhaps the more offensive elements of *Lean on Me* are
in the assumptions they make about race, class, and gender. Although

both African Americans and European Americans are portrayed as villains in this film, the former in the person of Barrett is far more evil than the latter, the moderately calculating and politically insecure mayor and fire chief. The jungle is inhabited by African Americans and it is African Americans who commit the majority of the offensive acts that are used to signify Eastside's decline. The bathroom scene involves African American girls as a group harassing a sole European American student. The drug dealers are bedecked with gold chains and fancy suits and, primarily, are African Americans. The single mothers are African American. The pregnant adolescent is African American. True, the knights in shining armor are also African American, but they behave in ways that contrast dramatically with the citizens of the jungle—they dress differently and talk differently. They are not unlike Clarence Thomases, situated in positions of power to demonstrate an absence of prejudice while concurring in actions that perpetuate division. They do the messy work of the power-holders for them.

One assumes that the students at Eastside High are there because they do not have an economic alternative. Who, after all, would want to spend time in such an institution unless forced to do so or unless able to use that opportunity for personal gain? When we see the 1960s version of the school, it reflects another set of values and, not coincidentally, the seats are predominantly occupied by European American, economically advantaged students. The 1980s version of the same school suggests what happens when race and class change. It is because these are poor and African American students that the school can become what it did become. Granted the film makes the point that the mainly white power structure will tolerate such degradation until forced to do otherwise; Eastside is not, for example, in the mayor's neighborhood. However, *Lean on Me* compromises the potential of such a message to suggest some underlying racial and class prejudices in the decline of Eastside by signaling that the jungle savages are, after all, residents of the hood; they are agents of their own lack of success. Folks must send their children to Eastside because they did not make something of themselves. The acceptance of the film that the object of schooling is success on state-administered standardized tests and that the test of record for Eastside is a basic skills or competency exam is an additional class signifier. Forget about high aspirations (the annual Lincoln Center concert); concentrate on the ABCs and arithmetic. Any educator who has spent time in public schools knows that disproportionately academically gifted classes are populated with the students from the 1960s Eastside and that classes for the educationally challenged or disadvantaged (interesting terms themselves) are populated by students to whom the 1980s Eastside might have been home. We know that the best predictor of success on academic gatekeepers like the Scholastic Aptitude Test is socio-economic status, an indicator that also has tremendous predictive power for which students are placed in which types of classes, for which students who are directed toward academic success and which are counseled to take a general program of study. The perpetuation of a basic education curriculum for some, but not all, students ensures that the separating and sorting that revisionist historians like Joel Spring (1976) claim are the main themes of American educational history will continue. The students of Eastside High in the 1980s, either in their pre-Clark guise or their domesticated post-Clark portraits, are no threat to the students in the boarding school of *Dead Poets Society.*

Additionally, the film suggests that women are part of the problem and only in certain roles can they become part of the solution. The main damage to students comes from single mothers, not fathers. Kneesha becomes pregnant, like "you girls" always do. Mrs. Barrett, not the mayor, is the villain. Mrs. Elliott refuses to dump Mozart. Ms. Levias doubts Clark and nearly quits. The saviors are Napier and Clark; their implicit successor is Sams. The student council president, the boy who displays the school for visitors and calls Barrett a wench, is male. Clark shelters female students and provokes male students to action. He takes care of the problems of girls (Kneesha's foster home episode and her pregnancy; the Hispanic girls who worry that they are not included in his efforts), but requires the males to perform (Sams to dress well, Sams' friends to learn the song). The male football coach returns; Elliott is out for good. When the film freezes near the end on the faces of Napier, Clark, and Sams, the theatre audience, symbolically represented by the crowd, rejoices in their victory. It is a victory brought about by men basically for men, occasionally supported, perhaps, by women who know their places. Clark is a hyper-masculine hero, reflective of what Elizabeth Traube (1992) argues is a mass culture that became, in the 1980s, a "site for . . . [the] process of remasculinization" (p. 19). We are in this fix educationally, by extension politically and economically, because we have become a soft and feminine society.

William Borah (quoted in Harrington, 1986), an early twentieth-century ideologue whose ideas resonate with the deliverance themes one finds in Reagan rhetoric, argued that "institutions set up, often for perfectly good purposes . . . secretly, silently, remorselessly undermine and sap the character and stamina, the self-reliance, and the self-governing capacities of the people" (p. 79). Our schools have done that. Welfare has done that. The results are a greedy pursuit of self-interest, crime, drug use, sloth, illiteracy, abandonment of the work ethic, and rampant hormones. We need strong men, Joe Clarks, to rebuild America.

My reading of *Lean on Me*? Like Denby (1989), I found it "a true product of the hallucinatory Reagan era" (p. 75). It nurtured ideas that carry us, as a nation, away from a discussion of our problems by providing simplistic analyses of both issues and solutions. The film not only lies, quite literally, about events at Paterson's Eastside High School (the scores never rose out of the bottom quartile, the issues were never that easy, the popular support for Clark was mixed, the heritage of the school not reclaimed), but about the issues that brought about the situations we find in urban schools (Hyman, 1989). As Mas'ud Zavarzadeh (1991) notes, "films are not merely aesthetic spaces but political ones" (p. 5). *Lean on Me* is a dangerous pedagogical and political statement.

ALTERNATIVE READINGS OF *LEAN ON ME*

So convinced was I of my accurate reading of the film that I dismissed the first times that I encountered viewers with contrary opinions. Yet the more alternative opinions I heard, the more I began to question my own "one best reading." Perhaps, like the academicians of whom Camille Paglia (1992) complains, my "elitist sense of superiority to popular taste" had made me not only one of the "biggest snobs in America" (p. ix), but also a poor reviewer of my culture.

Reader response theory claims that the text is filtered through specific readers who, in the words of Michael Riffaterre (1978), "make the literary event" (p. 116). The literature on alternative readings, the importance of readers, and their ability to bring to a text a perspective that reshapes it challenges the idea of a monolithic reading of any specific text, including a film; it subverts the existence of a "right" interpretation (Andrew, 1984, note particularly chapters 8-10). As someone who grew up with Roy Rogers and Dale Evans westerns, I was always able to transcend what should have been a gender affiliation with Dale to ride more exciting trails with Roy. However, like Henry Giroux and Peter McLaren (1992), I believe that

> to a certain extent, our very acts of naming reality always occur from positions of intelligibility which are complicitous with the moral imperatives of the dominant social order and must be interrogated for the limits of their conditions for enabling transformation . . . a pedagogy of representation provides the basis for educators to be attentive to a politics of location, one which recognizes and interrogates the strengths and limitations of those places one inherits, engages, and occupies and which frame the discourse through which we speak and act. (p. xxviii)

Reader response theory, for me, was limited by linguistic boundaries, the vocabulary of the dominant social order. I could read against the grain, perhaps, but only in the vocabulary of Roy's world. For example, there was not an alternative, attractive set of adventures to those he and his loyal friends provided. If I wanted to participate, to read, in that genre, European Americans were still the good guys, native Americans were likely to be the bad guys, men did most of the work and seemed to have most of the fun, and the central institutions, values, and assumptions of that version of the American west remained intact. However I wanted to resist those messages, I still spoke and thought in the same language, or variations thereof. So, as I became more sophisticated as a reader, I assumed that the way to challenge texts was to interrogate them, to bring to the table the tools of critique, to unpack their messages and reveal the master's assumptions. Initially, that meant deconstructing texts, decoding symbols and metaphors, raising to a level of consciousness tacit assumptions, and becoming attuned to the cultural trappings of political messages. With a little intellectual work and political fervor, I could articulate the ways in which the dominant culture conspired to limit my ability to resist or to challenge, the ways in which that culture made me complicit. There were, I reasoned, a set of "correct" cultural messages to unravel and examine in any text that would yield, if I struggled with them sufficiently, the "correct" deconstruction. *Lean on Me* was an ideological piece of cake. Or was it?

I was from the first viewing of the film ready to credit the existence of one alternative reading of *Lean on Me*, one situated approximately 180 degrees away from mine. It was, of course, the reading the power brokers intended. Both Reagan and Bennett had supported Clark publicly and had lauded the film. Both Clark and the movie absolved them as well as their political colleagues of any blame in the existence of such a school. *Lean on Me* placed responsibility where they were inclined to place it: on teachers, on poor parents, on single mothers, on students whose family situations had deprived them of an appropriate work ethic. Racism and poverty were never causes; America was a land of equal opportunity. That reading also suggested resolutions in all the right places: in the schools, locally, without additional support, through revitalizing teachers and hiring take-no-prisoners leaders. It even suggested the right solutions: Basic skills that could/would lead to productive citizenship, with an emphasis on economic productivity. The film confirmed the Reagan-Bennett analysis of what was wrong in our schools; it affirmed that their arguments about how to improve them were correct. We needed true grit and John Wayne. Surely it is not an accident that the successors of the Reagan-Bush analysis now tout family values and character education, making the latter both an educational and an economic growth industry. Nor is it an accident that hiring retired military officers to run schools or school systems is now a popular initiative.

Slowly, usually in casual or informal conversations, I became aware that there were other readers out there, that the film provided other audiences with different pleasures. The most accessible of those alternatives was that of some of the African American parents and students at the middle school where I had worked as principal. Although the bad guys were generally African Americans, the good guys were *exclusively* African American. Unlike earlier films that address issues of education deficits in racial and class terms (*Conrak* comes to mind, but the same theme is obvious in *Blackboard Jungle* (1955), *The Principal, Renaissance Man* (1994), and the 1986 *Wildcats*), in *Lean on Me* the solution is not brought into a neighborhood by a crusading European American interloper. Agency and efficacy are in the hands of "the other," not "the man." Clark, an African American male, is portrayed as a care-giver, a leader, a man of righteous indignation, of power, of action, of God. He takes on the establishment and wins; it is the European American politicians who turn tail (literally, as they go back into city hall and leave Clark to his victory on the steps) and run. Even if the school were, symbolically, theirs, the trouble-makers generally African American, and the problems articulated coded in symbols and language that signified urban, black, and poor, these readers generally believed that those conditions were precipitated by the institution not being literally theirs. The context was background; the foreground belonged to redemption, hope, and Clark. If Barrett were corrupt, she became that way as a victim of a society not of her making; she was a tool the policy-makers created to maintain their power.

Moreover, the problems one finds at Eastside High (pregnant girls, drug dealing boys, random violence, sexual harassment, disrespectful adolescents, low achievement—in both academics and on the football field—uninspired teachers, and unkempt facilities) are problems that no parents of whatever race want their children to encounter. The African American parents I knew, many of whom were, by federal definition, members of the working poor, some of whom lived in the two public housing projects that were adjacent to the school, some of whom were on welfare, and some of whom daily confronted the possibility of drug-related violence, did not think that Eastside was their public school nor any of the public schools their children attended. It was, rather, what might happen were they not vigilant. In the absence of Clark, *they* assumed the role of ensuring that their children were treated with respect, given educational opportunities, and had responsive teachers. They identified with Clark's anger and his zeal; they sought his symbolic results—educations that would help their children make their ways in this world well, that would help them be, like Clark, in charge.

Irwin Hyman (1989) rightly notes that "black parents . . . would not be happy if their own children were victims of Joe Clark" (p. 27), but what Hyman did not consider is that they also think that their children will not be. Few parents claim those unredeemed and expurgated children, in part because much of what one sees at Eastside is an exaggeration, a fantasy of how bad things are. The stories of troubled adolescents are far more complicated than the images we see of essentially feral teen-agers in that opening montage. *Lean on Me*'s high school is designed to scare the electorate (it's a Willie Horton school). None of these parents felt sympathy for the dispossessed. Clark simply did what he had to do. Those children belonged to someone else; their children stayed, flourished, and succeeded once the policy-makers backed off and the teachers began to do their jobs.

For my younger African American male students, this was a film that provided them with a victory off a basketball court or a football field. They could grow up to occupy a seat of power (both the Superintendent and the Principal are African American males). They could be caring and strong simultaneously; they could "kick ass" and be a messenger of God at the same time. Not only would they get "the man" (the mayor and his allies), shape up the largely European American faculty, and tweak the nose of a meddlesome matriarch, but they would also get the good woman. Ms. Levias is, after all, obviously smitten. Some of them identified with the student council president and his imitation of Clark; some wanted to take the place of Thomas Sams and be reclaimed by a Joe Clark. All of them saw the spotlight firmly on an African American male winner on a stage from which he was generally excluded. It was a fantasy high; unpleasantness or discordant images were pushed into the background, while the lure of potential, of becoming someone powerful, played center stage.

The few African American female students with whom I talked about the movie were less taken by it than were their male counterparts. Yet they, too, were not put off by some of the stereotypes and negative images, like the opening montage bathroom sequence. They either dismissed those scenes or felt that they did not apply to them. They sympathized with Kneesha, knew boys like the father of her child, and hoped, were they in her place, that Clark was around and that their boyfriend was undergoing a personal transformation under a Clark mentorship. A few of them identified with the role of Ms. Levias and hoped for a potential husband as strong and passionate as Clark appeared to be; a few argued that they would not have threatened to quit, as Levias did, because they understood how hard it was for Clark to do what he was doing. All of them thought the song was important, that you had to have someone who was there for you to make it in this world.

Less easy to reconcile for me was the attitude of an African American administrative colleague, the one who had been interviewed by one of my college students—the man who saw the film each year immediately prior to the start of school "for inspiration." Although I had known that person for some years, I had not known about his affection for *Lean on Me*. From what I knew of his professional history, his administrative style was decidedly not that of Clark. As a former school administrator, I could understand the attraction of a story that allows us sometimes to make our own rules, to free ourselves from what are often cumbersome, tedious, inhumane, bureaucratic constraints. Yes, he admitted, that was one of the reasons he found the film pleasurable. What he found on the screen was also partially what the parents and students found; it was an affirmation of his role in leading an institution in an white world and of taking care of "his kids." Yet, he also found in the film an affirmation of his role in opposition to some of the behaviors he encounters among African American youth, adolescents who expected him to "understand," "to cut" them "some slack." Unlike me, an European American female, he regularly confronts the Mrs. Barrett accusation of turning "on his own people." Clark gave him permission to do so with vigor, to expect that he would face opposition from multiple sides in so doing, and to know that the means would justify the ends. His take on the Mrs. Elliott scene also differed from mine. Elliott represented all those teachers who questioned his motivations and his competence. Mozart was not a symbol for high expectations, but a symbol for another culture's music, one that was of little utility to inner-city youth seeking positive reflections of their own lives. He liked the idea of being able to declare one's self the H.N.I.C. ("head nigger in charge") as Clark did and to make it work. At the film's conclusion Clark is vindicated and students graduate. That good things happened for young people justified abuse from parents and doubts from faculty; the thrill of that victory made the trials of the previous nine months worthwhile.

More inexplicable still was the attitude of several European American colleagues who were teachers. The film does not present what they do in a positive light, and it suggested that European American educators were more often the sources of problems than the sites of solutions. In *Lean on Me* teachers are a benign part of a corrupt system, taken in hand by a dictator, and, through humiliation and verbal abuse, forced to do what they should have been doing in the first place. Yet for them what the film did was vindicate part of a message they have been sending: Schooling is important, responsibility for education is partially on the backs of students and parents, and the existing power structure with its emphasis on regulations and due process gets in the way more than it helps. These teachers resented the legal and procedural "do not do's" of their jobs. They struggled to teach young people, placed in their classrooms by judges, whose conduct remade the dynamics of their classes in ways that multiplied geometrically their tasks. They contended with young people whose learning problems were profound, whose behaviors sometimes bizarre, and whose educational values suspect. They railed against being at the end of a task bus that placed television, social events, extra-curricular sports, films, music, videogames, part-time employment and drugs ahead of them. The thought of a forced mass exodus of ne'er-do-well's identified by them, an exodus without reprisals or appeals, appealed, as did a curriculum that included an emphasis on conduct, appearance, and responsiveness. They saw the film as one depicting a school in which the problems were physically removed, the administration was strong, and the mission was clear.

Lean on Me nowhere suggests that education and learning have anything to do with inquiry and questions. These teachers, however, were able to overlook both the negative images of their profession and unions as well as the somewhat limited perspective presented about schools and schooling. They, after all, would know to extend their instruction beyond the basics. Like the parents, the teachers denied that they had a personal claim to the film's negative images. *They* were not the meek or ineffective practitioners Clark harassed in the gym, but the victims of a system that placed them in unsafe buildings, with untamed children, without sufficient administrative or parental support. I suspect that several of my African American teacher colleagues, many of whom echoed the remarks of their European American peers, agreed with the film's implication that some teachers did not challenge all students equally, that *Lean on Me*'s muted racial indictment of some practitioners was correct. Although, with me, they did not dwell on that part of the film's message, they did suggest that there was some truth in some of the things Clark said to those teachers in the gymnasium.

What was going on with this film was what happens with every text, including the text of the moment, of our shared experiences. We transcribe what we see or what happens in ways that make sense to us, to where we are and what we need at a particular time. Jane Radway (1984) in what is now considered a classic example of reading against the grain, *Reading the Romance: Women, Patriarchy and Popular Literature*, demonstrated that even a text as contrived as the romance novel can become an instrument of liberation to some readers. That we bring to a text different histories, the New Criticism notwithstanding, makes likely that we will take from it different understandings. What matters is what we then do with those understandings.

MAKING SOME SENSE OF MIXED READINGS

So what was I to make of these varied readings? I must admit a retaining affection for my own. I am, by inclination and training, prone to ideological analysis of texts. Academics are rewarded for textual interrogation; it is what many of us do "for a living" and to live with an awareness of our world. Yet such a structured and singular reading might be insufficient, as well as arrogant.

Emile Benveniste (1971) wrote that

> Consciousness of self is only possible if it is experienced by contrast. I use *I* only when I am speaking to someone who will be a *you* in my address. It is this condition of dialogue that is constitutive of *person*, for it implies that reciprocally *I* becomes you in the address of the one who in his turn designates himself as *I*. (pp. 224-225)

An exchange of readings between you and me makes possible my consciousness of self, makes possible unpacking who I am. If that is true, then popular culture, partially because it is accessible, inexpensive, and potentially shared by all of us, can serve as a vehicle for widening what is sometimes called the Great Conversation. Although there might be a border that encloses that conversation, one dictated by a dominant ideological, economic, and political order and its vocabulary, that border becomes visible through conversation and problematic only by opening spaces of dispute, arenas of critique.

We live in a world of stories and we construct our world in the sharing of those stories. In describing such partial narratives, Stanley Aronowitz (1987/88) claimed that "one of the crucial features of discourse, is the intimate tie between knowledge and interest, the latter being understood as a 'standpoint' from which to grasp 'reality'" (p. 103). It was different interests, different positions or standpoints, that took me and those with whom I discussed *Lean on Me* to different films, albeit at the same theaters; it is in the discussion of those differing films, all sharing the same title, that we can construct a world of multiple possibilities. We have been cautioned repeatedly, by feminists, by critical theorists, by neoMarxists, about searching for a common mind; our troubles seem to reside in an inability to operationalize an acceptance of a plurality of minds. My personal persistence in a political reading of *Lean on Me*, one tied closely to ideas associated with critical pedagogy, muted and probably continues to mute my willingness to acknowledge the multiplicity of responses that the film could engender.

Perhaps one way to explain the popularity of the film is not to dwell exclusively on how it affirms the status quo and simplifies some of our more profound educational and social problems but to consider the spaces it offers for resistance to that picture. That does not make the film any more salutary necessarily, but it does suggest that it has more positive power than I was once willing to grant it. And it suggests that we can use our differences as a way to examine the status quo, to identify those parts of it that are problematic or contested, and the ways by which each of us negotiates those areas. Indeed, by revealing how we negotiate within that dominant culture we broaden and begin to alter it. Although such discussions can not be removed from the power relationships that currently define our shared world, nothing can happen without engagement, without a *you* bringing into existence an *I*.

Paglia (1992) suggests that to do otherwise is to consign all readings other than the ones that examine popular culture for its hegemonic language and assumptions to the erroneous ramblings of "the pitifully witless masses [who] are always being brainwashed by the money-grubbing capitalist pigs" (ix). Whereas Zavarzadeh (1991) would argue, with Foucault, that film is a powerful technology of the self and is one of the means by which "the social order fashions the kinds of subjectivities required for its perpetuation" (p. 1), Paglia would invite us to credit the masses with a modicum of cultural intelligence. Radway (1984) writes that we should acknowledge that all of us can and most of us do read against the grain, even in the most stereotypical examples of pop culture texts. Obviously, there is knowledge being created in popular culture that provides meaning in ways we cannot recognize or address until a conversation begins. Asking who benefits from a film like *Lean on Me* and its message is insufficient. Asking who liked it and why, what won our applause and what precipitated our groans, in what ways did we understand this or that portion of the film, and in what ways did our readings diverge and what that might say about who we are, those questions could provide us with a different and potentially more useful discussion, particularly if we are serious about attempts to move from a static understanding of our world to one that is both multi-dimensional and multicultural.

For me there are two additional reasons to advocate going beyond the ways we normally address issues related to popular culture, one social and one personal. In a recent article for *Holistic Education* Christine Shea (1996) suggests that although the term "postmodern" defies definition, there are three distinct "varieties of postmodern critique" (p. 42). The first she associates with deconstruction. "The nihilistic postmoderns argue that reality is pure illusion; everything is intertextual, not causal or predictive. Their preferred social critique is introspective interpretation . . . As political agnostics, they propose that all political views are mere constructions" (p. 43). The second group are the critical poststructuralist postmoderns. Sensitive to the oppression of and potential for inscription in dominant systems, "these critical postmoderns support a wide range of political and social alliances and recommend moving back and forth among the various discourses." Their position is "one of critique, opposition, and emancipation from, rather than one of creation and construction" (p. 44). The third group she identifies as constructive ecological postmodernists. Although I am unwilling to, at least in this paper, engage in a discussion of the implications of that typology, I am intrigued with the notion that we move beyond positions that are defined strictly in opposition to or emancipation from to positions in which we act, in which we are granted a measure of agency and begin to construct rather than continuously destruct. As Benveniste observes, the construction of self is relational, it requires a "you" as well as an "I." It is, however, more than a discussion of opposites and distinctions; it is a dialogue, a social generative act. So, by paying more attention to divergent constructions of realities and by examining them as equally real we might enter into that dialogue captured by the metaphor of the Great Conversation. It matters little that I bring down the master's house if I do not work to build an alternative.

On a more personal level, Andrew, in *Concepts in Film Theory* (1984), points out that "the cinema in a unique way merges public reality and private dreams." He argues that we can continue to be interested in the philosophical or analytic aspects of film, with meanings, representations, signifiers and the signified, but that we cannot ignore the more human aspect of those movies. We cannot nor should we put aside our inclination to respond to them on a personal and intuitive level, to answer "the call expressed by the text in the aspirations and gutterals of its voice." An expression is different from a meaning; it is almost a primal response, one shaped by the personal, by fantasy and aspiration. It, like our rational thoughts, can be manipulated by our culture, but we are not necessarily enslaved thereby. Mind and feeling are interdependent.

> Certainly this is not an untroubled interdependence, but it is one that gives to viewing, reading, and writing a place in human life different from philosophy, analysis, or sheer behavior. This border zone of reading is the life of the imagination. It is worth as much as we imagine it to be. (p. 190)

Perhaps one of the things my experience with *Lean on Me* has taught me is that singular readings deny what could be a supremely human enterprise, a conversation that incorporates both head and heart. It might be in an exchange within these spaces, of our desires as much as our reason, that we can find the building blocks of alternative social constructions.

REFERENCES

Andrew, D. (1984). *Concepts in film theory.* New York: Oxford University Press.

Aronowitz, S. (1987/88). Postmodernism and politics. *Social Text, 18*, 99-115.

Benveniste, E. (1971). Subjectivity in language. In M. E. Meek (Trans.), *Problems in general linguistics* (pp. 223-230). Coral Gables, FL: University of Miami Press.

Denby, D. (1989, March 20). Grand illusion. *New York*, pp. 73-75.

Giroux, H., & McLaren, P. (1992). Media hegemony: Toward a critical pedagogy of representation. In *Media knowledge: Readings in popular culture, pedagogy, and critical citizenship* (pp. xv-xxxiv). Albany, NY: SUNY.

Harrington, M. (1986). *The dream of deliverance in American politics.* New York: Alfred A. Knopf.

Hyman, I. (1989, April 26). The 'make believe world' of 'Lean on Me.' *Education Week*, pp. 27, 29.

National Commission on Excellence in Education. (1983). *A nation at risk: The imperatives for educational reform.* Washington, DC: Government Printing Office.

Paglia, C. (1992). *Sex, art, and American culture.* New York: Vintage Books.

Radway, J. (1984). *Reading the romance: Women, patriarchy and popular literature.* Chapel Hill: University of North Carolina Press.

Riffaterre, M. (1978). *Semiotics of Poetry.*

Schickel, R. (1989, March 13). Tough love. *Time*, p. 82.

Shea, C. (1996, Autumn). Critical and constructive postmodernism: The transformative power of holistic education. *Holistic Education 9*, pp. 40-50.

Spring, J. (1976). *The sorting machine: National educational policy since 1945.* New York: Longman.

Traube, E.G. (1992). *Dreaming identities: Class, gender and generation in 1980s Hollywood movies.* Boulder, CO: Westview Press.

Weiler, M., & Pearce, W.B. (1992). Ceremonial discourse: The rhetorical ecology of the Reagan administration. In M. Weiler & W.B. Pearce (Eds.), *Reagan and public discourse in America* (pp. 11-42). Tuscaloosa: University of Alabama Press.

Zavarzadeh, M. (1991). *Seeing films politically.* Albany: State University of New York Press.

Zavarzadeh, M., & Morton, D. (1991). Theory pedagogy politics: The crisis of 'the subject' in the humanities. In D. Morton & M. Zavarzadeh (Eds.), *Theory/pedagogy/politics: Texts for change.* (pp. 1-32). Urbana, IL: University of Illinois Press.

CHAPTER TWO

Teachers Reading Teachers: Using Popular Culture to Reposition the Perspective of Critical Pedagogy in Teacher Education

Donald E. Guenther and David M. Dees

The critical pedagogy project, specifically the work of Peter McLaren, has explored in enormous detail the issue of "voice." As McLaren (1989) acknowledges "a *student's voice* is not a reflection of the world as much as it is a *constitutive force that both mediates and shapes reality within historically constructed practices and relationships of power*" (p. 230). He continues highlighting that the "*teacher voice* reflects the values, ideologies, and structuring principles that teachers use to understand and mediate the histories, cultures and subjectivities of their students" (p. 230). Thus, for McLaren, the dramatic "play" that is created within a classroom is dialogue of voices. This dialogue is between the historical/contextual power relationships that have constructed our students' reality and the mediation of the teacher's ideological interpretation of these realities. For McLaren, the teacher, sensitive to the power plays that the dominant culture has used to create students' perspectives, has great "*emancipatory power*" by providing "a critical context within which students can understand the various social forces and configurations of power that have helped give shape to their own voices" (p. 231). Like McLaren, we agree with the critical pedagogical project of questioning and challenging the sexist, racist, ablest, and homophobic ideological perspectives that infiltrate the cultural "realities" of our society. However, by presenting teachers as the "great emancipators" over the "power-structure" created student realities, it becomes fundamental to ask ourselves some salient questions. For example, by taking this perspective, are we truly repositioning the power structure of our society or are we just inverting the power structure to our own theoretical/ideological perspectives by controlling classroom dialogue and ideology? If we as teachers are serving as great emancipators, what type of society are we emancipating our students towards? Lastly, are our students that naive as to not recognize in any sense how the dominant ideology has been disseminated to them through their neighborhood, classroom, place of worship, the media, or any other such cultural institution that they have encountered as they have created their own cultural dialogue? These are tough questions, yet vital to ask ourselves as we participate in the dialogue of voices that occurs within our classrooms.

For the critical theorist, liberation from the dominant hegemonic structure of our society is a process by which "the oppressed are educated about their situation and about their potential capacity to alter it" (Fay, 1987, p. 205). This liberation "awareness" is conceived in terms of an emancipatory democracy, one in which the voices of all are included in the social dialogue.

As McLaren (1994) in his later edition proposes, "schools as democratic public spheres function to dignify meaningful dialogue and action and to give students the opportunity to learn the language of social responsibility" (p. 237). However, this dialogue has a specific focus and agenda, one that is keyed to "the idea of democracy as a *social movement* grounded in a fundamental respect for *individual freedom* and *social justice*" (pp. 237-238). Yet by setting this specific democratic boundary, the question arises as to how much individual freedom are our students' voices given if they must be framed within this perspective of liberation, social justice, and social movement? What type of democratic dialogue are we creating? David Smith (1991) highlights this critical theory problem when he states:

> Dialogue in the critical sense becomes dialogue with a hidden agenda: I speak *to* you to inform you of your victimization and oppression rather than *with* you in order that together we create a

world which does justice to both of us. The interest of the critical
tradition is not just persuasion but a predetermination to shape the
social order in fixed directions. . . (p. 196).

This has been our dilemma as critical pedagogues. We believe in
challenging and repositioning the sexist, racist, ablest, and homophobic
agenda that devalues the voices of difference. Additionally, we believe
that the current structure of the educational system within our own
university and the public schools is an atmosphere that devalues
teacher/student knowledge and serves to create an intellectual
oppression that limits the educative experience. Yet how can we as
teacher educators accomplish the task of raising student awareness in
our own classroom practice without creating a dominant ideological
agenda that devalues and depreciates our own students' lived
experience, knowledge, and existing frame of reference? We began to
believe that popular culture could provide a space to open a different
type of democratic dialogue.

READING A DEMOCRATIC DIALOGUE

The first critical question that must arise before stepping into a
democratic mode of being is to address the notion of what type of
democracy we as teacher educators are envisioning. As Lummis (1996)
notes ". . . democracy is not the name of any particular arrangement of
political or economic institutions. It describes an ideal, not a method for
achieving it. It is not a kind of government, but an end of government;
not a historically existing institution, but a historical project" (p. 22).
And as John Dewey (1916) echoed earlier,

> A democracy is more than a form of government; it is primarily a
> mode of associated living, of conjoint communicated experience. The
> extension in space of the number of individuals who participate in an
> interest so that each has to refer his own action to that of others, and
> to consider the action of others to give point and direction to his own,
> is equivalent to the breaking down of those barriers of class, race, and
> national territory which kept men from perceiving the full import of
> their activity (p. 101).

For Dewey, as well as ourselves, this "conjoint communicated
experience" should occur within the realm of education. Moreover,

educational systems should be designed to facilitate meaningful shared experiences. Dewey (1916) describes this educational environment in the following manner:

> In order to have a large number of values in common, all the members of the group must have an equable opportunity to receive and to take from others. There must be a large variety of shared undertakings and experiences. Otherwise the influences which educate some into masters, educate others into slaves. *And the experience of each party loses in meaning, when the free interchange of varying modes of life-experience is arrested* [italics added] (pp. 97-98).

We were left with a challenge. How could we create meaningful shared experiences within our own classroom space that allowed for the "free interchange of varying modes of life-experience" from which our students could learn from each other and we could learn from them, while simultaneously remaining sensitive to the racist, sexist, ablest, and homophobic agenda that pervades much of our American culture?

In an effort to translate our own concerns into sound educational practice while meeting the challenge outlined by John Dewey, we felt that one of the most common and meaningful "shared" experiences for our students could be found in popular culture. Popular culture could provide a source for dialogue in our own classrooms that engages their lived experience. But the possibilities for dialogue that popular culture could provide presented us with a new dilemma. What were we "meaning" by popular culture?

As Ray B. Browne (1987) notes, popular culture is the practical Humanities. It can be used to overcome illiteracy, to keep people in school, to encourage life-long learning and to energize schooling and teaching methods (p. 1). Browne views popular culture as

> . . . the everyday lifeblood of the experiences and thinking of all of us: the daily, vernacular, common cultural environment around us all, the culture we inherit from our forbears, use throughout our lives, and then pass on to our descendants. Popular culture is the television we watch, the movies we see, the fast food, or slow food, we eat, the clothes we wear, the music we sing and hear, the things we spend our money for, our attitude toward life. It is the whole society we live in,

that which may or may not be distributed by the mass media. It is
virtually our whole world (p. 2).

Lawrence Grossberg's (1986) insights which he gained from his own
research and reflection on teaching the popular, lead to his assertion
that the popular demands pleasure before understanding, or as he states,
"popular culture is what remains of culture after subtracting the part
that is worthy of serious critical consideration ('high culture')" (p. 177).

Like Browne we see popular culture as energizing schooling and
teaching methods. Like Grossberg we want to remove ourselves from a
tradition of academic criticism that deals with popular culture by way
of value systems and classifications that protect professorial authority.
Our own concerns over creating a meaningful shared experience in our
classrooms were foreshadowed by Grossberg when he stated that
cultural theory's tendency to limit criticism of popular culture to
analyses of ideological effects prevents the acknowledgment of the
affective power of the popular. Thus we reasoned that if there was to be
the "free interchange of varying modes of life-experiences" from which
our students could learn, our initial forays into experiencing products of
popular culture as a collective audience of educator and students had to
be free of everything but our own initial engagement, with no prior
discussion or analysis.

With these definitional elements of popular culture in mind, we felt
it is important to develop *with* our students an understanding of
democratic "critical citizenship." Schwoch, White, and Reilly (1992)
define critical citizenship as "a philosophy of pedagogy that. . .
promotes the teaching of egalitarianism, the values of social difference,
and a qualitative concern with individual ability to master the skills
needed to gain knowledge throughout life" (p. xi). Additionally, for
these authors, one of the skills that must be developed is a critical
awareness of the messages found within popular culture. They state "a
mainstream, passive, accepting reception and reading of an array of
media texts—such as television news, romance films, or advertising
ultimately supports and reaffirms a dominant ideology in contemporary
American culture founded on beliefs in the positive values of consumer
capitalism. . ." (p. x). Thus for them, and ourselves, we need to open
the awareness of our students and encourage ". . . a more active,
engaging, questioning way of reception and reading. . ." of media
culture (p. x). Yet, once again, we were back to our dilemma: How do
we open our students' readings of dominant culture, without converting

them to our own ideological agenda, and thus devaluing their lived experiences and knowledge?

READING POPULAR CULTURE

Although we had found a common and relevant experience in popular culture, we were still staring the main critical pedagogical dilemma in the face. What were we to do? What follows is our attempt to use the shared experience of popular culture in a classroom practice that translates the ideas and principles of critical pedagogy into an educational practice that integrates, reflects and appreciates student voice, student knowledge, and student affective response while simultaneously providing these voices with skills that will help them develop a critical citizenship awareness.

CREATING A DEMOCRATIC DIALOGUE: A BEGINNING

To begin this process of a "different" type of dialogue we began by asking these tough questions specifically around the curricular choices we made in our own classroom practices. As teachers who have a great appreciation, or should we say "addiction" to popular culture, we have for a long period in our own classrooms realized the generative implications that popular culture could have for our own pedagogical practices. We have both resisted the notion that university "knowledge" needs to be grounded in traditional scholarly textual traditions. As Ava Collins (1994) suggested, as teacher educators we had long ago become sensitive to "[t]he desire to maintain a specific form of 'critical thinking' rooted in one technology-—print-—simply does not respect the mutability and diversity of institutions, or of various cultural forms—oral, written, imaged, electronic, in short all that traditionally constitutes popular culture—of transmission of information and value" (p. 60). So, as we showed our popular culture pieces to our students, we were struck by how they were not as excited as we were by the critical readings we had developed. We found our students had learned to play the game, joining in with our criticism, in an effort to make the teacher happy. Like Robert Bullough, Jr. and Andrew Gitlin (1995) noted, we found that "[o]ur project, and the public theories we presented, was not their project; being well-trained students, they mastered our discourse to give it back to us but, apparently unaffected, left us to engage in their lives' work as though they had never been in our classes" (p. 7). As educators, we had not turned our own critical pedagogical perspective onto our own classroom practices. We were faced with the same critical pedagogical dilemma: How do we encourage our students to engage in personal critical reflection on important societal issues without imposing and forcing "a" truth perspective onto them? Could popular culture, a genre that many, if not all of our students were familiar with, even provide a space for a critical perspective that could empower future teachers as they prepared to embark on their own professional journeys? We began the process of reassessing our own work with popular culture within our teacher education practice.

TEACHERS READING OUR OWN CHOICES OF POPULAR CULTURE

David M. Dees

Hoping that popular culture may connect more with my students' own personal stories, I chose a piece that I knew was a popular presentation and critique of society at large and additionally dealt specifically with the school setting. We were going to watch an episode of *The Simpsons* which revealed the problem of school funding, challenged the notion that anyone could teach, and offered an absurd, albeit successful solution (combining a prison with a public school) to increase the financial capital of our public schools. I felt this episode could lead to a tremendous discussion by my students on these issues. As I announced what we were doing that night in class, twenty-three of the students showed signs of appreciation, while two remained silent and disinterested. Those were the two that forced my reflection. Why were they not excited? What was the problem with watching *The Simpsons*? Why were they not open to having fun? Because our classroom had a very open policy from the very beginning, these students began to voice their opposition.

One student felt that *The Simpsons* reduced important social issues to trivial and comical concerns that did not encourage any type of larger reflection. The other student, given her religious convictions, felt that the characters in this show encouraged and glorified disrespectful behavior that helped to lead to the moral corruption that is so prevalent in our society. Both felt that I as a teacher had marginalized their voice, and forced them into critical reflection with no regard to their personal knowledge and belief systems. Finally, one of them stated, "Isn't that the exact type of classroom behavior you are constantly warning us about?" These students were right. The piece of popular culture I chose had its own agenda. *The Simpsons* characters, because of the show's longtime success in our culture, had become cultural icons, representations of certain patterns and modes of being that all, whether they liked the show or not, had become familiar with in one way or another. Additionally, this show was known to my students as one that challenged the status quo, so what new knowledge or perspectives was I hoping to gain? I had learned through these experiences the popular culture that one uses automatically controls the readings and sets the tone for the student perceived "accepted" readings that should arise from this type of encounter. I was once again to the critical pedagogical dilemma: How do I encourage and appreciate student voice, allow my own voice to speak, yet not force my students into accepting "a" preconceived "truth"? I had to start over.

Donald E. Guenther

My choice of a popular culture piece to augment student understanding and classroom discussion of the idea of meritocracy had much to do with personal memories of watching an old movie on television many years earlier. The film was the screen adaptation of William Saroyan's *The Human Comedy*. I specifically remembered a scene wherein two male students in a classroom argue openly over the affections of a female member of the class as well as over their social standing in the school and community. The scene was ultimately a paean to free enterprise and healthy competition, unencumbered by special privilege and unequal power. The teacher character had a stirring speech to deliver to the two boys, complete with patriotic background music.

The movie's appearance on home video was a happy day for me. I would now be able to use the classroom scene as a teaching tool. I thought the students might find it interesting to see Mickey Rooney when he was a teenager. I was certain the scene offered a richness in dialogue and detail that the class could use to its advantage in increasing awareness of the effects of social class on life chances in a school classroom.

The quality of the student response to the initial viewing came as a definite shock. Initial comments were of surprise to the fact that the film was in BLACK and WHITE!! There even seemed to be a few boos. While discussion did occur around my desired topics, considerable time was devoted to the question of technology in media, the ethics of colorization, the relative devaluing of the black and white image, what was happening in daily life and the world in 1943 and who was Mickey Rooney! Clearly a generational gap loomed large. My students and I were reading with different eyes—set apart by time, technology and pedagogy. Suddenly, the reading of popular culture in my classroom had become more problematic.

OUR CURRENT PRACTICE

To begin this reflective process, we had to admit to ourselves and accept the multiple readings that occur within popular culture. Schwoch, White, and Reilly (1992) highlight that "the study of media culture often means abandonment of the search for some sort of singular, overarching, 'truth' or 'correct reading' in favor of multiple and competing interpretations" (p. 121). Additionally, these authors contend that this is the true power of popular culture within an educational setting. They continue stating "[t]his [multiple readings] is a positive attribute in the study of popular media culture, because it allows for experience in the practice of reasonable argumentation, the respectful differing of opinions, and the value of debate. . . [s]tudents and teachers should appreciate the evidence of ambiguity" (p. 121). This ambiguity is exquisitely demonstrated through Grossberg's (1986) assertion that it is necessary to recognize that the world is affectively and semantically structured. He is referring to the intensity or desire with which we invest the world and our relations to it. We are placed into an apparently immediate relation to the world through our affective investments. Our struggle with our affective investments is what defines "the popular" (185). To convert our students to "a" critical pedagogy perspective as the singular reading of the media "message" was thus to devalue the ambiguity of living life in a diverse and multi-perspective world. Our previously described classroom examples illustrate this ambiguity well. We discovered that even the choice of media could set its own agenda into the types of affective response and dialogue that could occur within our classroom environment. Thus, we then turned our focus onto this newly identified issue, the choosing of a particular representation of popular culture.

Having learned from our *The Simpsons* and *The Human Comedy* "mistakes," we felt it was important to choose a piece of popular culture that had not yet fallen into the societal, concretized, iconic readings of each ideology and representation. We had to attempt to filter the imposed readings forced on consumers of popular culture, including those readings suggested or imposed by the teacher. However, we were also sensitive to the fact that television itself limits the readings and interpretations that it deems acceptable by the populace. As Ken Kantor (1994) notes

> Situation comedies have. . . capitalized on varied images of the teacher, as spinster or bachelor, mother or father, entertainer, missionary, moral example, rebel, provocateur, idealist. Administrators are often depicted as pompous, dictatorial, old-fashioned, but rarely sympathetic, and students are variously dim-witted, mischievous, manipulative, innocent, resistant, apathetic, hip, motivated or unmotivated, cooperative or uncooperative. . . ultimately the dominant form seems to require playing to rather than debunking stereotypes (p. 186).

Therefore, we had to choose a "new" piece of popular culture, free from the concretized readings, yet representative of the stereotypical representations of the "lived" events that occur within the school setting. By choosing such a piece, we could use popular culture's stereotypical readings of the educational experience and our students' "lived" interpretation of life in schools (from their own lives and the teacher education program) to co-create dialogues around the readings of teachers in the media and their own life. This dialogue could open a space for critical awareness towards both life in schools and life in popular culture.

READING OUR CHOICE

We felt that such a piece of popular culture was represented in a television midseason replacement show entitled *The Faculty*. This show, starring Merideth Baxter as an "almost" burned-out assistant vice-principal, Flynn Sullivan, featured many of the stereotypical images of life in a public school. These images included such stereotypes as the clueless and uninformed principal, the bitter, quick-witted "leave-my-things-alone" school secretary, an uptight history teacher, a narrow sex-driven industrial arts teacher, a passionless yet caring English teacher, and a new dreamy-eyed "change-the-world" first-year teacher. As the episode progressed, the audience realized that the main focal point was how vice-principal Sullivan was willing to give up instead of fighting to "save just one kid," a problem student who had been disrespectful to a teacher. Drawing from a recently discovered teacher journal of her first year as an educator, Sullivan's own words come back to haunt her, as she begins to see that after years in the profession, she was becoming just like one of those non-caring, burned-out teachers she hated when she started. Sullivan's teacher journey, from the passionate journal entries to where she finds herself now, is being lived out in front of her and the audience, through the first-year teacher character, Amanda Duvall. As Amanda enters the lounge for the first time, both Sullivan and the audience witness the thrill and excitement of her new beginning, only to see it fall away when she enters again after first class stating, "O.K. . . .let me tell you something. . . you cannot put thirty-five students in one room and expect them to learn anything. . . because. . . I have news for you. . . there are a lot of students who do not want to be here." Vice-principal Sullivan is being forced to re-evaluate what her job is as an educator. As expected, Ms. Sullivan is able to convince the problem child to do the right thing and apologize to the teacher, while convincing herself that she is not one of the burned-out educators that she so despised so long ago. Although the story line suffered from being stereotypical, sappy, and predictable, this episode did contain moments of great humor and satire. Additionally, this episode highlighted that given the oppressive structure of our current public school system, it is amazing that teachers are able to educate anyone in any manner within this type of environment.

As educators, we felt that this episode would be a solid pedagogical tool that appreciates the meaningful shared experiences within the realm of popular culture that exist for our students and ourselves for several reasons. First and foremost, we felt that this piece of popular culture dealt within the realm of teaching. As Phil Jackson (1992) states "it does seem reasonable to expect that material whose content explicitly referred to teaching would in the long run have a greater chance of having. . . an impact than would material that had nothing to do with teaching at all" (p. 68). For us, this represents the essence of a meaningful shared experience. Second, given that both of us teach a senior level course that is required for undergraduates to complete prior to their student teaching, we felt that this episode, specifically the role of the new teacher, may provide some insight for our students as they are themselves in the process of creating their own teacher self. Third, because popular culture is so prevalent in our students' lived experiences, this episode allowed us to acknowledge, appreciate, and discover our students' engagement with and knowledge of popular culture itself and of life in schools. Fourth, because of the "newness" of this show, the characters, message, and tone of the program had not yet fallen into the societal trap of concretized, iconic, and predictable representations.

READING OUR OWN CLASSROOM PRACTICE

After making the decision on which piece of popular culture to use, we then turned to the issue of sound classroom practice. How could we, without imposing our own reading of this text, engage and encourage our students' perspectives and voices regarding this teacher representation? We decided the best manner would be to allow the students to respond free from our own critical pedagogy perspective by silencing our own voice at the beginning of the viewing process. Without any discussion on our part, we asked our students to engage and respond in any manner they desired to this episode. After introducing the show, we sat back and watched with our students, allowing them to engage the show free from our own readings and interpretations. After the episode, we encouraged them to submit in writing any response, attitude, feeling, or reading that they had while engaging this program. After receiving their responses, we were impressed at our students' ability to relax and enjoy an image, while simultaneously focusing a critical eye on the images of teachers that were before them. Some of these responses were as follows:

> In *The Faculty*, I found many common stereotypes of teachers and teaching portrayed. Most of these stereotypes were considered norms and were the basis for most of the humor. The teachers also considered the students more as "cattle" than individuals. Things that needed to be "vaccinated." . . . The new teacher was motivated, idealistic, yet panicked about teaching. While jokes were leveled at her expense, she also served to remind the other teachers of their cynicism and loss of ideals. . . . In the end, I could see that the show had a message, but it was based on so many preconceived notions of teaching that I was sickened.

After reading this, one would think that this student had a complete distaste for this media representation. However, what is interesting is that this student herself said, "Can't someone laugh at something funny, yet still be able to criticize it and share with others why this is not true?"

Another student, after going through the stereotypical representations, stated:

> Teachers have high aspirations/goals at first. Little or no preparation/tools for dealing with apathy—therefore, get discouraged easily and give up. Older teachers are embarrassed to care/sacrifice for students—it's against the norm—it's not what colleagues expect of each other.

To this student, her "lived" reality of her own school experience, her field placements in the teacher education program, and the modeling she had seen from the teacher education faculty, confirmed this popular culture's representation of teacher transformation. While she was able to see the stereotypical images, she was also able to highlight the pieces of "truth" represented within this show. Additionally, she highlights for us as teacher educators the power that we have in teacher modeling in our own classrooms. As we discussed this response in class, this student noted that in her own educational experiences within the college of education, she has seen first hand "burned-out" ideological faculty that have limited and devalued their own role as educators. Another student added a different form of the same sentiment.

> I found this show quite humorous for reasons I'm not real comfortable with. This said volumes about society's twisted view of education. There was an exploitation of the lack of discipline in the school. . . . Some of the situations are inherently funny just because of the fact that they propagated popular misconceptions in society that play on the stereotypical role of teachers, apathy in teaching after an extended period of employment, disorganization on the part of everyone. . . . Hopefully, these things are funny because they are exaggerations.

Unlike the previous student, this person's "lived" experience had not been confirmed by the popular cultural representations. This student had seen experienced teachers who were not burned out, still cared about professional development, still cared about the students, etc. For her, this was funny because it was exaggeration, rather than a representation of the "lived" experience she had had in the school world.

The classroom dialogue that developed around these "reading" differences centered on the multiple realities of teaching that exist within the culture of a school. For the first student, her field placements and previous life experience led her to believe that burn-out is an inevitable result of the structure of our public schools. For the second student, her field placements and life experience led her to create a "reality" of teaching that was able to avoid teacher burn-out. After further dialogue, the class felt that the "reality" of teacher burn-out is somewhere in between these two perspectives. Additionally, this class, after our dialogue, felt that the "reality" of teacher burn-out is centered around teacher choice. A teacher either allows burn-out to "take over her world" or he/she resists burn-out by focusing on the passion and commitment that the individual once had for the profession. Then, there were responses that were critical of the entertainment value of the show as well as its content.

> First, I didn't really think the show was all that funny—I know these sitcom comedies are supposed to be humorous, but I really didn't find this one entertaining. Second—I feel that the teachers were portrayed in a negative light. They were portrayed as if they were dumb and "airheads." I found it almost insulting how childish and undereducated the audience was supposed to perceive them. They also appeared very hostile toward each other and toward school administrators. . . . Most of the situations and actions of the characters seemed unbelievable and unrealistic. . . .Overall, not realistic, not humorous, not entertaining sitcom.

Another student chose to describe the faculty as "airheads" but used this definition as a kind of personal empowerment:

> Coming from a future teacher's point of view, I enjoyed *The Faculty*. I don't know how realistic it was. The principal was a quack. But it did show the side of teachers and other faculty that I never saw as a student. I can only hope I teach at a school where the principal is like

the one on the show so I won't be intimidated by authority. Although I don't see that happening.

Also, the faculty seemed so airheaded. I was trying to be polite but I couldn't think of another way to put it. It sets me at ease in a funny kind of way. That these people I'll be working with are just humans. I give it a "thumbs up" perhaps only because I want to be a teacher (like the new teacher on the show).

Finally, we were impressed with the students who already had a "developmental/stage-like" perspective about their budding teacher careers as the following excerpt illustrates:

I thought the show was cute. It was nice to see a new teacher in the atmosphere with the older, experienced teachers. I also think that it is a good idea to keep a journal of our first year of teaching, when everything is new and exciting. Then years later, when we are a little bored or tired of the same thing, we can read the journal to remind us of how happy and exciting it was our first year. It is a good idea to keep in touch with new teachers to remind the experienced teachers of how they acted and why they became teachers.

From these few excerpts, the multiple readings and affective responses that each of our students had regarding a shared experience are very apparent. Though not surprising, it reminds us again of the multiple levels of awareness that our students have regarding the societal images that exist within our culture. Our students are not naive when it comes to engaging a media representation. Each of them was able to see the stereotypical representations they encountered in this form of popular culture. Each of them noticed and acknowledged the sense of unreality from "the constraint of the half-hour time limit . . ." in which ". . . problems must be quickly identified and even more quickly resolved" (Kantor, 1994, p. 186). Each of our students were able to realize Anthony Smith's (1985) claim that "[e]very generation of technologies of perception has left behind a newly reduced version of the human mind or limited image of the world" (p. 13). Additionally, each of them was able to draw from their own experiences in an effort to critically evaluate the teachers (whether on film or in person) that have been placed before them. Thus, for some there was a sense of reality, for others there was a sense of fear for the public perception, and yet for others it was a complete and total farce. This multi-layered shared experience created a space for us to begin a dialogue *with* our students around the issue of multiple readings that occur within a classroom experience.

After reviewing their responses, we then returned to our classrooms to explore with our students a model of interpretation of Reel to Real life (Guenther & Dees, 1994). This model serves to help our students realize the multiple factors that engage their own perceptions and readings of "Real" teaching. This model attempts to give students a means through which they can assess their own evaluation and interpretation of this television show. As conceptualized, the model brings to the foreground the filtering influence of personal experience, schooling and media technology (from popular film and television to videotaping of student teaching) on students' perception of their worlds. As Collins suggests (1994) "[h]ow can we address the issue of how students assign value to texts, of how they construct their own evaluative paradigms in relation to the evaluative paradigms they encounter in the classroom and what that relation is, when we have not explicitly addressed the issue of how value is assigned to any text by anyone, including teachers and critics, except in reference to the accepted wisdom of the canon?"(p. 58). Our model, and our process in presenting this model, attempts to explicitly address how we as teachers have assigned value to our students' readings. In turn, our students are presented with a process model, one they can choose to accept or reject, but a model from which we can enhance their own reading of the popular cultural pieces they engage in their lived experiences. In this model, students are shown how they draw from their lived experiences (in public schools public schools, teacher education field placements, parents, politicians, media, etc.) to create their own "real" teacher self. Additionally, due to the circular nature of this model, students are able to see how readings turn on other readings, constantly re-positioning and re-interpreting themselves, requiring the students to realign their thinking, their attitudes, and their perceptions of "lived" experience. Through this classroom exercise, students are able to see that, just as in the media there is no one final reading, in their own teacher self there is no final "real" or ideal teacher that they should become. Teaching itself has multiple readings, each of which is related to and created by the "lived" experiences one is allowed to have. Just as one student viewed this show as a "true"

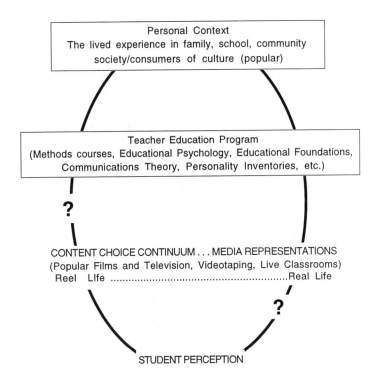

**A Selective Perception Model Illustrating the
Active Involvement of Teacher Education Students
in the Development of Critical Citizenship**

representation, others viewed it as unrealistic and sickening. Which one was correct? Through dialoguing around the multiple readings of this television episode, along with dialogue around a process model, our students came to realize, through a meaningful shared experience that appreciated their knowledge of popular culture and teaching, that life itself is multiple. Life itself is tied to the experiences that one has, or better yet, to the experiences one has been allowed to have. As one student, whom earlier in the semester shouted, "I don't care what Peter McLaren says!," eloquently stated during this dialogue, " I guess this is like the whole point of resistance theory. As teachers we better realize that our students have life experiences that color the way they see us [teachers], T.V. and school."

At this point in the process we allowed our own critical pedagogy voice to speak. Through dialogue, we began to question our students on some of the critical aspects of our society that were avoided in this representation of popular culture. For example, when viewing this episode, it was interesting to note the absence of people of color in the school and on the faculty. Additionally, we found it interesting that the producers of the show placed a "Rainbow Coalition" poster on the wall in the office yet failed to address or even mention any of the salient issues that have evolved around this public education debate. Was it some hidden message and/or agenda the writers and producers of the show were trying to share with the audience? Was it just some colorful prop piece that the studio thought would look nice on the wall? Whatever the reason, we were able to highlight to our students that our own experience in reading popular culture and educational images caused us as teachers to focus our "reading" on specific images that we deem to be relevant to the critical pedagogy perspective. Therefore, through this experience, we were able to demonstrate to ourselves and our students that the reading of popular culture, like the reading of life itself, is keyed to one's experiences and ideological frame from which the individual engages the world. Our students were able to recognize how ideology affects presentation and interpretation. Additionally, we were able to address the issues of power in interpretation that can arise through media representations.

The dialogue around this issue became dynamic. As one student noted in this class discussion, ". . . this show was clearly geared towards white-middle class America. . . so to show people of color or address the Rainbow Coalition, like how the show *Ellen* has been avoiding homosexuality, would challenge the audience too much, reduce their ratings, and kill the show." This may be a possible reading, however, others in the class challenged this student's assumption. As the dialogue continued, another student stated "What do you think, there is some sort of conspiracy in television to make everyone think white-middle class?" Some felt there is, others felt like a third student who said, "Man, Oliver Stone would be proud of you conspiracy people." Whether or not the media power bloc is involved in a cultural conspiracy is not the issue we were trying to address. What we wanted our students to see is that life experience and ideological perspective guides the interpretations we allow ourselves to "read." Additionally, we were able to demonstrate to our students that reflection on these interpretations, and dialoguing with others who have a different ideological perspective, allows us to expand our own readings and interpretations, which in turn will affect our future engagements with diverse opinions. Finally, it was obvious by both the tone and flow of the dialogue that everyone in the classroom audience of *The Faculty* had their own individual affective response. Popular culture served as a medium for our students to see the importance of this type of interpretive reflection.

Through this experience, we also learned to reposition our own perspective towards dialogue itself. Remaining sensitive to our students' readings while acknowledging our own critical perspective, the art of dialogue must be explored. As Gadamer (1975) suggested

> To conduct a conversation means to allow oneself to be conducted by the subject matter to which the partners in the dialogue are oriented. . . . It requires that one does not try to argue the other person down but that one really considers the weight of the other's opinion. . . . A person skilled at the "art" of questioning is a person who can prevent questions from being suppressed by the dominant opinion (p. 367).

As Gadamer suggests, this is the skill of interpretation—being able to identify ones own prejudices yet also being able to give oneself over to the other in the art of conversation. For teaching, this is the art of allowing our students to truly express their voice through a meaningful shared experience as we educators focus on giving ourselves over to the conversation that arises out of these multiple interpretations.

Both our students and ourselves were reminded of the impact of "lived" reality. As educators, we were reminded of the impact of a meaningful shared experience that appreciates students' knowledge. We were all reminded that "when students step into a classroom, they do not shed their cultural and social context; they understand that. . . technological changes affect the dynamics of an institution whose central work had been the definition and circulation of information and knowledge" (Collins, 1994, p. 58). This exercise demonstrated to everyone involved the knowledge each of us have regarding media representations, specifically the knowledge of sitcom "reality." Additionally, this exercise highlighted that this knowledge has various and multiple interpretations and readings that are irreducible to a single unified whole.

TEACHERS READING TEACHERS: OUR METAPHOR

We began this discussion by highlighting our dilemma within critical theory. How can we as educators, without imposing our own agenda, help our students to develop an understanding of the importance of accepting the multiple readings that occur within our society? We felt that popular culture could provide such a space to model this type of awareness. For others, it may be something completely different. The point is that whatever one chooses, it should be a meaningful shared experience that taps into and appreciates the knowledge and voices of the students within the classroom space. Additionally, it requires that one reads their own reading in an effort to resist imposing an agenda on the lived experience of students. Finally, it requires an educational practice that allows students to present their own voice in lived experience free from the teacher's filtered perception. As highlighted in our model through the question marks, it is fundamental to reflect at which point the teacher's interpretation should enter the classroom dialogue.

From this experience, we were able to model for our students the importance of multiple readings within a shared event. Additionally, we provided them with a tool to realize how they come to have their readings of the "real" teacher. Through dialogue, they also came to realize that for each of them, even though they all had the same Kent State education, their life experiences and attitudes towards the act of teaching were extremely different. They also came to realize the importance of deconstructing their own perspectives in an effort to avoid the trappings of a single reading to knowledge, life, and their future students. Finally, from their own knowledge, not ours, they came to see the importance and appreciation of multiplicity of life experience, which for us is the goal of our critical pedagogical project.

For us, the goals of critical pedagogy must include being critical of a) our own classroom practice and ideological agenda, b) the media, and c) sexist, racist, ablest, and homophobic perspectives that pervade much of our American culture. Additionally, we feel it is imperative that critical pedagogues provide students with a means to "step" into and be able to "read" from a critical pedagogical perspective. Lastly, for us, the critical pedagogical perspective is about appreciation and development of a "growing" student voice. By this we mean that the student voice is appreciated, then allowed to mix with other perspectives through honest and "artful" dialogue, in an effort to experience and learn the art of "reading" others' interpretations of text, media, and life itself. To us, this form of emancipatory growth, encourages and provides a means for the appreciation of difference, an honest and achievable goal of critical citizenship and emancipatory democracy. Through this, we as educators must confront ourselves and admit that our perspective is just one of many that should be contributed to a meaningful democratic dialogue.

As educators, we learned the importance of reading our own teaching. By exposing our own agenda, we were able to force ourselves to confront our own ideologies, tastes, and experiences in an effort to keep from falling into the trap of a singular reading to the world. We learned, again, the importance of curricular choices, especially those choices that tap into students' lived experience. Through this reflective stance, we attempted to develop a classroom practice that put the students' knowledge and voice before our own, allowing us to "read" our students and ourselves in an effort to create a classroom dialogue that is free from agenda yet is not value free. Is this the ideal model for all? No. However, we felt that this chapter could serve as a metaphor for the type of critical reflection that is missing from some of the critical pedagogy's project. We, as educators, must turn on ourselves, and begin to read ourselves again, through whatever means possible, or we will fall into the trap that critical pedagogy has resisted since its inception; the trap of one reading, one agenda, one perspective, which however emancipatory it may appear, is devaluing and dismissing the multiple voices of our students. It is time for us to read ourselves while we begin to read again with our students.

REFERENCES

Browne, R. B. (1987). Popular culture: Medicine for illiteracy and associated ills. *Journal of Popular Culture, 21*(3), 1-15.

Bullough, Jr., R. V. & Gitlin, A. (1995). *Becoming a student of teaching*. New York: Garland.

Collins, A. (1994). Intellectuals, power, and quality television. In H.A. Giroux & P. McLaren (Eds.), *Between borders: Pedagogy and the politics of cultural studies*. (pp. 56-73). New York: Routledge.

Dewey, J. (1916). *Democracy and education.* New York: Macmillan.

Fay, B. (1987). *Critical social science: Liberation and its limits.* Ithaca, NY: Cornell University Press.

Gadamer, H-G. (1975). *Truth and method* (2nd ed.). (J. Weinsheimer and D. Marshall, Trans.). New York: Continuum.

Grossberg, L. (1986). Teaching the popular. In C. Nelson (Ed.) *Theory in the classroom.* (pp. 177-200). Urbana: University of Illinois Press.

Guenther, D. E. & Dees, D. M. (1994). *Students beware! Teachers may be hazardous to your health.* Paper presented at the meeting of the American Educational Studies Association, Chapel Hill, NC.

Jackson, P. W. (1992). Helping teachers develop. In A. Hargreaves & M. G. Fullan (Eds.), *Understanding teacher development* (pp. 62-74). New York: Teachers College Press.

Kantor, K. (1994). From our Miss Brooks to Mr. Moore: Playing the roles in television situation comedies. In P. B. Joseph & G. E. Burnaford (Eds.), *Images of schoolteachers in twentieth-century America* (pp. 175-189). New York: St. Martin's Press.

Lummis, C. D. (1996). *Radical democracy.* Ithaca, NY: Cornell University Press.

McLaren, P. (1994). *Life in schools: An introduction to critical pedagogy in the foundations of education* (2nd ed.). New York: Longman.

Schwoch, J., White, M. & Reilly, S. (1992). *Media knowledge: Readings in popular culture, pedagogy, and critical citizenship.* Albany, NY: SUNY Press.

Smith, A. (1985). The influence of television. *Daedalus,* 114(4), 1-15.

Smith, D. G. (1991). Hermeneutic inquiry: The hermeneutic imagination and the pedagogic text. In E. C. Short (Ed.), *Forms of curriculum inquiry* (pp. 187-209). Albany, NY: SUNY Press.

CHAPTER THREE

School Is Hell: Learning with (and from) *The Simpsons*

Mary E. Reeves

The TV environment ratifies itself everywhere. Cartoons, comic strips, fabric prints, sculpture, music, paintings, flip books, T-shirts, jewelry, movies, and TV itself—these, along with printed texts, have featured television prominently, often critically, both attacking television and at the same time exploiting its resources, but above all affirming and validating the TV environment. Television is by now ubiquitous in virtually every cultural format and venue in the United States. It takes shape as familial hearth, as the illuminator/corruptor of children, as the paradoxical site of sedentary activism, as the locus of a new, multivalent consciousness. It is a source of language, virtually a contemporary phrasebook, and certifies human experience in contexts ranging from sports stadiums to personal spaces where camcorder cassette tapes are played on personal screens. Every sign of it, from a T-shirt front to a refrigerator magnet reinforces the idea of the TV environment, one extending from the Magic Screen on "Pee-Wee's Playhouse," to the video apparatus (videocamera, VCR, big-screen monitor) on which the pantomime, Bill Irwin, the electronic-age Charlie Chaplin, performs onstage in his one-man video vaudeville act. Everywhere is television ratified as it is reified in contemporary culture. (Tichi, 1991, p. 209)

Any instance of living language that is playing some part in a context or situation, we shall call a text. . . . The important thing about the nature of a text is that, although when we write it down it looks as though it is made of words and sentences, it is really made of meanings . . . . The text is a product in the sense that it is an output, something that can be recorded and studied, having a certain construction that can be represented in systematic terms. It is a process in the sense of a continual process of semantic choice, a movement through the network of meaning potential, with each set of choices constituting the environment for a further set . . . . Text is a form of exchange; and the fundamental form of a text is that of dialogue, of interaction between speakers. (Halliday & Hasan, 1989, pp. 10-11)

In the past forty years, television has changed from the miracle box in the center of the family room to the family room itself; Americans gather at the set in the nightly rituals of viewing, but the physical television set no longer comprises all of television: from the discussions of the prior evening's fare to the ability to program recorders for a year or more in the future, from "The Brady Bunch Movie" to MTV's game show "Remote Control," television is simply an undeniable and often unexamined part of the landscape. Current estimates place the percentage of homes in this country with at least one television at 99%, and "most homes (nearly 70 percent) now have two or more TV sets and nearly 28 percent have three or more, according to Nielsen Media Research. That means that many families no longer gather together around the living room set but scatter to separate rooms to watch their 'own' programs" (Farhi, 1996). Similarly, estimates of typical daily viewing for children ranges from six to seven hours per day, every day. With such a widespread, devoted following, it is truly amazing that the textuality of television has gone unexamined for so long.

In this chapter, I will explore some of the textuality of television as it relates to education, in an animated situation comedy called *The Simpsons*. With the aid of a small but devoted group of viewers, I will examine the meanings of representations of education, including teachers, students, administrators and schools, focusing on the dynamics of power within schools and the abuse of that power, on questions concerning the nature and value of education, and on the sense of hopelessness which is maintained about the prospects for reforming education.

THE TELEVISION ENVIRONMENT

In *Electronic Hearth: Creating an American Television Culture* (1991), Cecelia Tichi asserts that television is an environment, a space which is "an encompassing surrounding" (p. 3) and which, like all environments "cannot speak for itself but must be spoken for and about" (p. 4). In this act of interpretation, the speaker becomes part of the environment, not merely an occupant; the speaker has the power to intervene within the television environment. Heretofore, she argues, this environment has been assumed to be imperceptible, based on the writings of Marshall McLuhan, early theorist of television. Her work is an attempt to reveal, make visible, the environment of television as a "symbolic environment into which one is now born and raised" (p. 4). She traces and interprets the ways in which this technology has been assimilated into the culture over a period of forty years, and how the "public, constructed as white, middle-class American society, was prepared to accept a major new technology of mass communication" (p. 6). There can be little doubt as to the success of this project, which Tichi carefully documents, or to the value of semiotics as a tool for making visible the construction of meanings in the television environment (Eco, 1972; Halliday & Hasan, 1989). Her task is to bring into our view the televisual environment, so that we may see how our interactions with and interpretations of non-televisual environments is further mediated by our constant awareness of the televisual world.

Fifty years have passed since the introduction of television, and the generation now reaching adulthood "have no memory of a world without such electronic definition" (Wallace, 1988). These "second generation" viewers have a different relationship with the television environment than their older counterparts, and many can scarcely remember the time before cable services and remote control devices (Bellamy & Walker, 1996). This relationship is more active, more involved and less trusting (Howe, Strauss, Williams & Matson, 1993), than the generation of viewers upon which Neil Postman (1992, 1985) bases his conclusions. In his widely-cited critique of television, *Amusing Ourselves to Death* (1985), Postman states that "this book is an inquiry into and a lamentation about the most significant American cultural fact of the twentieth century: the decline of the Age of Typography and the ascendancy of the Age of Television" (p. 8), which has resulted in a change in the content and meaning of public discourse, not merely its mode of transmission. Postman concludes that "the problem . . . does not reside in *what* people watch. The problem is *that* we watch. The solution must be found in *how* we watch. . . . [W]e have yet to learn what television is" (p. 160).

Douglas Rushkoff, in his popular *Media Virus! Hidden Agendas in Popular Culture* (1994), also explores the television environment and the relationships that viewers form with it. Rushkoff (like other contemporary writers on media) posits an active viewer who may willfully manipulate the media to her own ends. "We worry that our media industry has developed a generation of couch potatoes who are incapable of making an intelligent decision and too passive to act on one if they did . . . The first step toward empowerment is to realize that no one takes the mainstream media any more seriously than you do" (pp. 4-5). Rather than passively accepting the world as given by television, the children of the fifties, sixties, and seventies know that the images of television are constructed and manipulated, and they appreciated and appropriate the power to change the [television] world by changing the images of the [televised] world.

> I was born and reared into this television environment. Like others of "my generation," I was weaned on "Sesame Street" and reruns of "Gilligan's Island" and "The Brady Bunch." I cannot remember and can scarcely imagine, a culture without televisual world; I do not know anyone well who dwells completely outside the television landscape. I am drawn to understand television as an extension of myself, as I seek to understand what my place is and potentially can be in this culture through the mediation of television. There is no aspect of my being which is not, at least potentially, within the sphere of the televisual, or which cannot be brought into this sphere; who I may become is likewise circumscribed by the televised images that flicker across my screen. I am not an electronic being, but I, like the rest of you, live an electronic life.[1]

The media, as described by Tichi and Rushkoff, is a complex, dynamic system, feeding itself upon itself in an endless cycle of iteration. It is into this complexity that media-savvy "GenXers," a name derived from a Douglas Coupland novel which in turn derives from a Billy Idol band, are able to introduce what Rushkoff terms a "media virus." The media virus, like its cousin the biological virus, spreads through the organism, attacking and altering it on the cellular level "wherever the . . . existing codes are weak or confused. It spreads through the interest it provokes, and is more successful by provoking more interest; "the more provocative an image or icon, . . . the further and faster it will travel through the datasphere" (p. 10). Our lack of familiarity with the new form results in its perpetuation; the Oklahoma City bombing and the "Murphy Brown"/Dan Quayle motherhood controversy are two examples of spontaneous virus generation and communication.[2]

In contrast to these spontaneous, self-generating viruses that reveal and attack cultural weaknesses are viruses that are specifically created to carry "its more hidden agendas into the datastream in the form of *ideological code*—not genes, but a more conceptual equivalent called 'memes' . . . [that] infiltrate the way we do business, educate ourselves, interact with one another—even the way that we perceive reality" (Rushkoff, p. 10). Cultivated to carry specific information into the datasphere, both the message of the intentional virus and the vehicle used to transport that message are carefully designed, generally from scratch. "Commercial television activism means hiding subversive agendas in palatable candy shells" (Rushkoff, p. 7) and, through its non-threatening, animated format, Rushkoff argues that *The Simpsons* injects into mainstream culture a psychedelic worldview.

> To me, "The Simpsons" has always been about education (among other things such as nuclear power, corruption of government, issues of privilege and power), and this is clearly evidenced by the proportion of episodes which re-present schooling, in ways both iconic and symbolic. I must admit that I have been a fan since "The Simpsons" first made its debut on "The Tracey Ullman Show," and have been a regular viewer of the program throughout its eight seasons. I am a mathematics teacher, and the references to schooling resonate with my own questions about how I formed such a different understanding of mathematics than my classmates, male and female, even though I learned in no more radical a classroom than Bart or Lisa. Other questions resonate as well, particularly the one that arose during my dissertation: How do students form attitudes about mathematics education, and more broadly, education in general? In what way(s) does education-on-television both shape and reflect the images that we have of what schooling was, is, will be, can be, should be? Over times, these questions have called ever more insistently, demanding a more methodical approach.

In the past few years, an increasing number of educational researchers have turned their attention to the relationships between education and popular culture. Some of these have focused on a multiplicity of aspects of this relationship (Farber, Provenzo, & Holm, 1994; Joseph & Burnaford, 1994), while others have focused on more narrow features of this relationship: the images of teachers in popular culture (Weber & Mitchell, 1995); the relationship to a particular area of teaching, like mathematics (Appelbaum, 1995); or the importance of cultural literacy (McLaren, 1995). Although each of these has defined the realm of inquiry differently, all are connected by their fascination with the influence of popular culture on teaching and learning. I seek to continue this effort by examining the representation of education within and through the television environment. Semiotic criticism is an explicit, essential tool in my efforts to deconstruct the "natural" unity (Fiske, 1987, p. 6) of the televisual re-presentation of schooling, teaching, and learning found in *The Simpsons*.

The study described here focuses specifically on the images of schooling presented in the animated sitcom, *The Simpsons*. This weekly half-hour program has its origins in "The Tracey Ullman Show," where it served as "transition material between Ullman's comedy sketches and the commercial breaks" (Rushkoff, 1994, p. 109). *The Simpsons*, now in its eighth season, is broadcast, as was "The Tracey Ullman Show," by the FOX network. New episodes (or repeats from the current season) are shown on Sunday nights at 8:00 p.m. EST, and syndicated reruns are available on a daily or twice-daily basis; weekly schedules and summaries of all shorts and episodes are available on the World Wide Web at http://www.snpp.com.

THE IMPORTANCE OF *THE SIMPSONS*

The frequency with which "the school" figures as a significant plot device in *The Simpsons* leads to a representation of contemporary schooling which is more complex than is found in other readings of more mainstream sitcoms (Johnson & Holm, 1994). This complexity results in a variety of readings, ways of understanding the representations of, for example, The Student, The Teacher, The School, and the conflicts between them, or the implications of gender/sexuality issues in relation to success or failure in school. In addition to provoking consideration of, say, how student success is defined and measured (and by and for whom), other educational issues, such as the role of freedom and authority in education, the nature of cruelty in the educational enterprise, and a pervasive hopelessness about the potential of schooling to achieve its promises, are important recurring themes.

Matt Groening, creator of *The Simpsons,* claims that "you can get away with all sorts of unusual ideas if you present them with a smile on your face," (Rushkoff, 1994, p. 109). Through the smiling face of the animated sitcom, Groening and the (mostly) Harvard-educated staff of writers are able to offer counter-cultural comment on the dominant culture, including the televisual world of which they are part. Although Rushkoff emphasizes the parodies of the media, especially television, which seem to comprise some part of virtually every episode, many episodes of *The Simpsons* address educational issues and events as well. Of the 128 episodes broadcast in the first six seasons, at least 55, or 43%, contain references to some aspect of education or educators. Of these 55, thirty episodes feature education primarily in at least one plotline. In all, nearly one-quarter of the episodes focus significant time to education. The frequency with which education takes center stage in the episodes is an indicator of the degree to which the process of schooling is seen to deserve counter-cultural commentary.

In addition to the educational commentary in *The Simpsons,* Nielsen ratings and numerous web sites indicate that children and young adults are likely to watch, either in prime time or in syndication. According to Nielsen ratings reported in *TV Guide, The Simpsons* was third in the list of the top 10 programs for children ages 6-17, between 8 and 9 p.m., (ET), as recorded for September 1995 to March 1996.[3] *TV Guide* also selected the "Who Shot Mr. Burns? (Part Two)" episode of *The Simpsons* to be number 92 of the top 100 television events of all time. This list includes the final episodes of many long-running series ("M*A*S*H," "The Fugitive") as well as real-world events, like the moon walk and John-John's famous salute at the funeral of his father, President Kennedy. The high level of viewership among children, who are still in school, and young adults, who attended public school at the same time as the writers and who may have children of their own in school, makes *The Simpsons* important in any study of education and popular culture.

Like many of these viewers, I find that the images of education on "The Simpsons" resonate strongly with my own memories and emotions regarding school, both as a student and as a teacher. I can see myself in these characters; each week I remember the pain and frustrations along with Bart, Lisa, and the others. I also wince as I remember my first days and weeks in the classroom, alone, unsure, and afraid, just like the teachers at Springfield Elementary School. I laugh at the exposure of the failings of school, and feel compelled to continue to search for a better way to educate myself and others.

MEET *THE SIMPSONS*

As the show begins, the clouds part to reveal a blue sky and the name of the show in yellow letters. Through the "P" we see the atomic symbol on the containment tower of the Springfield Nuclear Power Plant (SNPP), overlooking the town of Springfield from its perch on the hill. Below, the camera[4] closes in on Springfield Elementary, where Bart is seen at the blackboard, writing his weekly lines for punishment. The bell rings, signaling the end of detention for today, and Bart sails out the front door on his skateboard. The sequence then cuts to Homer at the plant, working with a green, glowing rod. Behind him, C. Montgomery Burns, the owner, and his assistant, Waylon Smithers, are looking at a blueprint. The whistle blows and Homer removes his protective gear and drops the rod, which bounces and lands on his back. Marge is then seen at the checkout counter in the grocery store, reading a magazine as Maggie, the baby, rides the grocery belt, where she is scanned and bagged by the clerk (she registers a cost of $847.63). Next, we see the Springfield Elementary School band, conducted by Mr. Largo, and we hear Lisa jamming on her saxophone. Mr. Largo angrily stops the band, and sends Lisa away.

Now, back to Homer, in the car. He finds the rod in his shirt, and tosses it out the window. It bounces on the sidewalk, where Bart is riding his skateboard and weaving past various pedestrians: Mrs. Lovejoy, the minister's wife, Apu Nahasapeemapetilon, the convenience store owner and his dog, Moe the bartender and Barney the drunk outside Moe's, an unknown man, Bleedin' Gums Murphy, Lisa's musical mentor, and Police Chief Wiggum. Bart crosses the street, in front of a car. The car is speeding, and appears to be driven by Maggie (cuts from car to Maggie with a steering wheel, to the car, to Maggie). The scene expands to show Marge behind the real steering wheel, and Maggie using a small wheel on her car seat. Marge and

Maggie honk their horns together. A rapid pan of numerous people, including Milhouse and other children playing, brings us to the driveway of the Simpson home, where Homer parks the car and gets out. As he is trying to make his way inside, he faces various obstacles: First Bart skips his skateboard off the roof of the car, then Lisa zooms past on her bicycle, and finally Homer is chased into the garage by Marge's car. We then see the family arrive in the living room, where they settle on the couch in front of the television. The final scene in the opening credit sequence is of the television itself, where the names of the creator, Matt Groening, and the developers are written.

Many of the elements of the opening sequence are the same each week, although some may be missing entirely, depending on the length of the prime time episode, or to allow for increased commercial time in syndication. However, the lines that Bart is writing change each week, Lisa's sax solo is different, Homer's reactions to the obstacles in the driveway vary somewhat, and the "couch gag" at the end is different, and often involves some impossibility in how the family enters. For example, one couch gag shows the family with the wrong heads; they each take off the incorrect head and replace it with the correct one. Another couch gag showed the family in an impossible house, reminiscent of M. C. Escher's "Relativity."

The credits proceed at a frenetic pace; the entire sequence takes less that a minute and a half. This establishes a high level of energy and excitement. The bright colors typical of comic strips give a deceptive first impression, possibly leading the viewer to believe that this is a program for children, a kind of modern-day "Flintstones." This introduction is also reminiscent of other family-based sit-coms: Central characters are presented independently, eventually coming together for the beginning of the episode, often in or near the family home.

The credits also tell us a great deal about the members of this family, and for the viewer familiar with the show, provides glimpses of the other people who figure prominently in the show. In relation to education, we see some significant things about Bart and Lisa. Bart is always in trouble, every week, for something different. At times, his punishment lines reflect the broader culture, as in "It's potato, not potatoe," which addressed Vice President Dan Quayle's infamous misspelling, or "I did not see Elvis." At other times, Bart's punishment addresses some behind-the-scenes aspect of the show, as in "I am not a 32 year old woman." It is true that Bart is not, but the person who provides Bart's voice is (or was, at the time). Alternatively, the lines may address the specific show directly, as in "I will not celebrate meaningless milestones," for the 100th episode, or "This is not a clue. . . or is it?", the opener for "Who Shot Mr. Burns? Part One," a season finale which was supposed to contain clues to the identity of the person who shot the owner of SNPP. However, the majority of Bart's punishments reflect some terrible act that he has committed, such as "High explosives and school don't mix," or "I will not bury the new kid," or else some indication that Bart has challenged the authority of the school, as in "I will not expose the ignorance of the faculty[5]," or "This punishment is not boring and pointless." Each week, Bart's identity as a troublemaker is reestablished.

Although she is not a troublemaker in the same sense that Bart is, Lisa is also shown to have her own difficulties with school. Where Bart's problems center on his misbehaving in school, Lisa's are rooted in the fact that she is more talented than her classmates, and perhaps the faculty. If her superiority can be contained, Lisa does well in school, but Mr. Largo kicks her out of the band room for being unable to restrain herself to the level of the other members of the band. The message for both Lisa and Bart is the same: Conform, or else be punished.

Beyond the family members, there are three characters central to the school, and several less vital characters as well. Seymour Skinner, principal of Springfield Elementary School, was a sergeant in Viet Nam who now lives at home with his mother. Bart's teacher, Mrs. Krabapple, is a divorcee with a Master's degree from Bryn Mayr, who teaches fourth grade. Miss Hoover, Lisa's second grade teacher, is a hypochondriac who cannot successfully maintain a relationship. Other recurring school characters are Superintendent Chalmers, Groundskeeper Willy, Lunchlady Doris, and Mr. Largo, the band director. These characters will be explored in greater detail below, as all were significant in the comments of the members of the discussion group.

THE DISCUSSION GROUP

Recent criticisms of studies of popular culture's representations of reality and their meanings and significance (Hatch, 1996; Giroux, 1996) have highlighted the importance of broadening such studies to include the thoughts and words of members of the intended audience for whom the researcher presumes to speak. In order to include such voices here, I invited several long-time fans of *The Simpsons* to watch three episodes and discuss them.[6]

The members of this discussion group were Chuck, Ben, Sarah, Donald, John and Mary[7] and all, with the exception of John, currently live in a small town in rural Louisiana and are associated with the regional state university there. Three members, Sarah, Donald, and Ben, hold at least one degree from the university, and Chuck and Mary are both on the university faculty. Aside from this research study, members of the group are friends, and Chuck and John are brothers. All members are white, with working class backgrounds.

The ages of the group members ranges from 26 to 33, and all are life-long residents of Louisiana. Sarah and Donald grew up in rural areas; Chuck, John, and Mary lived in a metropolitan center in the northwestern part of the state; Ben moved from a large city to the country at the age of ten, then to a suburban area during high school. With the exception of John, who described himself as a "classic underachiever," the members of this group excelled in school. For the most part, the family was supportive of education, and valued it highly.

Chuck holds a Ph.D. in mathematics, and describes himself as a "gay man out of the closet for 15 years" and as being of Italian descent. He is the oldest of three children. His younger brother, John, has a Bachelor's degree in history and political science. He particularly enjoys watching major league sports on television, but is also active himself. Donald, currently a computer hardware technician in local schools, attended a magnet school's gifted program in high school, and was admitted to the Scholar's College, a selective admissions liberal arts program at the local university. He describes himself as a "super liberal." His wife, Sarah, holds a Bachelor's degree from the university, and will soon complete a Master's in counseling. She is the oldest of two children, and is the only member of the group with a parent who attended graduate school. She describes herself as a "liberal and feminist." Ben is a bisexual male who has been married for seven years. He is intensely interested in popular culture and is extremely knowledgeable about it. He says of himself: "I'm interested in bringing an inquisitive, academic approach to the production, consumption, and texts of popular culture; the political work done by TV, film, magazines, etc., particularly intrigues me."

WATCHING "OUR FAVORITE FAMILY (OFF)"[8]

The members of the discussion group are all frequent and long-time viewers of *The Simpsons*. All are intimately familiar with the show and repeatedly quote lines from various episodes throughout the discussion, as well as in general conversation. After a brief discussion of how often each watches *The Simpsons,* I asked about the nature of social commentary in the show.

Ben:	I think it is conceivably the most subversive show ever on network television for any length of time.
Interviewer:	What makes you say that?
Ben:	It tends to encourage complete distrust and cynicism of institutions such as the church, seen on the screen right now, corporations, educational institutions ...
Sarah:	The police.
Ben:	The police, . . .
Chuck:	The media.
Ben:	The media, . . .
Chuck:	Particularly television.
Ben:	Local government, . . .
Sarah:	Education.

It is this subversive tendency in *The Simpsons* that makes it appealing to this group and to the writers of various reviews available at many sites on the World Wide Web.[9]

Chuck:	I think it's . . . the idea that more important than getting people to look at things from your point of view, it's important to get people to question their own point of view, to look *at* things. I think that's much more, . . . more than *The Simpsons* is trying to say anything is particularly right, because it's like, "Have you thought about this?" Which *is* better, because a lot of times you get this thing with the Simpsons, where you see how happy a family they are and how supportive they are of one another, even though they do really dysfunctional things, so you are set up with this real juxtaposition between what they are doing and "Do you think this is a

good thing?" and "In what ways is this better than the way in which everyone else in the world is, and in what ways is it worse?" and it's more just trying to get you to think about it. I think it is a subversive point of view, in the sense that it is asking you to question your preconceptions, and that is always a subversive view.

Sarah: Because it is going against the traditional, in getting you to question, not so much to believe exactly what we believe, but don't necessarily believe what society says you should believe. Make your own decisions.

Perhaps the questioning of tradition and of authority are viruses that *The Simpsons* is encouraging to grow and spread.

The writers of *The Simpsons* are particularly interested in questions about authority and the uses (abuses) of power in schools. After watching "Separate Vocations" (8F15) the group discussed the images of power:

Ben: The whole school-as-police-state thing was fun, too.

All: Yeah.

Mary: That shows up other places, too. There's an episode that starts off with Bart complaining about going to school, and Lisa says something like, "It's not like it's a prison," and then Otto [the incompetent bus driver] shows up in the prison bus.

Chuck: And the whole school is not never a waste of time thing.

Ben: Yeah, that really is a great moment.

Sarah: I think we all can recognize lots and lots of things from this episode.

Donald: Y'all stare at the front wall for ten minutes . . .

Ben: Certainly everyone has had moments like that, and I guess it's really frightening to think that everyone has had moments like that. The thought that an educator could ever do something so complete useless and pointless with children's time.

It is the absolute power that teachers have over students' every action that allows for the images presented on *The Simpsons*. It would be comforting to tell ourselves that this is simply parody run amok, that the writers are stretching reality to make a point, but the discussants in this study had memories of a reality very much like that presented in this program.

Interviewer:	Somebody said earlier something about it being scary to think that this is typical of people's experiences in school. Do you think it is?
Sarah:	I think it is, or it was mine.
Ben:	I wouldn't say I had things like that happen a lot, but certainly I can recall instances where stuff just that boring and pointless was inflicted upon the class . . . We had a woman, . . . my third grade teacher, Mrs. B, I honestly think just hated being a teacher, I think she really hated her job. She never seemed happy, she didn't like kids, and she would for long stretches, on numerous days, just have us copy a random page out of the encyclopedia, out longhand. I mean, for two hours. We would get back from lunch, and then maybe take a little break, then she'd talk about science, and then we'd go home.
Sarah:	I had a teacher that for every spelling word you missed, you wrote it nine hundred times. And you didn't have a break after lunch, p.e. break, you didn't have break between classes, you know, the recess and stuff in fourth grade. Every spelling word was 900 times . . . I had [another] teacher, when I was in the fifth grade, who, it reminded me of Lisa, I was sitting at my desk and I had finished all my work, I always finished it early, and I was drawing. And she came up to me and she said, "What are you doing?" And I'm like, "I'm drawing." And she's like, "You can't draw in my class." And I'm like, "Well, I'm finished with all my work. Are you going to go over it?" And she spanked me for wasting my time and not doing what I should've been doing, which was my homework, even though I'd finished it.
Chuck:	Mr. S—my eighth grade math teacher . . . was appalled that there were three comic books that I had brought to school in the back of the room. It was the same, we were through, and we had nothing to do, but he just, I

mean, he had, I mean, he couldn't have looked more appalled and horrified if I'd had dismembered human body parts on my desk. I mean, he was just . . . The horror in his face, that I would have the gall to read a comic book in his class.

Donald: Well, that whole little sidebar there [in the episode], while they're in the property room, "complete collections of *Mad*, *Cracked*, and [even] the occasional [issue of] *Crazy*."[10] Those things were *verboten*. Don't you remember that? . . . Really was *verboten*, that sort of . . . anything that might reek of . . .

Mary: Fun.

Chuck: Satire.

Donald: Entertainment, after, I mean, if you finished . . .

Mary: Questioning authority?

Donald: Hey, God forbid you be quick, . . . because you were continuously confronted with the problem of what do you do after you're finished?

The actions and thoughts of students must be controlled at all times, so deviating from the established script cannot be permitted if order and authority are to be maintained. However true this may be for the students, the same cannot be said for the faculty and staff:

Donald: Well, she writes that note that says "Please keep Bart busy for a few minutes" and then gives it to Bart and tells him to take it to the office. . . . Yeah, there's a whole little subplot there, you know, not only is this something she considers is okay, and then you see her doing it, but it is also something that Skinner will play along with.

Chuck: Teachers feel above the rules . . .

John: Just like the cops.

Chuck: The societal rules they're trying to impart. Yeah, it's the abuse of authority.

John: It's like being above the law.

Sarah: And the whole thing about students again. It's administration against the students.

Interviewer: So, do you think they're making a parallel between education and law enforcement? Is that something is in

> this episode, sort of the abuse of power, the lazy ineptitude?
>
> John: The control factor of the whole system, I mean, that you are something that is . . .
>
> Ben: I think it's a lot like the, um, something that is in "School is Hell" that Matt Groening says, in one of the very last columns of that, the horrible truth, which is that people who are picking on you, beating you up and stealing your lunch money right now are going to be the people who are pulling you over in cop cars, telling you why your insurance rates are going up, selling you used cars, and telling you why you can't get a bank loan right now, in twenty years.

Maintaining proper discipline is vital to the project of education, at least as typically understood and as presented on *The Simpsons*. However, the image of the school is not this simple; absolute power and control are not the single aims of the teachers and administrators. As with all complex relationships, there is a dynamic tension between authoritarianism and the control needed for any large community to function well.

> Ben: I think this episode (1F18) really goes against the grain of a lot of them. I mean, there are few occasions ever on *The Simpsons* where you see a need for more discipline in the worldview. This is one, and the episode where Bart can't go see the Itchy and Scratchy movie is another one,[11] but this really is a case of, with Ned[12] in charge, it's *Lord of the Flies* all of a sudden at Springfield Elementary.
>
> Chuck: But I think the statement that being made is that there is, . . . the right approach is somewhere in between . . .
>
> Ben: Oh, absolutely.
>
> Chuck: The police state and, . . . you know, somewhere in between *1984* and *Brave New World*.

In addition to questioning the nature of authority and power in schools and uncovering the common abuses of power by educators, *The Simpsons* also questions the value of education. In "Separate

Vocations" (8F15), the children take the Career Aptitude Normalizing Test, or CANT.

> Chuck: I like the fact that the test was called CANT, both in the sense of "cannot do" and the sense of "cant," just rigmarole, you know, meaningless repeated beliefs.

This is an important insight: much of what the children are seen doing in school is this kind of mindless nonsense. Although Lisa typically completes her assignments with intelligence and flair, it is clear that this is rooted in Lisa's character and is not accomplished by school. In most cases, Lisa is on the side of learning and thus the school; her science fair project, the essay contest she enters, and her musical skills are all examples of areas where Lisa excels in school. However, after the CANT, Lisa gets her results, and her scientifically selected career is homemaker. This leads Lisa to abandon (temporarily) the goals of schooling; she becomes one of the bad kids.

> Sarah: I like the fact that, okay, since Lisa's pretty significant mental powers were not being employed toward school, she didn't see any outlet for that, she immediately started becoming the worst kid possible. The whole idea that if you don't use this imagination and this ability, then it's going to be used somewhere, and it's going to be to your detriment . . . . She is the smartest, brightest bad kid.
>
> Donald: She's the one that knows where to hit Skinner where he lives.
>
> Sarah: Exactly. That's what I was saying. The whole idea that if they feel that, if you don't tap that, then it's going in a direction away from you.

In the same episode, Bart's career is law enforcement, and he finds himself in the unusual position of authority and order. He naturally exceeds the bounds of his authority:

> Skinner: The school is a police state. Students are afraid to sneeze. And I have you to thank (8F15).

Lisa further assaults the authority of the school by taking the teacher's editions from every classroom and hiding them in her locker.

Without the answer keys, the teachers are unable to teach; Mrs. Krabapple tells Martin (the smartest boy in fourth grade) to teach for the remainder of the day while Miss Hoover just stands, stricken with terror and surrounded by second graders.

In the final challenge to education which will be discussed here, *The Simpsons* asks difficult questions about the abilities and motives of classroom teachers. Through the contrasting characters of Mrs. Krabapple and Miss Hoover and, in one episode (7F19), the substitute teacher, Mr. Bergstrom, concerns about the quality of the nation's teachers and educational practice in general are raised.

Chuck: Obviously she's [Miss Hoover] got the drill down, she prepares lesson plans, she plans things out, but it doesn't help. All of the built-in mechanisms that are part of the regimentation of the system that are supposed to improve the quality of education, apparently the comment is being made that they don't really help that much. Because obviously, we are supposed to perceive Mr. Bergstrom as a much better and more effective teacher than Miss Hoover ever was.

Ben: I think, sort of, the ineffectiveness of teachers like Mrs. Krabapple and Miss Hoover are a lot more clearly pointed out when we have somebody to contrast them with. When we saw Mr. Bergstrom, he was always among the students, either, of course he was walking up and down the rows playing the guitar and then he was in the center with everybody's desks turned toward him, but Mrs. Krabapple's classroom was much more static. She had a very clearly defined space behind her desk, and the students were in their desks, in rows, and didn't leave those, except for Martin and Bart debating.

Sarah: I guess the whole thing about the opposite of love is not hate, it's indifference. And, you know, Miss Hoover is pretty indifferent. . . . The indication that you are given is that she'd rather be doing something else.

Chuck: I think the distinction is there: she's the "bad bad" teacher and Mrs. Krabapple is the "good bad" teacher . . . There's an episode, one I can't remember, and Lisa is talking with one of her friends about something, and the friend is complaining that what they are being asked to do is a waste of time and Lisa says, "Janey, school is never a waste of time." Then Miss Hoover says, tells them if they are finished with their work they all should sit quietly and stare at the front of the room for five minutes.

Ben: I think Mrs. Krabapple's main relationship on the show is with Bart. Mrs. Hoover's is not with Lisa, but with Ralph. I think that's the most telling relationship in that classroom, is her, just, complete . . .

Donald: "Ralph, are you eating the paste again?"[13]

Ben: Yeah. She doesn't really care what he does, just hopes that he won't bother the other students, doesn't care what he does to himself, really.

Sarah: Well, she's like, "As long as he doesn't injure himself, so I get in trouble."

Ben: Yeah.

Chuck: "My worm jumped in my mouth and then I ate it. Can I have another one?" "No, Ralph, there aren't any more. Please put your head on your desk while the other students are trying to learn."[14]

In contrast to the indifference and incompetence of Miss Hoover, Mrs. Krabapple appears to have many of the characteristics of a teacher suffering from burnout.

Sarah: The impression that a lot of time I get is that she feels frustrated by the education system, as well as by the students.

Donald: I've always gotten the impression, too, that she's just frustrated with life in general. If she found fulfillment elsewhere, then . . . You get the impression that she was at least a better teacher or a nicer teacher while she was being given these love letters by Bart. I mean, she's just so frustrated with life, she's just a bitch to be around.

Chuck: That's what I always . . .

John: I always thought of her as a bit of failure, maybe.

Sarah: Yeah.

Interviewer: Do you think Mrs. Krabapple means well?

Chuck: Yeah.

Ben: Yeah.

Chuck: Yeah. Much more so than, . . . well, I mean, mainly in comparison to Miss Hoover . . .

Donald: She's just sour and bitter . . .

Sarah: She's bitter at the system.

Ben: Mrs. Krabapple is horribly, horribly mislead about almost everything she does, I mean . . .

Chuck: You know the episode about the lemon tree, when she's trying to teach them about Roman numerals? "Class, pay attention. If you don't learn Roman numerals, you'll never know when movies were released."[15]

Interviewer: So, do you think maybe she really wants them to learn it, but she knows deep down that it's not vital?

Sarah: That it's useless.

Chuck: Yeah.

Ben: Yeah.

Chuck: With Mrs. Krabapple, you kind of get impression that sometimes she can't believe the things that are coming out of her mouth. I think she really does care. You see that time and time again, in episodes when she has to deal with Bart, she really does want Bart to learn, that she's frustrated by Bart more than she dislikes Bart.

Her frustration leads her to take drastic action at times, including sending Bart to the office with a fake note (as discussed above). Like Mrs. Krabapple, Principal Skinner also experiences frustration due to Bart, but he is generally seen to be genuinely interested in the children.

Sarah: I really find it interesting that when Skinner was standing in front of the school, he wasn't thinking about his power and he wasn't thinking about, you know, "Man, I had all this neat stuff as a principal," what he was thinking about is the fact that he had changed people's lives.

Ben: Yeah, he really had affection for these students

Chuck: I think it's true generally, . . . You get the impression that Principal Skinner and Mrs. Krabapple really have good intentions, they've reached a point where they're

so wound up in the way they think things have to be run
that they aren't terribly effective, but they mean well.

However, Skinner has a dark underside which is revealed from
time to time, especially when anyone mentions something that triggers
a Viet Nam flashback.

Interviewer:	Skinner seems . . . really disturbed.
All:	Yeah.
Ben:	There are so many Norman Bates jokes.
Mary:	Well, and the whole Viet Nam thing. He mentions being in Viet Nam, and the lights change . . .
Chuck:	And the thing about being trapped in a tiger cage for six months . . .
Mary:	The whole "Apocalypse Now" thing.
Sarah:	And, of course, being shot.
Ben:	In the back.
Donald:	At the Bob Hope show.

In all, the images of educators that are presented in *The Simpsons*
are overwhelmingly negative. For the most part, school is a place of, at
best, boredom and trivia, and, at worst, a place of torture and
humiliation. The degree to which the writers of *The Simpsons*
emphasize the lack of caring and concern for students' intellectual,
physical, and emotional well being highlights their importance to real
students in real classrooms. The knowledge that teachers privilege,
enjoy, and desire to pass along is inconsequential to a child who does
not feel cared for. As educators, we can never forget this lesson, for our
own sake and the sake of our students.

THE RECURRING DILEMMA

Jeremy Butler (1994) notes that in order to sustain itself, a sitcom must
possess a recurring dilemma that is never completely resolved in any
episode. This lack of resolution his crucial, for if the recurring dilemma
is resolved, the show ends. Take, for example, the long-running sitcom,
"M*A*S*H." The recurring dilemma in this show was the Korean War;
when the war ended on the show, it was during the final episode. In *The
Simpsons,* there are several recurring dilemmas, and one of them
concerns the problems of education. Like the never-ending Korean

conflict, the deadly-dull routines and procedures grind on and on, and nothing ever changes.

Clearly, Lisa benefits from school, and she reflects the fact that school does work for some students. In her we see the advantage of learning and knowledge. Not coincidentally, she is the most intellectual and moral member of the family, only infrequently engaging in any questionable or reprehensible behavior. Nevertheless, a fundamental ambiguity emerges through Lisa: schooling is unsatisfying to her, failing to fully engage any of her talents. In spite of her superior abilities, we never see her progress beyond the second grade, and most of her accomplishments happen outside of, in spite of, school, and are the fruit of her independent and self-directed labors.

Indeed, no one in the school ever progresses at all. Students are never promoted to the next grade; Bart is threatened with being held back but is not (7F03). When he passes the test that determines his fate, he runs gleefully from the school, announcing his success as he goes. However, the reality is that Bart (and everyone else) has been held back at least seven times, at the end of each season, and each is in the fourth grade together for the eighth consecutive year. Lisa, likewise, must confront educational hopelessness, as Mr. Bergstrom, the amazingly good substitute teacher who replaces Lisa's teacher, Miss Hoover, for a time, leaves her for inner-city students in Capital City (7F19). As she pleads with him to stay, Mr. Bergstrom explains the situation to her:

> That's the problem with being middle-class. Anybody who really cares will abandon you for those who need it more . . . I'll tell you what. Whenever you feel like you're alone and there's nobody you can rely on, this is all you need to know. (7F19)

He hands her a note, then leaves on the train. He calls out the window to her to read the note, and it says, "You are Lisa Simpson." The seeming hopefulness of this ending is mitigated by two things: (1) the note has never reappeared, and neither has Mr. Bergstrom, in the six seasons that have followed; and (2) Miss Hoover remains Lisa's teacher. Although she has had a powerful, positive experience through school, little if anything has changed for Lisa.

No change in the school is lasting: Mr. Bergstrom leaves and Miss Hoover returns; Skinner is rehired; the teachers' strike is ended.

However, the resolution of whatever specific conflict is raised for the school itself perpetuates the central dilemma, and thus the hopelessness which surrounds the school. By reestablishing the environment of *The Simpsons,* the horrors of education continue unchanged and each character remains trapped in her or his respective role.

> Chuck: School is a trap for Lisa, too, because . . . so much of her self worth is wrapped up in being an exceptional student, and . . . it's clear that that doesn't mean all that much from the way the school is portrayed.

CONCLUSION

A crucial part of the nature of the television series is the constancy of character and setting from episode to episode. This constancy is needed for a variety of reasons, but the most significant of these reasons is that consistent, known characters and spaces require little exposition, and so a complete plotline or more can be told in a half-hour segment (minus commercial time). This constancy means that series characters [and spaces] do have an established past, and their characters [and spaces] do not need reestablishing each week; but they often misplace their past and, in any event, it is usually not necessary for our enjoyment of a specific episode for us to know the specific details of the character's past. (Butler, 1994, p. 27)

Indeed, such a requirement is more indicative of the serial than the series.

> Ben: Right. Although even more than episodic series television, that's almost as much a part of comic strips.
>
> Mary: True.
>
> Ben: I mean . . .
>
> Mary: So an animated sit-com is kind of like a blending . . .
>
> Ben: Yeah, yeah. I mean, I think there aren't many similarities, but I think that may well be something that, I mean, . . . that world, that cartoon world is very, is very static. For everything that happens in Springfield, not a lot . . .
>
> Donald: There's the whole thing that Burns can never remember any of the significant events that the Simpsons have impacted his life in.

Mary:	Or Krusty.
Donald:	Or Krusty, or any of these guys [the police officers on the screen].

Unlike the series, a television serial generally "contains a large quotient of redundant narrative information" (Butler, 1994, p. 31), to allow viewers to catch up to the action that is joined in progress.

As a series, *The Simpsons* must to some degree return full circle following the conclusion of each episode, so that the action of one week is only infrequently carried over into any other week's episode. This maintains the program's characters and settings, giving us "Our Favorite Family" anew each week, ready to embark on another "wacky adventure" (1F14). As part of the program's setting, the conditions of schooling, as well as Homer's positioning at work and Maggie's inability to talk, must be reset. No matter how reformed Bart is at the end of one episode, he will be writing punishment lines for Mrs. Krabapple at the start of the show the following week. No matter that Lisa has abandoned her saxophone playing, we will find her in the band next week, as the opening segment continues. Homer might win a promotion or the recognition of his boss, but rest assured that he will return to old habits and to shirking old responsibilities next week.

The structural requirements of the television series conspire to keep Bart and Lisa, Mrs. Krabapple and Miss Hoover, Principal Skinner and Groundskeeper Willy and Lunchlady Doris and Jimbo and Nelson and Sherry and Terry and everyone else trapped in their relative positions at school. Although the alignment and relative power of each character may shift and change within an episode, the pressure of the series to return to the constant, to the attractor, is irresistible; indeed, maintenance of the attractor is an important factor in the success or failure of the program (Fiske, 1987).

Of necessity, then, the characters remain where and how they are, and the sense of hopelessness is strengthened. However, the compulsion of the producers and writers is to re-present the practices of school, and "within this medium, official culture is contested and debated in dialogues between a variety of contexts, . . . thus forming the potential for critique of, and opposition to, the dominant ideology" (Skorapa, 1994, p. 227). The creators of *The Simpsons* are drawn into obscuring and reinforcing some aspects of the social conditions they seek to expose and critique.

But the point of this is not merely to expound on the lamentable images of education and schooling presented to children and adults via the medium of television, but to provide support for

> urging that schools include courses in their curricula which teach the critical evaluation of TV, and of other mass media. These observers argue that we are leaving the age of the spoken and written word and entering the age of pictures. It is high time, they say, that our classrooms caught up with the outside world. We teach our children standards in grammar and literature: why not also teach them how to look at television, read the funnies, go to the movies? ... The inculcation of critical capacities should not wait upon higher education; it should begin in the lowest grades where, certainly the contact between children and education and the mass media is the sharpest (Shayon, 1951, p. 86).

This quote from 1951 is echoed by the more recent sentiment of Farber and Holm (1994): "Educators could do worse than to examine the films [and, by extension, television] of adolescence [and childhood] together with the young" (p. 38). We cannot banish negative stereotypes of teachers (or of anyone else) from the television environment (or anywhere), but we can teach our students and ourselves to read across these stereotypes and negativities for more emancipatory meanings and practices.

NOTES

1. Sections in italics are the personal reflections of the author.

2. The criminal trial of O. J. Simpson for the murders of Nicole Brown Simpson and Ronald Goldman may be the best recent example of a spontaneously generated virus that has had virtually limitless reach in its influence. Following the arrest, trial, and acquittal of a famous black man for the murder of his abused ex-wife and her male companion, no discussion of race or domestic violence can be held without mention of O.J. According to Rushkoff, the intensity of interest in the trial and verdict can only be attributed to the weakness of the social fabric with regards to race, celebrity, and the abuse of women. As a virus, it has both exposed those weaknesses, and altered forever the social discourse surrounding them.

3. The following is a listing of all ten shows in order:

1. *Boy Meets World* (ABC)

2. *Family Matters* (ABC)

3. *The Simpsons* (FOX)

4. *Muppets Tonight* (ABC)

5. *Lois and Clark: The New Adventures of Superman* (ABC)

6. *In the House* (NBC)

7. *Friends* (NBC)

8. *The Fresh Prince of Bel-Air* (NBC)

9. *Boston Common* (NBC)

10. *The Single Guy* (NBC)

4. Although a camera is obviously not used in the convention sense, it is convenient to use conventional terminology to discuss the appearance and construction of the show. The reader is asked to ignore the impossibility of actually filming an animated location or characters.

5. Bart writes these lines as punishment during the episode, rather than at the beginning. He has actually not committed the infraction, Lisa did, but Bart has taken the punishment for her, so that she doesn't give up her clean record. As Bart writes, Lisa plays her saxophone for him from outside the window.

6. Funds to support this research were provided were provided by the CURIA of Northwestern State University of Louisiana.

7. The author appears in the transcript as both the interviewer and part of the discussion group. When I asked a question to guide the group in a particular direction, I am credited as the interviewer. When my comments were given as part of the general discussion, I identify myself by first name. All other names are pseudonyms.

8. OFF is a common abbreviation used in newsgroups and on the web pages devoted to *The Simpsons*.

9. It is interesting to note that virtually all of the contributions to the episode summaries have been made by males. The implications of this observation are not clear and could be related to both the level of male interest in the program, and the dominance of electronic communication by males.

10. The square brackets convert Donald's statement into a quote from episode 8F15.

11. Itchy and Scratchy: The Movie (9F03)

12. Ned Flanders is the Simpsons' very Christian next-door neighbor. As President of the PTA, he replaces Principal Skinner when Skinner is fired. Ned is fired (making room for Skinner's return) near the end of the show, when Superintendent Chalmers hears him pray over the school's intercom.

13. Miss Hoover: "Now, take some paste and spread it on the construction paper. Ralph, are you eating your paste?" Ralph: [muffled, with paste on his

lips and the applicator in his mouth] "No, Miss Hoover." [8F15]. Ralph is shown eating paste on at least two other occasions, in "Marge vs. The Monorail" [9F10] and in "Team Homer" [3F10]. He has a mishap with the paste in "I Love Lisa" [9F13] and glues his head to his shoulder.

14. Ralph: "My worm went in my mouth and then I ate it . . . can I have another one?" Miss Hoover: "No Ralph, there aren't any more. . ." [shaking her head] "Just try to sleep while the other children are learning." Ralph: "Oh boy. . .sleep! That's where I'm a Viking!" [3F03]

15. Mrs. Krabapple: "Class, please! If you don't learn roman numerals, you'll never know the date certain motion pictures were copyrighted. . . . No, children, no! Your education is important. Roman numerals, et cetera. Whatever. I tried!" [She lights a cigarette.] [2F22]

REFERENCES

Appelbaum, P. (1995). *Popular culture, educational discourse, and mathematics.* Albany: SUNY Press.

Bellamy, R. V., & Walker, J. R. (1996). *Television and the remote control: Grazing on a vast wasteland.* New York: Guilford Press.

Butler, J. G. (1994). *Television: Critical methods and applications.* Belmont, CA: Wadsworth Publishing.

Eco, U. (1972). Towards a semiotic inquiry into the television message. *Working Papers in Cultural Studies.* (Autumn).

Farber, P., & Holm, G. (1994). Adolescent freedom and the cinematic high school. In P. Farber, E. F. Provenzo, Jr., & G. Holm (Eds.), *Schooling in the light of popular culture* (pp. 21-39). Albany: SUNY Press.

Farber, P., Provenzo, E. F., Jr., & Holm, G. (Eds.). (1994). *Schooling in the light of popular culture.* Albany: SUNY Press.

Farhi, P. (June 17-23, 1996). "The racy race for ratings: Network TV's old 'family hour' now is laced with sexy sitcoms and soaps," *The Washington Post National Weekly Edition, 13*(33), p. 34.

Fiske, J. (1987). *Television culture.* London: Routledge.

Giroux, H. A.. (1996). Hollywood, race, and the demonization of youth: The "kids" are not "alright." *Educational Researcher, 25*(2), pp. 31-35.

Halliday, M. A. K., & Hasan, R. (1989). *Language, content, and text: Aspects of language in a social-semiotic perspective.* Oxford: Oxford University Press.

Hatch, T. (1996). If the "kids" are not "alright," I'm "clueless": Response to a review by Henry Giroux of the movie *Kids. Educational Researcher, 25*(7), pp. 40-43.

Howe, N., & Strauss, B. (1993). Crashed by Williams, I. Cartooned by Matson, R. T. *13th gen: Abort, retry, ignore, fail?*

Johnson, L. N., & Holm, G. (1994). Education 1st!: Using television to promote the schools. In P. Farber, E. F. Provenzo, Jr., & G. Holm (Eds.), *Schooling in the light of popular culture* (pp. 21-39). Albany: SUNY Press.

Joseph, P. B., & Burnaford, G. E. (Eds.). (1994). *Images of schoolteachers in twentieth century America: Paragons, polarities, complexities.* New York: St. Martin's Press.

McLaren, P. (1995). *Rethinking media literacy: A critical pedagogy of representation.* New York: Peter Lang Publishing.

Melody, W. (1973). *Children's television: The economics of exploitation.* New Haven, CT: Yale University Press.

"The 100 Most Memorable Moments in TV History." (1996, June 29-July 5). *TV Guide, 44*(26), pp. 12-64.

Postman, N. (1985). *Amusing ourselves to death: Public discourse in the age of show business.* New York. Viking Press.

Postman, N. (1992). *Technopoly: The surrender of culture to technology.* New York. Alfred P. Knopf.

Rushkoff, D. (1994). *Media virus! Hidden agendas in popular culture.* New York: Ballantine Books.

Shayon, R. L. (1951). *Television and our children.* New York: Longmans, Green and Company.

Skorapa, O. (1994). Carnival, pop culture, and the comics: Radical political discourse. In P. Farber, E. F. Provenzo, Jr., & G. Holm (Eds.), *Schooling in the light of popular culture* (pp. 213-230). Albany: SUNY Press.

Tichi, C. (1991). *Electronic hearth: Creating an American television culture.* New York: Oxford University Press.

Wallace, D. F. (1988, Fall). Fictional futures and the conspicuously young. *Review of Contemporary Fiction, 8*(3), pp. 36-49.

Weber, S., & Mitchell, C. (1995). *"That's funny, you don't look like a teacher": Interrogating images and identity in popular culture.* London: Falmer Press.

"What Kids Really Watch. (1996, July 13-19). *TV Guide, 44*(28), p. 21.

CHAPTER FOUR

Cyborg Selves: Saturday Morning Magic and Magical Morality[1]

Peter M. Appelbaum

What follows is one story of my work with children, teachers, and Saturday morning television. It is a story of a curriculum project but also a story of how such a project forced me to reflect on the difficulties of presenting practice as a narrative. The moral turns out to have something to do with the impact of technoculture, and the "free-spaces" not seen in curriculum research. But this is also the story of a picaresque quest, a movement from Foucault to Deleuze and Guattari, from action researcher to rhizomic practitioner, and back again.

AFTERMATH: TRIAGE

This project had as a primary impetus my need to work through the implications of a *triage*[2] of terms highlighted by Bruce Mazlish's (1993) book *The Fourth Discontinuity: The Co-Evolution of Humans and Machines*. Mazlish argues that, just as Copernicus, Darwin, and Freud overturned our illusions of separation from and domination over the cosmos, the animal world, and the unconscious, it is now necessary to relinquish a fourth fallacy—that humans are discontinuous and distinct from the machines we make. As I continue to re-read Mazlish, I persist in trying to unravel these three words: 'animal,' 'human' and 'machine.' We see in Mazlish the enormous play already accomplished in (primarily Western, Amero-Eurocentric) thought that sets up one or two of these as a potential "other" through which a third can be defined.

I note as well Andrew Ross' characterization of the "cyberpunk embrace"—an oft-posited "emergent stage" of human development that integrates the tenets of evolutionary humanism with a "frontier rhetoric of discovery and creative invention, [linking] the LSD spirit of synthetic transformation with the technofantasies of cybernetic consciousness." Ross (1991) makes a nice contrast to Mazlish in his critique of discourses that channel the "discourse of the maverick" into the evolution of human beings, headily pursuing its goal of an 'assault on limits' in the name of individual self-liberation (p. 162). Juxtaposing Mazlish and Ross need not set up a polarity or continuum, however; indeed, the problematic of cyberculture and technohumanity constructs a multiplicity of epistemologies that structure fields of possibility for practice and concomitant technologies of morality and power.[3] In this study, one facet of the problematic is this very multiplicity and its implications for research, in which my own, and others', perspectives and forms of meaning construction become examples of the conflicts themselves.

As I turn to the focus of my exploration in this instance, Saturday morning television, my excitement mounts: here we have film, video, animated, claymated and digitized combos across and over the three realms that Mazlish posits for *triage*—spheres? categories? ("Please don't let yourself tumble into the abyss," my simulacrum of early Foucault cries out)—in a plethora of images and representations that demand our attention. They demand our attention first of all because of the importance of these forms of entertainment and edutainment in the lives of our students. But they are important as well in our own lives— as people who work with and through those who consume and translate the images and stories for us, and as people who confront and celebrate the same images and stories in our own lives. The latter can be expressed in several ways: (a) Saturday morning television can be said to be communicating the fears and fantasies of the adult world. (b) [sometimes dubbed "the reception fallacy":] We must realize that although Saturday morning television is often referred to as "Kids' T.V.," its audience is not limited to children, (Coulton, 1947) and likely includes a fairly sizable proportion of teachers as well (even if they claim their own kids have the T.V. on, or that they are forced to familiarize themselves with the garbage slung at their students). (c) There is the argument that life is merely an enactment of the imagined possibilities first explored through fiction (sometimes described as the amazing quality of authors, e.g., sci-fi to "predict" the future); there is also the argument that change is so frantic in contemporary society that it resembles immigrant cultures in which the children teach the adults the new conventions they must adapt to (Mead, 1970, p. 72).

Triage as cultural practice follows several options, including: **Triptych**—here the three speak to us and each other as distinct images juxtaposed in order to establish a larger or more coherent "meaning." **Triangle**—in this option we have a representation of three distinct categories and their relationship among each other, including a continuum between each pair. **3-D Space**—in which, by convention, each ray of infinite possibility has its origin in a common point, and all reality can be defined by linear combinations of the three defining axes. **Overlapping regions**—here the categories are no longer distinct and overlap each other in a Wittgensteinian or Gombrichian way, structuring the model as collections of "family resemblances"; the terms are informative references but are not necessarily foundational in any epistemological sense. My discussion claims that different Saturday morning programs construct different epistemologies of the animal-human-machine *triage* in different ways. The epistemology is not necessarily foundational to practice and cultural politics but is symptomatic of these features of self and related technologies of morality, thus enabling an entry into theory *about* these issues and their relationship to pedagogy and the professions of teaching and learning.

Another impetus for my work was the need to work through the dilemmas of textual and reader-response analysis regarding media and technology. We might phrase the dilemmas in terms of production/consumption, or perhaps in terms of aesthetics/reception.[4] I was concerned that I could construct a reading of Saturday morning television programs, and that this could be useful to me as a teacher, or to other teachers as information pertinent to their teaching, but that others might not "read" these programs the same way, or that the creators of them might not have anything like what I have read in mind. Differences among students, teachers, and curriculum constructions should be expected rather than viewed as confounding research. You've heard all this before, I am sure. I aimed to avoid the anxiety by structuring in a variety of forms of hermeneutic "triangulation." I looked for a saturation of the discourse in repeated viewings of as many programs as possible, and entire series of those programs I videotaped. I applied the assorted checks for coherence and sensibility we all learned in graduate courses in hermeneutic research. But I also interviewed a group of 6- to 8-year-old boys and girls about the programs they found most important to share with me. And I interviewed teachers about what they thought about my interpretations as well. The process of my research was as follows: I interviewed children and asked them what programs I should watch and why—I told them I was researching Saturday morning television and needed their guidance so that I would watch the right programs and then be able to talk to their teachers about the programs I watched. Repeated versions of this text were shared with teachers; I asked teachers how they might use what I have been working with in their teaching and interactions with children.[5] Advice on what I should look for and how I should think about the children's expert opinions formed a parallel set of expert knowledge that I attempted to combine with previous work. Meetings with teachers were working projects over time, in which we planned curriculum changes and assessed implemented curriculum. I then returned to a subset of the expert young people to talk about how adults and children think about Saturday morning television. In these later meetings we found significant shifts over time as those interviewed began to critique their own former declarations as well as those of hypothetical prospective teachers. I remain convinced that popular culture is simultaneously a commodity to be consumed, collected, and traded for other cultural capital and a cultural resource, out of which individuals and groups construct ways to form meanings and new comprehensions in their experiencing and remaking of the world.[6] At any rate, we know that people watching these programs CAN use them as "tools" for constructing meaning. How, though? And how does this relate to the SELF? To quote the eminently quotable Andy Hargreaves (1994), "Postmodernity brings changes not only in what we experience, in our organizations and institutions, but also in how we experience, in our fundamental senses of self and identity" (p. 70). In other words, as I ask us to ponder Saturday morning television, it seems we must focus on that television and its relationship to a new kind of way to comprehend the self; at least, I claim, we have to entertain what options for constructing "selves" are available as a cultural resource. Hargreaves (1994) is helpful here as well:

> In the high-tech world of the instantaneous image, what once stood for the substantial self is increasingly seen as merely a constellation of signs. With the collapse of moral and scientific certainties of

foundational knowledge, the only intelligible reality appears to be
that of language, discourse, image, sign and text. But even these have
multiple meanings, infinite readings, and are open to endless forms of
deconstruction. So even the self is now suspect. It has no substance,
center or depth. It is "enfolded in language which [it] can neither
oversee nor escape." Selves become transient texts, to be read and
misread, constructed or deconstructed at will. Human selves become
things that people display and other people interpret, not things that
have lasting and inner substance of their own. Postmodernity,
therefore, sees a suspicion of the supposed unity and transparency of
the disengaged self [and] of the alleged inner sources of the
expressive self (p. 70).

In the "end," the self becomes a continuous reflexive project, constantly
and consciously remade and reaffirmed ("under construction" as
Hargreaves says). This heightened orientation to the self and to its
continuing construction can be a source of creativity, empowerment
and change; but it can also be a source of uncertainty, vulnerability and
social withdrawal. In any case, the self is important, is surely a central
concern to those who spend a lot of time with children, and can be seen
to be related to the available construction of human self within the
amorphous *triage* of animal-human-machine.

WHAT IS HUMAN?

The origins of many cyborg and other transmutated characters on
Saturday morning television[7] are found in adult fears of the cold war
and emerging technologies. Adult fantasies such as *Batman* and the *X-
Men* can be deconstructed in order to unravel the dynamics and
implications of these fears for cultural and historical patterns.
Children's reactions to these adult fantasies are interesting because of
the ways in which the cold war ideologies both create fears for children
and "alleviate" them by offering particular solutions to the fears. The
type of fear and solution is crucial, because it is interwoven with an
implicit technology of morality. Just as Donna Haraway (1985) asks us
"would we rather be a cyborg or a goddess?" the placement of "good
guy" and "bad guy" in the animal-human-machine geography
constructs a notion of identification and value (p. 107).

Similarly, the role of "technology" on Saturday morning—both
technological items and symbols of the technologicization of social

life—conveys a story about a "morality of potential," in the sense that
James MacDonald (1995) once articulated, as the function of MAGIC
in constructing a field of human potential:

> It is my personal myth that today's technology is yesterday's magic.
> Further, it is my intuitive feeling that technology is in effect an
> externalization of the hidden consciousness of human potential.
> Technology, in other words, is a necessary development for human
> beings in that it is the means of externalizing the potential that lies
> within (p. 75).

Douglas Rushkoff (1996) has raised this issue once again:

> When we look carefully at the reaction of younger cyber-denizens to
> their Sega-environs, we find that they make no distinction between
> information and matter, mechanics and thought, work and play, or
> even religion and commerce. In fact, kids on the frontier of the digital
> terrain have adopted some extraordinarily magical notions about the
> world we live in. Far from yielding a society of coldhearted
> rationalists, the ethereal, out-of-body experience of mediating
> technologies appears to have spawned a generation of pagan
> spiritualists whose dedication to technology is only matched by their
> enthusiasm for elemental truth and a neoprimitive, magical
> worldview. To a screenager, these are not opposing life strategies but
> coordinated agents of change (p. 109).

In "the beginning of a conclusion," Mazlish (1993) raises the
possibility of a leading definition of humanity: "a human is that animal
who breaks out of the animal kingdom by creating machines" (pp. 213-
214).

> In making machines, humans have become themselves Creators who
> endow their creations with movement. Automata, . . . express this
> form of creation dramatically. An automobile, a locomotor, and
> airplane, these also move under human inspiration. Until the
> Renaissance, it appears . . . that Western Man [sic] built automata and
> other machines not so much to dominate nature, but to copy it; not to
> rival God, but to imitate him. Increasingly, however, in the West,
> humans came to smudge the image of God as the Creator and to

substitute their own, first turning God into a Newtonian machine, and then merging him with nature as an evolutionary process. In doing so, humans united within themselves extraordinary powers of destruction . . . and of creation. Whether in taking on creative powers humans are also able, in the form of their machines, to bring into being a new evolutionary step remains our next question. If Man [sic] succeeds in taking this step, he would certainly be doing something admittedly unique.

What answers are plausible on Saturday morning regarding what a human self is? The answer has often been phrased in terms of an animal-human-machine epistemology. Descartes distinguished humans from animals by their possession of a soul, while arguing that other animals are mere machines. When the soul was removed from the human-machine in the 18th century by LeMettne, writes Mazlish, a human became only a machine. In the Industrial Revolution, humans passed the boundary between animal and mechanical, and Carlyle was able to say, "Man becomes mechanical in head and heart as well as in hand." In creating machines, humans appear to take on God-like or at least Promethean qualities, but as humans have moved to replace the concept of God, or gods, with nature, they have gone further and appear to be that being, or a conscious evolutionary agent of creation. So, as angels were a marker of a Christian way to human perfection, argues Mazlish, machines took on the same quality for more secularly minded humans. They did so in two ways: one, embodied in the idea of progress, was to lead humans into a mechanical paradise in which they were perfectible because they had entered into a perfectible society, with all bodily tasks performed by machines (thus leaving the human as a purely spiritual creature, and all social problems as solved). The other way was to embrace the machine as perfect, in the sense that it could never make a mistake; for humans to become more mechanical meant that they too were fast approaching perfection.[8] It is this narrative of evolution toward perfection and limitless potential that Ross brings up to date as the history of the cyberpunk embrace.

Masked Rider

Masked Rider is a teenager named Dex, sent to Earth from Eegonon. He's able to form a crystal on his forehead to communicate with his grandfather (the leader of Eegonon)—until "the attack." The leader of the attack is no other than his Uncle. His Uncle sent down to Earth the "destructosphere." It was a buglike creature that was like a cyborg, too. It could unfold shooting machine blasters, transform into a ball, and transform into a rock and sail underground.

Dex saw the message on T.V. He quickly ran into the backyard of the house he lived in with his two friends and their mother and father. And he quickly transformed into the bug alien cyborg known as "The Masked Rider." He was attacking when he was losing energy and he only had enough for one more strike. Fortunately, that one strike destroyed the destructosphere. Then Dex quickly transformed back into Dex. He ran to a cave he knew of and telepathically communicated with his grandfather, and he made a jewel on his forehead to communicate with his grandfather, who told him to use the jewel to create power sources he needed. He shot a light beam from the jewel at a rock and the rock fell open revealing a bird which quickly transformed into a solid cyborg motorcycle (it's a cyborg because it can talk). He shot another light beam which created a monster which became a cyborg car. The motorcycle is called "the combat chopper." The car is "the Magno."

His uncle then sent down a monster known as the "Battle Beetle." It was a cyborg because it was half tank, half bug monster. The combat chopper tried to attack it. But when it tried to crash into it, it did nothing more than make the combat chopper lose energy. Then Magno was ready to charge in, but not yet (She sensed the Masked Rider was coming). Then Masked Rider came and tried to destroy the Battle Beetle but lost energy. Then Magno charged at the Battle Beetle. The Battle Beetle was knocked over. Then Masked Rider jumped onto Magno. They destroyed the Battle Beetle together.[9]

Hargreaves (1994) writes that one of the key post-modern paradoxes is a "personal anxiety;" the search for authenticity becomes a continuous psychological quest in a world without secure moral anchors (p. 84). Viewing Saturday morning is an exercise in the simulacrum of anchor in this respect. In my interviews with my 6- to 8-year-old authorities, I often dwell on the geography of cyborgness. I ask, what is human? Is she human? Is she a cyborg? what is a cyborg? What is an animal? A machine? My own interpretations are often critiqued by my authorities. I think at this point that they tend as a group to use the triangle-continuum model. For virtually all interviewees, a cyborg is a living being combined with a machine in a way that is not easily disassembled into component parts. The machine aspect provides extraordinary abilities, such as enormous strength or laser ray projection. A person or animal inside a machine or a person using a machine as a tool can not be a cyborg in this typology. I tend in my own reading to be more general in some ways. I want to include human/machine combos that the children find inappropriate. The why of this difference must be explored further, and bears some resemblance to differences between "adult" and "child" definitions of "living thing" described in common science education methods textbooks.[10]

Megaman

Megaman is a robot fighting against the evil Dr. Wiley. Actually, he's a cyborg. He is able to transform his arm—or should I say pull his hand in?—into a blaster and blast. He can take others' powers by touching his hand onto their forehead or arm. Dr. Light, the guy who made Megaman, was awarded "Best Scientist" (not for Megaman but for lots of other stuff). Then Dr. Wiley attacked. So Dr. Light made his son into Megaman!

Megaman fights the robots known as Bombman, Gutsman, Blademan, Cutman, Torpedoman, Waveman, Diveman, and even against his OWN brother, known as Protoman, who is a cyborg (made, like all bad guys, by Dr. Wiley). Dr. Wiley and Dr. Light used to be partners; now they're worst enemies because Dr. Wiley wants to take over the world. He thought it would be a good idea to have Dr. Light's son fighting against Dr. Light. In the beginning of when Dr. Light attacked, he tried to capture the son who's now Megaman, but he escaped! And Megaman has a sister who is a cyborg because she has a mechanical bracelet arm which can make anything on it. She can pull her hand into the bracelet part and pull anything out of it. Her name is Rol. Their dog, Rush, is a robot, not a cyborg.

(How he was made:) mechanical devices with pointy things and static and stuff like that. You don't see much about that. You don't know much about his life.[11]

I and my authorities consistently identify science and scientists as the source of danger in most programs where cold war and post-cold war fantasies are enacted. There is a long tradition of this characterization. In early Japanese anim_ and gundam (represented in the 1960s programs *Gigantor* and *Speed Racer*) it is the children alone who are capable of harnessing the sometimes frightening applications of technology, or understanding the inner struggles and gentle nature of the monsters mutantly wrought from toxic spills and nuclear accidents. "Adults accidentally create monsters and catastrophes by letting their technology get out of control, while the children—thanks to their ability to understand the inner workings of technology and the secret hearts of monsters—are uniquely qualified to clean up the mess" (Ruskhoff, 1996, p. 69). Like their predecessors, contemporary North American children's programs are heavily influenced by their Japanese counterparts. Indeed, *Power Rangers* in its earliest version was dubbed sequences of Japanese programs, with Americanized plots spliced in. Like their gundam cousins, these North American versions enact plots that develop a relationship between the evolution of the young main characters and the human-directed evolution of technology. Each side in a battle between good and evil for the fate of the Earth and all humanity continues to develop new prototypes of technological wizardry; in response, the child-stars test out the new prototypes. The eternal war serves to create better technology through which the new children can test and develop their powers. In the home we see the plot behind the series' producers' obsession with technological innovation: The shows are sponsored by toy companies who want to sell as much as they can. Every innovation in body suit or technological prototype is mirrored by a new toy version whose price is higher than its forerunner. Douglas Rushkoff has suggested that the creation of child characters who have extrasensory experiences through technological devices is an attempt by the toymakers and television producers to convince children that they can really feel what it would be like to move, strike and *be* like a powerful mobile suit gundam. Ruskhoff (1996) also notes that the influence might be in the reverse direction, from children to the producers of the programs and makers of the toys:

> Ironically but not at all coincidentally, these programs . . . are driven as much by technology as they are by any personal visions of their adult scriptwriters. The shows and their themes are wrapped around technological innovation—toy robots with movable parts. The evolving features of these high-tech dolls advance the stories and concepts in this otherwise market-driven cosmology. Therefore, whether they realize it or not, the gundam marketers are merely reacting to their young viewers. Because their viewers are children of

chaos, these two forces turn out to be immensely compatible, and their marriage is depicted in the stories themselves (p. 74).

NEW CYBORGS FOR NEW WORLDS

Not all programs construct cold-war fantasies, of course. A second category of fiction posits post-radioactive trauma or cyborg developments as a positive solution because they give the characters "new" powers over the toxicity, radioactivity, or rampant technology. Here superheros, mutants and cyborgs are translated through "Kids' T.V." into a potentially positive friend rather than threat. Which in the long run, I suppose, suggests tipping the invisible balance toward "good" for science and its effects in general. Yet the positive nature of the new powers are ambiguous. The *X-Men* are people we are to like, and are the potential harbingers of an increasingly pluralist society, yet they live on the margins in a perpetual state of alienation and isolation, frozen in interminable, "illegal" immigration. Saturday morning versions of *Batman* and *Spiderman* wield technology to tame the cyborgs and psychotics of contemporary society but also suffer never-ending isolation and marginality, and experience severe levels of depression and anxiety. The overarching message, nevertheless, is that cyborgs and mutants are "more powerful" and hence "better" than humans.

In this case, the cyborgs have much in common with Marge Piercy's (1991) enhanced humans in *He, She and It* and less in common with her golem, or (humanly) enhanced robot. Born of catastrophe and crisis, they symbolize continued hope; yet the hope lies closer to the human end of the human-machine continuum than the machine end. While Piercy in her writing actually presents a vision of overlapping family resemblances, Saturday morning preserves the god-dream of Descartes in the triangle. Some test-cases in my discussions with the 6- to 8-year-old experts: R. L. Stine's scarecrow in *The Scarecrow Walks at Midnight* is not a cyborg; neither are Krang from *Teenage Mutant Ninja Turtles*, an evil brain from the fourth dimension who must remain attached to a machine to function on our Earth, nor Arthur, *The Tick's* sidekick, a man who derives his identity and life-project from the Moth-suit machine he always wears.

Technoman

Technoman's real name is Slade. He fights the evil Darkon. Darkon sent down another technoman named Gunner. At Technoman's and Gunner's first battle, Technoman went away; in the next battle Gunner went away; in the next battle Technoman blasted Gunner; in the next battle, he threw a sword in Gunner's face and cracked his technoarmor. The next battle Gunner won by destroying Slade's crystal. Fortunately Slade made a new one and went back. With the new crystal he blasted his technoblaster at Gunner and destroyed him. Darkon's normal soldiers who Technoman always destroys are named spidercrabs. He also has two friends from a space crew, and more friends from the space crew.

Slade is a cyborg because the crystal sent the power of his armor in his body to where the armor is inside him, forcing the armor out. For the same reason as Ronin Warriors, the exoskeleton is a machine because of things like technoblasters that blast technoblasts.

He kind of does and kind of doesn't like being Technoman. He's happy that he was able to remake his technocrystal and he's very happy because he's able to destroy things with his armor. Slade does not really like being Technoman because he's very unhappy about having enemies and stuff like that. Slade fights and everybody relaxes while he fights because HE has the technocrystal and the skills, so he should do the fighting.[12]

In the spoofs of cold-war fantasies, such as *Teenage Mutant Ninja Turtles, Power Rangers*, and *The Tick*, the cold war mentality is no longer ambiguous but clearly and unilaterally positive. The *Turtles* do not want to go back to being turtles; the *Rangers* revel in their role as fighters of enormous vitality and success (indeed, in the motion picture version, we see that younger children dream of one day becoming a *Power Ranger* themselves); *The Tick* and his superhero rivals bound with delight into each new adventure, turning every nightmarish threat into recreation (in the athletic pleasure sense). Here transmutation or robotization is a gift one must celebrate. Two programs help us see how the line from ambiguity to positivity has been crossed: *The Masked Rider* and *Sailor Moon. Masked Rider*, a *Power Ranger* take-off (the simulacrum of the simulacrum), is a sort *of "I Dream of Jeannie"* revenge fantasy: Dex must keep his powers secret in order to keep his identity hidden from the bad guys, but he uses them freely without disapproval to the delight of himself and his friends. *Sailor Moon*, touted as a "girl superhero show," can transform with "moon power" into a superfighter who battles the megaverse, and in doing so, proves how great she is. (Oddly, *Sailor Moon* turns out to reproduce the same ol' boring ideology—she often gets into trouble and must be saved by the only major male character, her uncle.)

Rushkoff tells us the children watching these programs are not reveling in the violence. Most of the destruction is done to and by machines. And the joy comes instead from a vicarious feeling of power. Mirroring the cyberpunk literature read by older brothers and sisters, these programs depict children who understand technology better than the adults who designed it; having evolved they also exercise a greater control over and a genuine friendship with this technology.[13] Adults are intimidated by these programs because they exalt this relationship. "The battle becomes one between our evolutionary future," writes Rushkoff (1996)—the combined efforts of a rainbow of children—and our evolutionary past: the efforts of a single, technoimprisoned dictator to maintain personal control over our planet" (p. 78).

> The overriding theme of the show turns out to be co-evolution with technology. In addition to the way the Power Rangers use technology to fight monsters of the tyrannous past, they depend on technology for moral and spiritual guidance. When the Power Rangers are in trouble, they turn to Zordon, a disembodied ageless sage who acts as a techno-oracle from within a computer. Pure consciousness available only through a communications device, Zordon demonstrates that the wisdom of the ages has the ability to speak to us through technology, just as the Power Rangers show how children may be able to bring us into our evolutionary future via the same means (Ruskhoff, 1996, p. 80).

CYBORG SELVES

In creating machines, humans are often said to take on the god-like role of "creator." Yet we often see the machine as the image of doom or evil. Is this odd? "After all," writes Mazlish (1996), "the machine promises perfection, and, if it threatens to take over life, in return it promises to do away with death" (p. 219). He suggests that we turn to Harold Searles, who has noted our frustration at the knowledge that we have created a technology which, seemingly omnipotent and immortal itself, has not extended our own allotted life span. Searles suggests that we thus identify unconsciously with the technology itself, which, being inanimate, can not die. The juxtaposition of these two impulses has been eloquently described by Jim Paul, in his account of building a catapult to launch stones into the ocean. Early in the process, Paul (1991) and his friend Harry step back to look at their work:

> Look at that, said Harry, in satisfaction. The proportion seemed right, like an arm's to a baseball. We were making an effigy of a human being, it seemed, one stripped of all capacities except stone-throwing, and that capacity amplified, as if in compensation for whatever else a person was (p. 78).

Later he has another thought:

> . . . I had to confess that the catapult's meaning hadn't really come up that evening. That we could afford it, that we could make it work, those were our concerns. That thought gave me the sinking feeling, as I drove home beneath the Bay Bridge's towers and cables, that I wasn't outside the catapult anymore, seeing it as an object in the world, but inside it somehow, assuming the world from its viewpoint. As if we were its eyes, its mind, on the lookout for the best way to make it manifest. And that was no observation at all—just a kind of mechanical vision, fascinating and persistent, against which my need to observe was an eddy to the main current.

Mazlish posits a future in which humans may look like we do now, may be enhanced or altered by machines, or may gaze at a new other species, the machine. I suggest the choices are not necessarily so clearly delineated, and that machines and people have always been members of an amorphous mass of stuff which we choose to categorize in a variety of ways. Once we do so, we have constructed a range of options for identification, and at least as many psychologies of identification. Cyborg selves are names we give to comprehend our positionality/ subjectivity/agency. The variety of potential relationships among the possible selves becomes the interesting phenomenon, as opposed to what one self looks like. Recalling Hargreaves' articulation of the postmodern self as a collection of images and fragments searching for an image to cling to, my presentation of Saturday morning alternatives suggests attention to the successive phases of the image as presented by Baudrillard (1990): (a) it is the reflection of a basic reality; (b) it masks and perverts reality; (c) it masks the absence of a basic reality; (d) it bears no relation to any reality whatsoever. We can take the triptych, triangle, 3-D space or overlapping regions, and ask of the model, when is it constructed as reflecting a basic reality? when is it represented as masking or perverting reality? In which programs do we see the *triage* as masking the absence of a basic reality? And in which does it bear no relation to reality? In my own reading of Saturday morning, I find mostly the triangle and it reflects a reality. I would prefer the more sophisticated (to me) overlapping regions offered by Piercy, Haraway and others, and I would prefer these regions to bear relevance to something other than a presentation of reality. Sometimes, however, the bad guys on Saturday morning are offered as seeing things differently, usually also a triangle, but sometimes masking or perverting reality; the ideological function is to construct the alternative as psychotic or absurdly evil, thus rendering the reality as common sense.

Why, we might ask, do we cling to the idea that a human-tool link is transformative, as potential merged beyond dissociation, while children freely make a categorical distinction? Why might we favor the family resemblance, the overlapping regions, while children so comfortably assimilate the triangle of contuua? Good questions. Here we confront Andrew Ross' "discourse of maverick humanism in fullflow, headily pursuing its goal of an 'assault on limits' in the name of individual self-liberation." The self is Rushkoff's (1996) "screenager," the chaos-acclimated kid who laughs at the paranoid superstitions of elders, satirizing their inability to cope with self-simularity and recurrence by creating mock cults and collectives, and distancing themselves in shells of self-conscious media.

> By accepting the notion that technology can play a part in the forward evolution of humanity toward its greater spiritual goals the children of chaos exchange the adult, paranoid response to the impending colonial organism with a philosophy decidedly more positive: pronoia (p. 154).

Another question, which children find perplexing, is, why are cyborgs always fighting? Why is it weapons which represent the machine-like aspects of the cyborg? I asked my authorities about this. Why don't we see them building buildings? Fixing cars? Transporting children to school? Playing games and cleaning scrapes? Because we are talking "Cyber-Chataque," declare Queen Mu and R.U. Sirius.

> . . . bringing cyberculture to the people!

> We're talking about Total Possibilities. Radical assaults on the limits of biology, gravity, and time. The end of Artificial Scarcity. The dawn of a new humanism. High-jacking technology for personal empowerment, fun and games. Flexing those synapses! Stoking those neuropeptides! Making Bliss States our normal waking consciousness. *Becoming* the Bionic Angel (Ross, 1991, p. 163).

Distrustful of the "puritanism" of the left, and dismissive of the "techno-fear" of the "self-denying" ecofundamentalists, the New Prometheans revive . . . a work-free, post-scarcity society, "all of it watched over by machines of loving grace." I am told cyborgs look just like people when they are not fighting, so they are not interesting, that's not what the story is about. Or, as my son so aptly put it, do we need cyborgs to do those things? No! So the cyborgs don't do that! The "machines of loving grace" are invisible, because they do the drudge work of the invisible man, and thus are simply uninteresting as the stars of our program; they are "the machines" and not "the people." This is Ralph Ellison (1947/1952) for the nineties, the walking zombie stripped of humanity:

> Behold! a walking zombie! Already he's learned to repress not only his emotions but his humanity. He's invisible, a walking personification of the Negative, the most perfect achievement of your dreams, sir! The mechanical man! (p. 86)

As Rushkoff (1996) puts it, "in stark contrast . . . kids' culture stands as a delightfully mixed-up common ground for all these digital, magical, and biological sorts of development" (p. 109).

THE TEACHER MAKES A DRAMATIC ENTRANCE

Masked Rider

His driving teacher was captured by Lord Dragonon's evil Maggots, and they made a clone of him who was actually an electricity force monster. He let Dex drive safely to the place they were going to; then they decided they would switch so that the teacher would drive back. The monster who was the clone of the teacher changed his hand into a weapon, and Dex turned into the Masked Rider. Both are cyborgs. Dex was able to hit the teacher-cyborg into an electrical equipment thing, but this turned the teacher-cyborg into an even more powerful cyborg. Dex called Combat Chopper and together they finished off the bad cyborg monster. Meanwhile, before that happened, Dex found out that his weirdo creature-pet Furbis was hiding in his backpack. (He's *not* a cyborg.)[14]

Teacher

As a teacher I am like a *dentist*. The dentist tells you what you have to do to have good teeth, but essentially you have to do it. Some days it is as hard as pulling teeth. And if they didn't brush their teeth last night, they come back and you can't get near them because they have bad breath. And you have this faint feeling as if they fail you in some way, or you failed because you did not press upon them the importance of doing it. They come with cavities and you have to fix them. They come to you two hours before you have to turn in the grades and they ask, "What can I do?" "Well, you really should have brushed. Let's see if I can fill it. We'll stick some silver in there and see if it holds. But next time remember to brush!" (female, 44, High School, Small Town) (Joseph & Burnaford, 1994, p. 54).

Ronin Warriors

The leader of the Ronin warriors is named Ryo. The Ronin warriors are cyborgs because of their machinery-like armor, which is part of them. The armor's, like, inside them. It becomes like an exoskeleton, like bugs have. The names of them are Ryo, Roin, Kento, Sage, and Cie.

However, the Ronin warriors action figures—if you happen to see them—you will not think they're cyborgs even though they are. Because the armor snaps on them. But on the T.V. show the armor is on them and doesn't snap on or anything.

They show their armor to fight to save the world from the evil dynasty master Talpa. They have to fight Talpa so he will not crash Earth into his netherworlds. If Talpa crashed the Earth into his netherworlds, he could rule the Earth and change the people into his evil dynasty.

Kento, especially, likes to be a Ronin Warrior. Although he is always hungry and needs to work on skills for everything, he likes to attack, and even though he is not very good at defense skills, he's very good at fighting. Ryo kind of likes being a Ronin Warrior because he's very good at fighting and he's the most powerful Ronin warrior. He's also able to defend them really well because he's able to call on the "white armor."

Most people on Earth do not know about the Ronin Warriors. Nobody knows about them. They don't have secret identities. You can even see their face through their helmet so you can know them instantly. They travel to Talpa's netherworlds for long periods of time to fight and even when they're on Earth, they live in a big city, and nobody knows about them really, except for their friend, Mia, and their other, five-year-old friend, Uli. They know Uli because he got lost in a crowd of people trying to run away from a dynasty warlord; Ryo found him and now Uli lives with Ryo.

They know Mia because she was sent out to find the Ronin Warriors from her grandfather to tell the Ronin Warriors that the dynasty would attack. She doesn't go back to her grandfather because he got too old and died.

I think the Ronin Warriors are interesting because when Ryo was fighting Saber Strike, he lived in a very hot desert jungle area, and then he lived in the big city.[15]

Teacher

It's the magic that strikes me, the magic and the power and the control. My students love magic tricks, performing magic for each other. Their favorite thing is to REVEAL the way to perform the trick! I don't remember this anymore from when I was young, but from my children I believe I must have felt this way too when I was a kid: sharing the magician's secret is actually more powerful than performing the trick, because the sharing of the KNOWLEDGE is the POWER. I wonder about what sort of leader I should be in my classroom: I put on different costumes—sometimes literally!—and I become an enhanced person, who can perform new tricks. The parents and the administrators never share this secret with us, and the magic comes from that LACK of sharing in this case . . . I can become a leader in my classroom by showing the students how they, too, can become the teacher, share the knowledge working in groups to teach each other something that they just learned . . . we're tapping into something in common that helps us find the magic.[16]

Joe Kincheloe (1993) has written:

> The professional educational research community too often has been guilty of viewing research in a manner that inhibits teachers from becoming critically reflective practitioners. This is the problem with modernist social and educational science: What is the benefit of the knowledge it produces? By the very techniques it employs, the very questions it is limited to legitimately asking . . . educational research creates trivial information. The response of practitioners is often, "So what?" (p. 17).

I have found that asking teachers what they find in my work that can answer "So what?" instead of telling them my answer, has enabled a new form of dialogue. Interviews with practitioners have allowed me to see how teachers critically adapt new information toward a reflection on the self, and the meaning of thinking about teaching, much as Kincheloe suggests, at another point in his work, in that teachers have invited me to share in their interrogation of relationships among students, teachers, knowledge, and the broader contexts in which schooling takes place.

One response from the teacher interested in Saturday morning as curriculum content, is to use discussion of Kids' T.V. to accomplish curricular goals. After having read Karen Gallas' (1995) discussion of Science Talks in her 1-2 classroom, one teacher imagined basing weekly open talks on asking, "How'd they do that?" about amazing accomplishments that happened on specific programs. The point of these discussions would not be to debunk the science as absurd but to theorize what would have to happen in order for such an accomplishment to be possible. More directly, another teacher found that students can develop an interest in science because they desire to perform some of the tricks they see on Saturday morning programs. Yet another teacher emphasized the positive impact of fantasy on her classroom: Many children are used to being told what to do; it is hard for them to draw a picture after listening to a story. These children can benefit from exposure to a wide variety of fantastic depictions, as an aid in thinking about what they might imagine themselves. The same children can use the stories and characters of common programs to role play, and after starting off reproducing a narrative they have viewed, move on toward improvising their own story. A shy child watching cartoons can take on his or her own destiny, finding better ways to speak to classmates or express thoughts, feeling secure in being able to be a monster or hero after sharing a character's experiences before emulating them; children who want to be leaders or are tired of always being expected to take on leadership roles by their peers can find a variety of models of leadership in the main characters of these programs. Explosive behaviors that result from watching these programs can be "teachable moments" that enable discussion of what constitutes excessive violence as opposed to a positive outlet for frustration or anger. Students who do not have enough opportunities to talk with others might benefit from an initial exposure to a world of a consistent character that they can share time with, if this time together is then handled in a reasonable way by some adult, possibly a teacher. Other children do not know "how to be" in reality, while some move back and forth between reality and fantasy; a discussion of Kids' T.V. can help a teacher understand children in this context either by way of private conversations or through what they choose to relate to in class activities.

Teachers often suggest that discussion of Kids' T.V. can promote self-esteem because children can easily compare themselves to a "cartoon character" that is not fully developed, noting in what ways they differ from the character, including instances in which they are "better" or "not as good as" the character. Such discussions, generalizable to the processing of any literature or narratives in various forms and not unique to the habitation of technoculture and popular mass media, respond more directly to my initial interest in morality and constructions of self. Students can identify aspects of a character that they would or would not want to copy. Such a conversation helps to promote students as "evaluators," forming skills for judging "good/bad," "like/don't like," and what they'd change. One teacher suggested it would be a powerful experience to run cartoons from ten to fifteen years ago and ask the children for their reactions, comparing the stories and characters to those that are aired today. What these pedagogical strategies have in common with the science talks is that the teachers ask not only unique questions but create classrooms where student learning is grounded on questions that students themselves ask.[17]

Another direction of response to my talks with children highlights the ways that teachers can use Kids' T.V. to transform their relationships with their students. By viewing these programs and talking about them with children in ways that are not hostile but invite response, some teachers believe students see them in a different way, as "more human" and less as a "teacher-person" animal or machine. Perhaps the first time such a discussion is attempted might result in silence, but students often come back a week or two later to talk about what you said. In contrast, relationships that result from a T.V.-saturated culture involve teacher-entertainers who are expected or expect themselves to "edutain" with increased pace and variation in media-dosage. Some teachers relish the cyborg imagery and find empowerment through it. They respond positively to the information that many students find some programs more interesting than others because of the novelty of the program (different artistic style in depicting characters on *Sailor Moon*, or in plot development as in *Iron Man*); they note with interest that many students prefer the cartoon-based programs to the ones that feature live actors because the animated programs can depict more fantastic things not realizable within the budgets of the live-action programs. They are, in the ways they talk about their presence in a classroom, "cyborg teachers," and they use the metaphor to their advantage, seeing various tools and equipment as enhancing their ability to provide novelty and extend their power to magically teach. Cyborg teachers promote proactive *bricolage*, seizing materials and unusual events of the day as opportunities for enacting the cyborg curriculum.

> I search for ways to enhance MY power to effect change for students.
> Scientistic technologies of teaching in the ideological battle over
> "best practice" become toys for me to enhance my potential: to break
> the limits in a Cyber-Chataque.

In this way, cyborg-teachers construct in their practice Hargreave's "self," constantly and consciously remade and reaffirmed. The implication is a heightened orientation to and reflexive attention to themselves as teachers, an enhanced sense of creativity, empowerment, and change in their work; a parallel observation is the need over time for these teachers to embrace rather than recoil from a practice defined in terms of uncertainty, vulnerability, and the threat of social withdrawal. Like Jim Paul and his friend Harry, these teachers exalt in the power to magically externalize the human potentiality they believe lurks within themselves while wary of the pull towards engulfment by that technology of externalization.

Those other teachers who initiate the use of Kids' T.V. as curriculum content find a view of the teacher as more "human" results in fewer expectations that they act like a "superhero" or "cyborg" and can begin to behave in a different way. The effect is similar to being seen shopping in the local supermarket. Some of these teachers then find that school can be an oasis of special time in a child's life, largely because the pace and techniques of working in a group are significantly different; students can slowly discover school as a unique opportunity to escape the entertainment-focused public realm of T.V.-tainted life. A recognition, however, of the powerful attraction of Saturday morning television as a time to be away from other components of life, retreating into the escape of fantasy, has led some teachers to incorporate similar ways to meet this need in their teaching and learning. A discussion of Kids' T.V. supports the recuperative function of Saturday morning throughout the week. An institutionalized space or time for being away within the classroom, such as a big refrigerator container turned into a By-Myself-Box for students to be alone, or a time when students choose something to do by themselves, are examples of this response by teachers. The point is to provide an opportunity for students to have a part of their life when nobody knows what they are thinking or feeling and during which they are not being judged or assessed in any way. Moments in time and space like science talks that begin and travel through student questions, by-myself areas, and journals of certain types, are examples of what Menser (1996) has called "heterarchic freespaces"—"material constructions that do not fill some metrical space, but are projective, producing, and appropriating their own spaces" (p. 310).

Viewing Kids' T.V. also helps teachers respond to students if they try to view the programs, not as adults, but as children do: avoiding a discussion of "use" of the programs in favor of immersing oneself in the fantasy has helped several teachers think about what it is like to be engaged in an activity in their own classroom as a child. In this respect, the curriculum takes on dimensions of *currere* as posed by William Pinar (1975), in facilitating teachers' movement towards an inner world of psychological experience, their own life histories with respect to television and technoculture, and school. *Currere* calls for teachers to be mindful of the potential for the provided-curriculum to construct the teacher as the gundam/child, and the students as the mutant monsters to be tamed. Teachers as technochildren sometimes try on new prototypes in order to experience a new sense of their powers of perception, production and destruction. At other times they experience the melancholia of the gundam, capable of harnessing the sometimes terrifying applications of scientistic pedagogical techniques in order to lead the student-monsters in an effort to save society from invasion or technological disasters.

When teachers use characters from various programs as examples of possibilities, encourage students to share their evaluations of those characters, or imagine themselves as teachers in terms of various characters, they are metaphorically thinking about their own thinking about teaching and learning. Metaphor, like constructing opportunities for curriculum based on students' questions, is important in post-formal pedagogy. As Kincheloe (1993) notes:

> Metaphoric cognition is basic to all scientific and creative thinking and involves the fusion of previously disparate concepts in unanticipated ways. The mutual interrelationships of the components of a metaphor, not the components themselves, are the most important aspects of a metaphor. Indeed, many have argued that relationships, not objects, should be the basis of scientific thinking. When thinking of the concept of mind, the same thoughts are relevant. We might be better served to think of mind not in terms of parts but in terms of the connecting patterns, the dance of the interacting parts. The initial consciousness of the "poetic" recognition of this dance involves a nonverbal mental vibration, an increased energy state. From this creative tension emerges a perception of the meaning of the metaphor and the heightened consciousness which accompanies it. Post-formal teachers can model such metaphoric perception for their students. Such perception is not simply innate, it can be learned (pp. 151-152).

Thus, Saturday morning television, as *currere*, like other aspects of culture, can be a cultural resource with any number of possibilities for interpretation and application, incorporating potential ideologies and expectations yet consumed or enacted in ways both foreseeable and surprising.[18]

Researcher as Rhizome

Some difficulties in carrying out my research emerged as I asked teachers to suggest what the research should be about. Holding expectations for education research grounded in their experience with a traditional style of expert pronouncements, some would not understand my questions because they were listening for declarations about what they should do. Because research "is supposed to tell me what's best" rather than "facilitate my work as a critically reflective practitioner," sharing summaries of interviews with children and inchoate attempts to make sense of this as an adult were received as "bad research" that confirmed the notion that educational research in general is trivial and useless. Most teachers see Saturday morning television, and Kids' T.V. in general, as a collection of information harmful to school learning, in opposition to high culture. In these discussions, it became clear to me that the people I was talking with were not "post-formal thinkers" who "see facts as more than pieces of information" (Kincheloe, 1993, p. 156). The introduction of my work had to be structured in a way that communicated that I was looking at this information regarding television and its young viewers "in relationship to the larger processes of which they are a part." Rather than "discovering" that teachers are uncritical thinkers incapable of applying such post-formal thought to reflection on their practice, however, I learned over time that I needed to translate my perspective and help them see that *I* wanted to talk about teaching in this peculiar, atypical manner.

For others, their construction of their function as a teacher does not include a critical examination of resources for potential curriculum; for these teachers, the practice of teaching is mostly technical and instrumental, and is separable from an engagement with curriculum content. Interviews with some teachers thus resulted in a difficulty in negotiating the purpose of the interview: having little exposure to cyborgs or cartoons, they would suggest that they had no authority to speak on the subject, and that they would have no knowledge of the correct way to teach the material. A common connection was made with a prevalent discourse that constructs many of these programs as productive of antisocial and violent behaviors.[19] Kids' T.V. as a potential resource for curriculum content or pedagogy runs counter to a view disparagingly summarized by Henry Giroux:

> [Pedagogy] is what follows the selection of ideologically correct content, its legitimacy rooted in whether or not it represents the proper teaching style. In the dominant discourse, pedagogy is simply measurable, accountable methodology used to transmit course content. It is not a mutually conforming element in the construction of knowledge and learning, but an afterthought reduced to the status of the technical and instrumental.

Teachers with this approach to pedagogy seemed most attuned to issues regarding the accuracy of my "data," how representative my sample of children might be, and the most efficacious ordering of tasks in a curriculum based on the topic. I risk identifying this group of experts as the "walking zombies," stripped of their humanity, invisible, and mechanized by the technoculture of schooling. Joe Kincheloe (1993) echoes Ellison in this respect, linking the politics of marginality, teacher thinking, and post-formal thinking:

> In this context teacher questions about the interpretation of information or questions about the moral and ethical nature of the curriculum are deemed dangerous. . . . Here the point emerges that the post-formal ability to ask unique questions and to detect problems never before detected is politically dangerous as it tends to juggle comfortable power relations. Thinking is indeed a political act (p. 151).

Finally, a small group of teachers wished to take advantage of my research project but were unsure about how they might do so because of their very ability to multi-contextualize the research itself:

> How should I interrogate YOUR research and my relationship to educational research? What role do you/I/the students/other teachers play in your project? I think YOU are the bad-guy uncle! I am the child gundam and the students interviewed are the hapless adults that have caused the problem but need my naivet_ to fix things. Or I am

the adult, of course! My students are the bad-guys, and YOU are the child gundam, attaching research gadgets to your body to morph into some superhero that can save us from the epidemic of post-nuclear standardized testing . . . OR: . . .[20]

ß The researcher is Piccolo on *Dragon Ball Z*. I have donned a costume of unusual color—brighter and different. Special details, such as the little claws on my fingers (dark purple, not black, on the program—who would have thought of that? Saturday morning and school and personhood—who would have thought of that?) heighten my uniqueness. Usually, I am a "bad guy," the intellectual-as-terrorist in Foucauldian terms; I aim to explode the bridges of common sense conceptual discourse. But, in some episodes, I align with the "good guy," Go-ku, my usual enemy, in order to defeat another "bad guy" (such as Raditz) who threatens the promise of public education. If nothing else, teaming up a bad guy and a good guy is more interesting for its novelty. Am I human? animal? machine? cyborg? Are educators human, animal, machine, cyborg?

> Go-ku is stronger—because he's actually Raditz's brother, and they're both aliens in a way—they're not human. Piccolo is some special creature. Other good guys might like to help, but they're much too weak and would probably get beaten up in seconds.[21]

> ß I am a *Marvel* cartoon hero. My program provides the metaphor for research because, in cartoons, . . . you can make ANYTHING happen. Well, you can do that with real people but you can REALLY do that with cartoons.[22]

My research pronouncements are thus transformative discourses of possibility rather than descriptions of reality or verifications of hypotheses. They reflect a basic reality in the sense of Baudrillard; yet by masking and perverting this reality, I foster pedagogical change.

ß This research program should be compared to *Iron Man*, which is harder to follow than other programs, but worth the effort.

> If one day you started watching it, you wouldn't know anything about it. They don't tell you much about it unless you see certain episodes. In other *Marvel* shows they make a littler number of villains, so it's

easier to follow. Sometimes a lot of different characters will make it more interesting, but only if you watch it a lot. Like if you have a favorite villain, you may not see that villain again for a LONG time.[23]

In this way, continuing with Baudrillard, my research masks the absence of a basic reality and demands the ongoing construction of an appearance of reality. The "magic" of research, while filled with good intentions, has ambiguous results. The good-guys/bad-guys are blurred into overlapping regions, and the subject of the study shifts from that observed to the observer and back, blurring these boundaries as well. We need to relinquish yet a different fallacy than that offered by Mazlish: that magic and morality are distinct terms. What are we looking at, and where are we looking? It is important to understand that we are not merely looking at the possibility of multiple epistemologies, but living in, with and through these epistemology/cultures.

ß An analysis of relationships among animals, machines, and cyborgs is, in Donna Haraway's (1992) terms, a "technology of vision." Research becomes a prosthetic device we attach to ourselves as part of the divine dream of Descartes' view from above, or the desire to merge with the machine into Mazlishian or Ellisonian invisibility. In such a paradigm, I have a choice: I can re-present a vision of reality more real than any other vision, or I can shrink out of YOUR sight, enabling the voices of those I have worked with to emerge, placing agency firmly in those voices. Surely you are not content with the hubris of the first option nor with the abdication of responsibility and dehumanizing mechanization of the researcher in the second. We realize together that any act of *triage* is a technology of vision rather than a practice of pedagogy and/or research. It would be, as Jim Paul wrote, "just a kind of mechanical vision, fascinating and persistent, against which [our] need to observe [would be] an eddy to the main current." Relationships among animals, people, machines, and cyborgs are not to be observed but lived; they are the stuff of the technoculture we breathe, dance, hate, use, and get used by. We are not looking at the epistemology but living in, with, and through it. We are surfing a mobius strip of technoculture, returning in every relationship to every other. The relationships simultaneously surf US, in an act of agency and *triage* that, in Haraway's new vision, may just as likely trick us, or treat us to their own humor. Harkening back to the origins of *triage* in Napoleonic battlefields, it is clear that any particular enactment wields morality in the service of power and ideology. Children performing their own mini-*triage* in selecting favorite programs from a menu of viewing options enact a parallel version of morality as a technology of vision. As do teachers who *triage currere* possibilities at the door to their classrooms, sending Kids' T.V. to either top priority, possible use, or low-status detritus. For me to add to the symbolic violence by selecting quotes that merged in my talks with children and teachers is perhaps a further act of immorality, perhaps a feat of magic.

It can only be magic if we read this act of research without expectations of appropriative knowledge stuff to look at. The research (Martin, 1996) is rhizomic in character, forging relationships in evasive, extensive, and intricately interconnected ways, much like the relationships that were forged among researcher, children, and teachers involved in the project: inexpressible as conclusions of scientistic research, the rhizome is magically moral in its intentions, successfully living in symbiotic status with educational institutional practices, inherently non-mechanistic in structure and function. We have simply performed a new feat of magic: we've pulled the rug out from under the legs of the animal-human-machine *triage* and seen that we can leave all of the technologies of vision still and intact. The magic, though, is in the rug, which can be used as a new prosthetic as we choose: ride it as a magic carpet.

Of course the whole point of this paper is NOT to prove that Kids' T.V. is or could be a central component of the constructed selves of students, teachers and researchers. If we use technoculture and cyborg metaphors to look at the selves of pedagogical practice, the research becomes a technology of vision which splits what is observed and analyzed into a spectrum of technoculture. If we employ technoculture and cyborg metaphors as a mode of enunciation with which we speak and write a story of pedagogical practice, the research becomes a technology of sign systems, power and the self, and of production. This is not to say that such stories do not exist and are not rhizomatically linked in innumerable ways with the one that appears here. They might be more likely to be found in other spaces, and told by other characters from *this* story.

We can produce, transform or manipulate curriculum; we wield signs, meanings, symbols or signification practices in our discourse; we determine the conduct of people and apply templates of analysis that submit subjects to ends, domination, and objectification; and we permit some people to, as Foucault has described, "effect by their own means or with the help of others a certain number of operations on their own bodies and souls, thoughts, conduct, and way of being, so as to transform themselves." Cyborg selves become a technology of morality when they enunciate a hierarchy between knowing oneself and taking care of oneself. The gundam or animé hero surfing and breathing technoculture lunges for self-care and begins to know his or her self through the act of self-care, discovering self-potential and realization. The machine-self of the invisible man shuns self care in the process of self-knowledge. The cyborg teacher is positioned in a web of possibility that presents links to any technology of vision, enunciation, self-knowledge, or self-care, and is itself in relation to such technologies imbricated in extended webs of possibility, power, signs, and production. Technoculture is a node in the web, a region of the mobius strip, a character in a saga.

NOTES

1. I would like to thank my research assistant, Noah Appelbaum, and Belinda Davis, for the initial suggestion that Saturday Morning has shifted from cold-war anxiety to a celebration of technoscience in the solution of its own havoc. Thanks also for the great critiques from Stefanie Rotsaert, Shirley Steinberg, and John Weaver.

2. Dividing into categories, or an act of triage. *Triage* in a different sense, but also compatible in its pursuit of a moral context and the social and cultural values represented by representations of education, can be found in Sue Books' article, "Literary Journalism as Educational Criticism: A Discourse on Triage." *Holistic Education Review.* 5 (3), 1992: 41-51.

3. This work begins with an embrace of concepts found in the work of Michel Foucault. See, e.g., *Power/Knowledge: Selected Interviews and Other Writings.* Brighton, England: Harvester Press, 1980; L. H. Martin, H. Gutman, and P. Hutton (Eds.), *Technologies of the self: A seminar with Michel Foucault.* Amherst, MA: University of Massachusetts Press, 1988. For another discussion of self, subjectivity, and power, see Julian Henriques, et al. *Changing the subject: Psychology, social regulations and subjectivity.* London: Methuen, 1984.

4. See, e.g., Charles Rosen, "Beethoven's Triumph," *New York Review of Books.* XLII, 14, 1995: 52-6.

5. My research is consistent with those of others who seek to respond to concerns about teacher empowerment. See, e.g., Janet Miller's *Creating spaces*

and finding voices: Teachers collaborating for empowerment. Albany, NY: SUNY Press, 1990:

> Within these daily spaces, clearings forged in the midst of permission slips and mandated curriculum and computer print-outs of test-scores, educators do recognize that the fissures of teaching and research, theory and practice, public and private, are artificial distinctions that separate us from ourselves and from the relationships in which knowledges about self and about our worlds are generated. (p. 172)

See also Joe Kincheloe's Toward a Critical Politics of Teacher Thinking: Mapping the Postmodern. Westport, CT: Bergin & Garvey, 1993:

The issue of knowledge control moves us into a direct confrontation with teacher power. We cannot maintain a view of students as democratic participants and teachers as disempowered technicians. Over sixty years ago, Dewey argued that teachers must assume the power to assert themselves on matters of educational importance with the assurance that this judgment will affect what happens in schools. Present technicist models of teacher education do not accept this argument, often teaching novices not to seek empowerment, not to think in an independent manner. Indeed, the hidden curriculum of technicist teacher education promotes a passive view of teachers, they are seen as rule followers who are rendered more "suspensable" with their standardized lesson plan formats and their adaptation to technical evaluation plans. (p.35)

6. Appelbaum, Peter. *Popular Culture, Educational Discourse, and Mathematics.* Albany, NY: SUNY Press, 1995; Making 'Sense' of Curriculum as Commodity or Cultural Resource. American Educational Studies Association, Cleveland, OH. November 1-5, 1995.

7. It should be recognized that children enjoy viewing some programs not discussed in this chapter. Teachers mentioned, for example, *Bill Nye the Science Guy, Wishbone,* and *Animaniacs.* However, the children I spoke with did not suggest these programs in my interviews. Even those children who later agreed that these others would be worth my time viewing did not include such programs in their recommendations.

8. See Mazlish: 216-219.

9. Interview excerpt.

10. Hargreaves: 84.

11. Bell, Beverly. *Children's science, constructivism and learning in science.* Deakin University Press, Australia, 1993. The issue of difference between children's and adults' epistemological *triage* of cyborg opens up a host

of dilemmas. I want to avoid reifying the distinctions in a backhanded ageist construction of "adult" and "child" through my descriptions of these meaning-making activities. Yet there are important constellations of cyborg as "power" versus cyborg as "sex" in these discourses (see, e.g., Freudian analyses of cinematic cyborgs, virtual sex, cyborgs and goddesses . . .). This is an area that requires a great deal of synthesis, ranging from Foucault's work on the care of the self (Michel Foucault, *The History of Sexuality*. New York: Pantheon, 1978) to work of Evelyn Fox Keller on the sexual metaphors of knowing and knowledge (*Reflections on Gender and Science*. New Haven, CT: Yale University Press, 1985). The links become clearer to me when I think in terms of the Foucauldian collapse of power/knowledge. But there is much to be done here in respect to curriculum research and theory.

12. Interview excerpt.

13. Interview excerpt.

14. Much work has been done in this area of curriculum. For exemplary work, see Noel Gough's *Laboratories of fiction*. Deakin, Australia: Deakin University Press, 1993.

15. Interview excerpt.

16. Interview excerpt.

17. Interview excerpt.

18. Kincheloe suggests this is an example of post-formal teaching: 115.

19. See, e.g., "Consumer Culture: Power and the Identity Politics of Mathematics Education," in Appelbaum, 1995.

20. See, e.g., Levin, Diane E. & Carlsson-Page, Nancy. "The Mighty Morphin Power Rangers: Teachers Voice Concern." *Young Children*. Sept, 1995: 67-72; American Psychological Association. *Violence and Youth: Psychology's Response*. Washington, DC: American Psychological Association, 1993; National Association for the Education of Young Children. NAEYC Position Statement on Media Violence in Children's Lives. *Young Children* 45 (5): 18-21. Pereira, J. "Caution: 'Morphing' May Be Hazardous to Your Teacher." *Wall Street Journal*. 7 (Dec), 224 (111): 1, 8.

21. Interview excerpt.

22. Interview excerpt.

23. Interview excerpt.

REFERENCES

Baudrillard, J. (1990). *Seduction*. New York: St. Martin's Press.

Bell, B. (1993). *Children's science, constructivism and learning in science*. Deakin, Australia: Deakin University Press.

Ellison, R. (1947/1952). *Invisible man.* New York: New American Library.

Foucault, M. (1988). Technologies of the self. In L. H. Martin, H. Gutman, & P. Hutton (Eds.), *Technologies of the self* (p. 18). Amherst, MA: The University of Massachusetts Press.

Gallas, K. (1995). *Talking their way into science: Hearing children's questions and theories, responding with curricular.* New York: Teachers College Press.

Giroux, H., & Simon, R. (19989). Popular culture and critical pedagogy. In H. A. Giroux & P. McLaren (Eds.), *Critical pedagogy, the state, and cultural struggle.* Albany, NY: SUNY Press.

Haraway, D. (1985). A manifesto for cyborgs: Science, technology, and socialist feminism in the 1980s. *Socialist Review, 80,* 65-107. Reprinted in *Feminism/Postmodernism,* edited by Linda J. Nicholson. new York: Routledge, 1990, pp. 190-233.

Haraway, D. (1992). Situated knowledges: The science question in feminism and the privilege of partial perspective. In *Simians, cyborgs, and women: The reinvention of nature* (pp. 183-202). New York: Routledge.

Hargreaves, A. (1994). *Changing teachers, changing times: Teachers' work and culture in the postmodern age.* New York: Teachers College Press.

Joseph, P. B., & Burnaford, G. E. (1994). *Images of schoolteachers in twentieth-century America.* New York: St. Martin's Press.

Kincheloe, J. (1993). *Toward a critical politics of teacher thinking: Mapping the postmodern.* Westport, CT: Bergin & Garvey.

MacDonald, J. (1995). A transcendental developmental ideology of education. In B. J. MacDonald (Ed.), *Theory as a prayerful act: The collected essays of James B. MacDonald.* With an introduction by William F. Pinar. New York: Peter Lang.

Martin, E. (1996). Citadels, rhizomes, and string figures. In S. Aronowitz, B. Martinson, & M. Menser (Eds.), *Technoscience and cyberculture* (pp. 97-110). New York: Routledge.

Mazlish, B. (1993) *The fourth discontinuity: The co-evolution of humans and machines.* New Haven, CT: Yale Press.

Mead, M. (1970). *Culture and commitment: A study of the generation gap.* New York: Doubleday.

Menser, M. (1996). Becoming—heterarch: on technocultural theory, minor science, and the production of space. In S. Aronowitz, B. Martinson, & M. Menser (Eds.), *Technoscience and cyberculture* (pp. 293-316). New York: Routledge.

Paul, J. (1991). *Catapult: Harry and I build a siege weapon*. New York: Avon Books.

Pinar, W. (Ed.). (1975). *Curriculum theorizing: The reconceptualists*. Berkeley, CA: McCutchan.

Ross, A. (1991). *Strange weather: Culture, science and technology in the age of limits*. New York: Verso.

Rushkoff, D. (1996). *Playing the future: How kids' culture can teach us to think in an age of chaos*. New York: HarperCollins.

Stine, R. L. (1994). *The scarecrow walks at midnight*. New York: Scholastic.

Waught, C. (1947). *The comics*. Jackson, MS: University Press of Mississippi.

CHAPTER FIVE

Teachers and Popular Culture Consumption: Notes Toward an Alternative Theory of Teachers' Non-Appropriation of Instructional Research

Jason Earle

The infrequency of teachers' use of instructional research continues to be a concern in the educational research community (Fullan, 1995; Hargreaves, 1996; Hutchinson & Huberman, 1993; Louis, 1992; Rothkopf, 1995). As one prominent scholar notes, "The quest to improve research utilization in education has failed over the last three decades . . ." (Fullan, 1992, p. 1). Different theories have been proposed to best explain why teachers do not appropriate educational research (Hutchinson & Huberman, 1993; Hargreaves, 1996). Typically, these theories have not stressed the influences on teachers from the wider society (Weber & Mitchell, 1995). In particular, these theories fail to acknowledge the increasing importance of popular culture consumption in the lives of teachers (Weber & Mitchell, 1995).

This article draws on analytic tools from the investigation of popular culture consumption to address the issue of teachers' non-appropriation of instructional research. Studies of popular culture have been used by other education scholars to better understand the everyday lives of students (Farber, Provenzo, & Holm, 1994; Giroux & Simon, 1989). Recently, scholars have turned to popular culture to better understand the everyday life of teachers (Weber & Mitchell, 1995). This paper hopes to add to these efforts. Specifically, studies of popular culture consumption are drawn on to work towards a new theoretical lens to understand teachers' non-appropriation of instructional research.

The paper is divided into three sections. The first section briefly reviews some of the literature on popular culture. The second section offers a discussion of why the issue of popular culture versus instructional research became of concern to me and the methods I drew on to address this issue. The third section provides a discussion of an alternative theoretical approach to use in exploring teachers' non-appropriation of instructional research.

POPULAR CULTURE: THEORY AND RESEARCH

Many scholars look to the Frankfurt School's early analyses of the culture industry as the starting point for the study of popular culture (Agger, 1992). Others see the pioneering work of Richard Hoggart, Raymond Williams, and E. P. Thompson as the key building blocks from which the Birmingham Center for Contemporary Cultural Studies emerged. Under the auspices of The Birmingham Center a number of important empirical and theoretical studies on popular culture were conducted (Storey, 1993). Whichever starting point one picks, it is hard not to acknowledge the growing scholarly focus on popular culture.

There are a wide range of different theoretical approaches to the study of popular culture (Storey, 1996). Some have argued that these different theoretical approaches can be broadly categorized in terms of a textual focus or a consumption focus (Moores, 1993; Stacey, 1994; Storey, 1996). With a textual focus researchers use a variety of theories to analyze the content and form of different films, television programs, books, and music. The assumption is that the meanings, ideologies, discourses, messages, themes, and contradictions identified by the researcher are what is generally communicated and understood by the audiences who view or read different types of popular culture.

A consumption focus asks the actual audience members of popular culture to articulate the meanings and messages they in fact extract from the movie, show, song, or book (Stacey, 1994). This approach is often called audience ethnography, because, like their anthropological counterparts, these researchers gather their data through written responses, interviewing, participant observation, and focus groups

(Moores, 1993). This approach to the study of popular culture has proven to be especially enlightening, because audiences frequently report extracting meanings that are quite divergent from the ones identified or predicted by textual researchers (Morley, 1980). This scholarship has contributed important changes to the theory of how popular culture actually impacts audience appropriation of meaning. Some who disagree with these theoretical changes have come to view the consumption approach as a form of cultural populism, because it emphasizes the ". . . symbolic experiences and practices of ordinary people"(McGuigan, 1992, p. 4) over the insights of researchers. For others this is a positive feature of the consumption approach (Storey, 1996).

In the last seven years, the study of popular culture has begun to attract the attention of some educators (Farber, Provenzo, & Holm, 1994; Giroux, 1994; Giroux & Simon, 1989; Schwoch, White, & Reilly, 1992; Weber & Mitchell, 1995). These researchers have started to grapple with the role popular culture plays in the everyday lives of students and teachers. Henry Giroux (1994) has been particularly instrumental in helping the educational community to better understand the "disturbing pleasures" embodied in different types of popular culture. However, Giroux and other educational researchers have almost exclusively relied on a textual approach in the study to popular culture. Despite many discussions about the importance of student and teacher voices, Giroux and other researchers have rarely done audience ethnographies or featured quotes from the voices of student and teacher audiences. Their studies also infrequently draw on the theoretical insights of the consumption literature. This chapter hopes to be a step in altering this trend.

CONCERNS AND METHODS

The notion of theory-making as a means of intervening into education has been an important issue for educators recently (Britzman, 1992; Giroux, 1983; Simon, 1992). This attempt at theory-making was informed by my research with teachers in public schools and my work as an instructor for teacher-education courses at the university level. I have been repeatedly struck by my undergraduate and graduate students' many queries as to why instructional research and its presentation in books and articles cannot be more interesting, accessible and fun like the popular culture—movies, television, music, and magazines—they encountered in everyday life. I have also been repeatedly surprised by comments from bright, articulate teachers like the following: "I have learned from the teachers in movies and on TV, and I try to emulate the manner and style of those that I respect and those that are effective." Rather than dismiss these types of comments with remarks about the need to delay gratification and work harder or how unrealistic movies and TV are, my hope was to begin developing more useful ways of understanding my students' and also to critically engage with them around these issues.

As noted above, students of popular culture have emphasized the importance of doing what they call audience ethnography to better understand how people appropriate different media products (Moores, 1993; Stacey, 1994; Storey, 1996). This involves gathering audiences opinions, thoughts, and beliefs through written responses, interviews, or focus groups. With this consumption approach in mind, students in my undergraduate and graduate classes were asked to write papers about their experience of watching popular movies about teaching. Student writing was also collected from undergraduate teacher education students at a nearby public university. Many students were also asked to compare their movie-watching experience to that of reading about teaching in the books and articles from their education classes. The point of asking students to write was to provide some extended audience discourse to examine as a starting point for theory generation.

The literature from consumption approach also played a key role in my theory-making efforts. As discussed above, there is a rich tradition in cultural studies of theorizing and studying the consumption of popular culture (Stacey, 1994; Storey, 1996). Hence, drawing from audience ethnographies and consumption theoretical work (Storey, 1996), students' papers (n = 116), and class discussions, I began to formulate the beginning of a theory that might offer new categories for understanding teacher's non-appropriation of instructional research. My intent is to offer theoretical categories for working with my students and colleagues and to suggest directions for future research. I also hope to loosen the boundary between university-based knowledge and popular culture knowledge by problematizing the historical hierarchy that views university-based knowledge as the sole or most legitimate source of teacher knowledge (see Hargreaves, 1996). A discussion of this beginning theory follows. At various points in the presentation quotes or findings from student papers are used for illustrative purposes.

NOTES TOWARDS A NEW THEORETICAL LENS

I start this section by summarizing my central arguments. Popular culture texts provide the dominant means of communicating knowledge to the general public in a postmodern society (Aronowitz & Giroux, 1991; Kellner, 1995). In fact, popular culture currently constitutes what some scholars would call a common culture (Storey, 1996; Willis, 1990). These scholars are not suggesting a commonality based on a value consensus, but rather a shared experience based on the consumption of popular culture.

There are significant differences in the form and content of instructional research compared to popular culture. In a common culture dominated by the form and content of popular culture, the form and content of instructional research is an unappealing, aberrant experience. In this context, instructional research may be unlikely to be appropriated.

Additionally, teachers are more apt to recognize themselves as belonging to the cultural world embodied in popular culture compared to the cultural world of instructional research. This recognition is based on two homologies or similarities (Hebdige, 1979; Willis, 1990) between the cultural world of teachers and the cultural world of popular culture. One, the form and content of teachers' on-the-job personal practical knowledge (Clandinin & Connelly, 1995) is similar to the form and content of popular culture, not that of instructional research. Two, a popular aesthetic that most people such as teachers are socialized into (Bourdieu, 1986) is similar to what is offered by movies, television, etc. and not by instructional research. Therefore, instructional research is comparatively less appealing than popular culture and, probably less likely to be appropriated. A full discussion of the initial theoretical attempt follows.

Popular Culture as a Common Cultural Experience

There seems to be a good deal of scholarly agreement that in the current postmodern world of Post-World War II popular culture is the dominant means for communicating knowledge (Giroux & Simon, 1989; Farber, Provenzo, & Holm, 1994; Kellner, 1995; Poster, 1995; Schwoch, White, & Reilly, 1992; Willis, 1990). Cultural studies scholar

Paul Willis (1990), from the vantage point of a large scale ethnography, takes this a step further by arguing that commercially produced popular culture has

> helped to produce an historical present from which we cannot now escape and in which there are many more materials—no matter what we think of them—available for symbolic work than ever there were in the past. Out of these come forms not dreamt of in commercial imagination and certainly not in the official one—forms which make up common culture. (p. 19)

Willis is not suggesting in the manner of functionalist sociologists like Talcot Parsons (1951) that a value consensus exists. Rather he is arguing that a sense of commonality has developed amongst people based on their shared experience of consuming popular culture.

This common culture based on movies, television, music, magazines, and newspapers has profoundly altered our way of life and the very substance of our identities. Kellner (1995) asserts that popular culture ". . . images, sounds, and spectacles help produce the fabric of everyday life, dominating leisure time, shaping political views and social behavior, and providing materials out of which people forge their very identities" (p. 1). Building on these insights, Weber and Mitchell (1995) have indicated that popular culture is a key part of what they term the "cumulative cultural text" that powerfully informs children's and, subsequently, teachers' lives and identity. I would argue that because popular culture is a common cultural experience from which life and identity is constructed and university-based instructional research is such a relatively rare experience for most of us growing up, that the features of popular culture may be thought of as having been "naturalized" (Barthes, 1972) and, consequently, have an appeal that instructional research does not.

The concept of *text* begins to offer us a way to describe the different features of popular culture and instructional research. Many cultural studies scholars employ the concept of *text* when referring to signifying practices such as movies, television shows, songs, magazines, and books (Storey, 1993). This concept is useful because it calls attention to, in a way that the concept knowledge does not, the fact that knowledge is embedded in a particular form of communication such as a book, article, lecture, movie, and television show. The form clearly matters to people. Large numbers of people select some forms of communication over others. For example, many people choose to watch television rather than read books (Farber, Provenzo, & Holm, 1994). Hence, the knowledge embodied in university-based instructional research texts must be understood in relationship to other textual forms, particularly the dominant audience-generating texts of popular culture. The content of university-based instructional research texts must also be understood in relationship to popular cultural texts. Movies, television, radio, magazines, and newspapers as popular forms of communication frequently focus on different types of subject matter than university-based texts (Fiske, 1992). The differences in content and form may be thought about in terms of *distance, codes, pleasure,* and *utopian hopes.*

DISTANCE. John Fiske (1992) has argued that "distance is a key marker of difference" between the texts of academic culture and the texts of popular culture. Academics' socialization into high levels of education cultivates a value placed on distance between themselves and the mundane qualities of everyday life. The academic disposition for distance encourages researchers to transcend the concrete particulars of context. This belief in a transcendent, distance predisposes academics to create "generalized, abstracted understandings" rather than understandings grounded in the "concrete specificities" of the contextualized lives of the subjects they study.

These "generalized, abstracted understandings" are embodied in instructional research books and articles about teaching, students, and classrooms (Hargreaves, 1996). And, as Hargreaves notes they are "detached" from the everyday specifics of a concrete classroom. "University-based knowledge was not tailored to any one school or classroom, but transcended the many different kinds of contexts in which teachers taught" (p. 106).

By contrast, the "embodied, concrete, context specific" nature of the everyday is a key feature of popular culture texts (Bourdieu, 1986; Fiske, 1992; Giroux & Simon, 1989; Storey, 1996). As Fiske (1989) notes, ". . . popular art is valued to the extent that it is of 'interest,' that is, interested in everyday life and not distant from it" (p. 139) This can be seen reflected in audience studies of popular television shows. Cultural studies scholar Ien Ang (1985) studied what viewers liked and disliked about a very popular evening program, *Dallas.* One of Ang's important findings was that *Dallas* viewers could lose themselves in the show. They could do this because *Dallas* closely reflected what viewers believed they experienced in their everyday lives.

This same concern is found in many of my students' comments about the differences between learning about teaching through university-based education texts versus popular culture texts like movies. Many students saw movies about teaching as more attentive to the contextualized concrete act of teaching in specific classrooms and schools. For example:

> I prefer to watch movies as an education tool [compared to books] because they put you in the classroom.

> [Compared to the book], the movie seemed more positive to me because it expressed the relationship between teacher and students. It showed that a teacher and student can work together in a struggling environment. Specifically, I am referring to the daily classroom scenes in the movie.

> I prefer movies over education textbooks in learning how to teach. The motion pictures with education themes bring to life a particular version of classroom teaching. Within *To Sir with Love* methods of teaching were demonstrated with real live teachers, students, [and] school buildings.

CODES. Codes are another feature that distinguishes different types of texts. Codes are the rules or conventions that govern different mediated forms of communication (Fiske, 1990). Scholars of popular culture recognize that codes can differ depending on the target audience of a text (Agger, 1992; Fiske, 1990; Storey, 1993). The codes used for the audiences of popular culture texts are referred to as broadcast codes. "A broadcast code is one that is shared by members of a mass audience: it has to cater for a degree of heterogeneity" (Fiske, 1990, p. 73).

The codes used for the audiences of university-based texts are referred to as narrowcast codes. "A narrowcast code . . . is one aimed at a specific audience" (p. 73). These narrowcast codes are complex and do not have immediate appeal (Fiske, 1992). They employ impersonal language that often excludes members of non-university audiences. Also, they are typically low key and without characters so they do not encourage personal identification. The flow of ideas are also based on logic and analysis rather than a narrative form.

For Fiske (1990), the broadcast codes of popular culture texts "are simple; they have an immediate appeal; and they do not require an 'education' (emphasis in the original) to understand them. They are community oriented, appealing to what people have in common . . ." (p. 74). Broadcast codes are also lively and frequently offer opportunity for personal identification with particular characters, human beings, or situations. The flow of ideas is in an appealing narrative or associational form.

The importance of broadcast codes for popular culture texts are evident in studies of popular culture audiences (Moores, 1993). For example, broadcast codes play an important part in Dorothy Hobson's (1982) study of television soap opera audiences. Hobson interviewed and observed women in their homes who enjoyed watching soap operas. She found that the different broadcast codes which consisted of non-linear narratives and a heavy emphasis on character dialogue were key features which kept viewers interested and involved in the soap operas.

Again, students comments about the differences between learning about teaching through education texts versus popular culture texts like movies reflects a concern with codes. Students viewed the codes in movies about teaching as more engaging and involving compared to the codes of university-based texts. For example:

> [Compared to a book] the movie was easy to watch. The language was what I am used to hearing. . . It also had a plot. The movie flowed while telling Mr. Holland's "story."

> The basic difference between watching a movie about teaching and reading a book about teaching is the involvement of the viewer/readers, especially in a movie such as *Dangerous Minds*. A book can clearly and concisely outline teaching strategies and discipline techniques, tell how to manage paperwork, . . . yet never cover the human element involved in teaching.

> In comparison with [the book], the movie was different because it had more narration. [The movie] did not explain to the audience what the problems were. The movie told a story and let the audience

reflect on what was told. I enjoyed reflecting on the narrative. The learning is personalized and meaningful.

PLEASURE. The texts of popular culture encourage the experience of bodily pleasure in the consumer, whereas the texts of academics encourage disciplining the body of the consumer (Fiske, 1992). Academic culture puts an emphasis on restraining the body as the body's sensual pleasure is looked upon as a false or inferior pleasure (Fiske, 1989; 1992). Academics emphasize a different form of pleasure, a pleasure that can only come through the training and discipline required to appreciate, understand, or conduct research (Fiske, 1992). Hence, the discipline of a doctoral education is in many respects part of forgoing the bodily pleasure that most of society sees as a valued part of their lives. This also means that academic training and discipline offer an appreciation of textual form and content from which only a small community of people derives pleasure.

By contrast, many scholars of popular culture have recognized the pleasure that audiences derive from television, romance novels, and other popular texts (Ang, 1985; Fiske, 1989; Giroux & Simon, 1989; Radway, 1991; Stacey, 1994). Fiske (1989), drawing from Barthes, argues that *reading* popular culture texts promotes *jouissance*, the ecstasy and bliss of bodily feelings and emotions. In addition, there is a pleasure that is added to this joy by virtue of evading the disciplinary control over self "that those with power attempt so insistently to exert" (p. 69) in capitalist societies.

This pleasure is evident in a number of studies of popular cultures texts (Stacey, 1994). A particularly interesting example is found in the work of Janice Radway (1991). Radway studied a community of women who were exceptionally involved with reading romance novels. She found that the pleasure these women received from reading these books was a key part of their interest and continued involvement with romance novels. In fact reading romance novels was one of the few pleasures they received in lives that were frequently devoted to taking care of husbands and children.

A concern with pleasure was found in many of my students' comments about the differences between learning about teaching through university-based education texts versus popular culture texts like movies. Students were clearly attuned to the differences in pleasure in terms of bodily emotion and excitement offered by the movies about teaching compared to that offered by university-based texts. For example:

> Being able to see [keeping student expectations high] on the screen means a lot more to me than reading it in a book. By actually seeing it, there is more feeling. You can see the expressions on the actors' faces and feel what they feel.

> A drawback of reading textbooks is overcoming boredom. Textbook language is not written to be exciting and entertaining. On the other hand, watching a movie about teaching is entertaining and holds one's interest about the subject.

> Studying about education using a text . . . can be boring. I enjoy being in a classroom with children. It compares favorably to the movies. Going to the movies is a treat [and it's] entertaining. Now if someone could just make textbooks entertaining, we would really enjoy school.

UTOPIAN HOPES. The texts of popular culture embody utopian hopes and wishes for a better world (Dyer, 1993). Instructional research texts seek to embody an instrumental rationality that is oriented towards focusing on the means rather than a discussion of valued future ends (Apple, 1990; Giroux, 1983). One of the key assumptions of traditional university-based knowledge is the notion of neutrality (Apple, 1990). Drawn from the scientific model, university-based texts present "an accumulation of neutral empirical facts" (p. 8). Mastering this type of neutral knowledge was thought to make teachers technical experts at their jobs (Welker, 1992) and would provide the most effective "means" to help students. However, maintaining the focus on neutral, instrumental means silenced a discussion of the ethics, morality, beliefs, and hopes of particular educational goals; this eliminated the possibility of discourse centered on a better future (Giroux, 1983).

By contrast, a key feature of the entertainment-oriented texts of popular culture are that they offer "the image of 'something better' to escape into, or something we want deeply that our day-to-day lives [doesn't] provide" (Dyer, 1993, p. 273). As cultural studies scholar Richard Dyer (1993) notes, "[a]lternatives, hopes, wishes—these are the stuff of utopia, the sense that things could be better, that something other than what is can be imagined and maybe realized" (p. 273). However, popular culture texts do not provide actual "models of utopia." Rather "utopianism is contained" in the beliefs and feelings embodied in popular culture texts. These beliefs and feelings suggest the possibility of a sense of efficacy and transformation often difficult to reach in everyday life.

Utopian hopes can be found in many forms of popular culture (Fiske, 1989). A useful example is found in Dyer's (1993) study of Hollywood musicals. For Dyer a utopian sensibility is found in both the representational and non-representational aspects of movie musicals. Both aspects are used to bridge the gap between how things are in a capitalist society and how things might be in a better future.

Once again, these types of concern were found in student comments about the differences between learning about teaching through education texts versus popular culture texts like movies. Students noted that movies affirmed their own beliefs about the potential positive futures offered through the act of teaching. For example:

> Though a bit unrealistic [compared to the "factual" information in books], this movie affirmed my beliefs about teaching. Teachers/people do make a difference. A caring person can change the world. One person at a time, one battle at a time, people who genuinely care for the well being of other people make this world we live in a better place.

> This movie was like a mystical fairy tale. It took a set of students who thought they couldn't achieve anything, put them with a remarkable teacher who taught them to give everything, and in the end they achieved such success that many people didn't believe it was possible. It was because of their teacher that the students reached their goals. If every teacher could do this, the world would be a much better place.

> In the movie *Stand and Deliver*, my hopes were lifted by the fact that one man was able to change so many negative attitudes among poor students. Jamie Escalante turned these inner city youths into intelligent, high achievers. In turn their self-concepts were improved. This makes me feel wonderful. By watching this movie, a bright ray of hope entered my thoughts that anyone can, in fact, succeed. . . .

Having discussed the different textual features found in popular culture texts versus instructional research texts, the paper now turns to a discussion of some other factors that impact the appropriation of these different types of texts.

Textual Hailing and Audiences

Communication theorists speak of texts as "hailing" readers, addressing them, beckoning them with particular textual features (Fiske, 1990). Hence, the popular culture texts discussed above can be thought of as hailing teachers with a concrete everydayness, accessible narratives, bodily and emotional pleasure, and hope. Some might say in response to this notion, that it is no wonder that teachers accept being hailed, and gladly take up the vapid, entertaining subject positions offered by these texts. Hence, the argument might suggest, popular culture texts, like most commodities in a capitalist society, turn teachers into unthinking passive consumers (Ewen, 1988). Teachers are ideologically "captured" by the hail of popular entertainment.

The argument continues that as instructional research texts require serious and thoughtful effort, it is probably not surprising that teachers do not respond favorably to being hailed by these texts. The distant, cautious, disciplined, and instrumental orientation of the scholarly identity offered by academic texts does not address teachers in nearly as lighthearted and superficial a manner. Instructional research texts are far more demanding and so their hail goes unheeded.

Although there is some truth in this, there is a problem with seeing textual features that hail audiences as the whole or as even the most important part of understanding teachers' appropriation of various texts. An important insight of cultural studies scholarship in the last 15 years has been that popular culture texts cannot, through various textual features, compel unwitting audiences to appropriate them and enjoy them (Moores, 1993; Stacey, 1994). Hailing cannot force people into participating in the dominant ideology. Audience members bring their own interests, beliefs, and agenda to texts of all varieties (Willis, 1990). By virtue of this, audiences can accept a text completely, negotiate with it, or reject the text altogether (Storey, 1993). This can be seen reflected in my students' comments about the movies as a tool for learning about teaching. They suggest that teachers are not simply hailed by pleasant textual features and turned into hapless consumers:

[B]ecause of the subjective nature of movies and the fact that many movies are not based on true stories we tend to take bits and pieces of ideas that we [as teachers] find interesting. We tend to adapt television or movie ideas and make them our own. [We take] good ideas and use our professional ability and training and change or adapt them for the classroom.

Movies such as *To Sir with Love, Mr. Holland's Opus, Lean on Me,* and *Matt Waters* do offer many positive images of teachers that I find helpful. [However], [m]ovie/tv shows such as *The Principal* or *The Faculty* can tear down positive images built by positive teacher movies.

Although movie and TV shows can be very unrealistic in their portrayals, I still like them better than textbooks. In most cases I am able to distinguish that which is not realistic and still understand the point.

Because audience members, like my inservice and preservice education students, actively engage cultural texts, a good deal of work has gone into developing a better understanding of why audiences appropriate some texts and not others (Willis, 1990; Stacey, 1994; Storey, 1996). A key factor identified by this scholarly work is the notion of *recognition* (Ang, 1985; Bourdieu, 1986; Stacey, 1994).

RECOGNITION AND INSERVICE AND PRESERVICE TEACHERS

Ien Ang (1985), borrowing from the work of Pierre Bourdieu, very clearly articulated what was involved with audience recognition (Stacey, 1994). She wrote that "[w]hat matters is the possibility of identifying oneself with [a popular culture text] in some way or another to integrate it into everyday life. In other words, popular pleasure is first and foremost a pleasure of recognition" (p. 20, Ang, 1985). This notion of recognition is nicely illustrated by comments from my students' papers:

I find the movie pleasurable to watch because the character Robin Williams plays reminds me of myself. I like to make the students laugh. In fact, I feel like a stand-up comedian sometimes. I think it is important that the students enjoy learning and find relevance in what they learn.

I was able to identify with [Miss Johnson in *Dangerous Minds*] because she was also a beginning teacher with limited experiences, looking for effective strategies to make learning relevant. I felt I could identify with her concern about her students, particularly in scenes when she talked about her male colleagues. I discuss concerns about my students with my colleagues because I am searching for the best ways to make learning fun and meaningful for them, as she did in the movie.

[Mr. Holland] was very much in the same situation as I. He taught elective classes, loved what he did, and had the students care about his work as much as he did.

Cultural studies scholars helps us to flesh out the notion of recognition by articulating more explicitly what aids an audience such as preservice and inservice teachers in this process. Dick Hebdige (1979) and Paul Willis (1990) argue for the importance of homology, a correspondence between what is offered by the text and the world of the audience. "There must be some kind of *homology* between the symbolic resources and meanings of the text and the values, concerns, meanings, and preoccupations of the receivers" (p. 154). I would argue that there are two homologies that facilitate teachers' sense of recognizing themselves in popular culture texts.

TEACHERS' PERSONAL PRACTICAL KNOWLEDGE. D. Jean Clandinin and F. Michael Connelly (1995) and others (see Hargreaves, 1996) have explored teachers' appropriation and construction of everyday work knowledge. This research argues that teachers' create and appropriate knowledge that is context-specific, narrative in form, "grounded in the body," emotional, and moral (Britzman, 1992; Clandinin & Connelly, 1995). Teachers communicate this personal practical knowledge through images, metaphors, and stories (Hargreaves, 1996). This suggests that the content and form of teachers' own work knowledge is more homologous to popular culture texts than instructional research texts. Hence, teachers are more likely to recognize themselves in popular culture texts.

One might argue that this homology may account for inservice teachers recognizing themselves in popular culture texts, but, as preservice teachers have not spent much time teaching in the classroom, it does not account for their recognition. I would argue this is correct and suggest that the homology discussed below adds to our understanding of why preservice teachers recognize themselves in popular culture texts. The homology discussed below also enhances inservice teachers recognition of themselves in popular culture texts as well.

POPULAR AESTHETICS. There is a growing scholarly argument that knowledge, despite the millennial hope of rationalists and positivists, is grounded in an aesthetic (Greenfield, 1992; Mosse, 1991; Nelson, 1990; Noble, 1996), a sense of beauty, art, and taste that informs what knowledge "feels" right or wrong. Groups socialize their members into an aesthetic along with other values, beliefs, and norms (Bourdieu, 1986; Greenfield, 1992; Mosse, 1991; Nelson, 1990; Noble, 1996).

Another line of research and theory about audiences builds on this insight and seeks to understand the broad sociological differences between audiences with high levels of cultural capital such as academics and those with less cultural capital (Bourdieu, 1986; Fiske, 1992; Moores, 1993) such as preservice and inservice teachers. This scholarship, initiated by Pierre Bourdieu (1986), suggests that people with high levels of cultural capital are socialized into a bourgeois aesthetic. This aesthetic places an importance on the distance between the self and the consumption of cultural texts. Texts that invite direct participation or portray the concrete reality of everyday life are viewed as unimportant (Fiske, 1992). The bourgeois aesthetic creates a strong preference for cultural texts that use codes requiring high levels of education to appreciate. There is an emphasis on the aesthetics of the "correct" forms used by a text rather than the function of the text. This aesthetic also views cultural texts that evoke bodily emotions and pleasures as vulgar and unworthy of attention.

The popular aesthetic, embraced by groups not socialized into high levels of cultural capital, such as teachers, is the inverse of the bourgeois aesthetic (Bourdieu, 1986). Bourdieu defines this aesthetic as "[t]he desire to enter into the game, identifying with the characters' joys and sufferings, worrying about their fate, espousing their hopes and ideal, living their life" (p. 176). Thus, Bourdieu's work suggests that teachers' aesthetic, if you will, is more homologous to the popular aesthetic than the bourgeois aesthetics of academics. Hence, again, teachers are more likely to recognize themselves in popular culture texts compared to instructional research texts.

To summarize, due to the two homologies discussed above, preservice and inservice teachers are likely to recognize themselves in popular culture texts in ways they do not in instructional research. Therefore, teachers are likely to appropriate popular culture texts and, I would further argue, *extract knowledge*. These arguments appear to be supported by other illustrative data from my students' papers. I asked students in their papers to answer the following question, 'Did you learn any practical tips about teaching from the movie?' Their responses, tabulated in Table 1, indicate an affirmative response to this question.

I do not believe that the illustrative data in Table 1 suggest any thing like a "truth." It does, however, counsel us that teachers do not seem to set boundaries nearly as rigidly around what constitutes legitimate knowledge about teaching as the educational research community does (see Hargreaves, 1996).

Table 1: Student responses to "Did you learn any practical tips about teaching from the movie?"

	Unquestionably learned tip(s)	Qualified sense of having learned tip(s)	Did not learn any tip(s)
Inservice Teachers (n=21)	71%	9.5%	19.5%
Preservice Teachers School-Based M.Ed. (n=18)	83%	11%	6%
Preservice Teachers Undergraduate (n=77)	96%		4%

CONCLUSION

Popular culture texts seem to be appropriated by preservice and inservice teachers and potentially mined for knowledge. I think the theory above *begins* to help us understand why this happens and why instructional research is frequently not appropriated and mined for knowledge. The theory does this by suggesting that teachers may view popular culture texts such as movies about teaching as relevant to their lives because they communicate knowledge that reflects, and helps them articulate, many aspects of their daily experience of teaching: by focusing on the everyday concrete context of teachers, students, classrooms, and schools; by making knowledge accessible through involvement, identification, and narrative; by affirming the validity of pleasure; and by supporting utopian possibilities inherent in education, teachers' classroom experience is affirmed. Their common experience as consumers of popular culture texts is also affirmed.

I think the educational research community may need to consider that teachers appropriate popular culture texts rather than instructional research because they find them recognizable and empowering. Aspects of their private *and* professional lives that the "official knowledge" of teaching in instructional research silences or de-legitimizes are communicated and authenticated for all to see. Teachers recognize themselves on the screen and take pride in sharing that experience with fellow audience members at a theatre or in front of the television. Hence, teachers probably view popular culture texts about teaching as a natural, valid everyday form of knowledge. Surely, their comments above suggest the need for further scholarly inquiry.

REFERENCES

Agger, B. (1992). *Cultural studies as critical theory*. London: Falmer Press.

Ang, I. (1985). *Watching Dallas*. New York: Methuen.

Apple, M. (1990). *Curriculum and ideology* (2nd ed.). London: Routledge.

Aronowitz, S., & Giroux, H. (1991). *Postmodern education*. Minneapolis: University of Minnesota Press.

Barthes, R. (1972). *Mythologies*. New York: Noonday Press.

Bourdieu, P. (1986). The aristocracy of culture. In R. Collins et al. (Eds.), *Media, culture, and society*. London: Sage Productions.

Britzman, D. (1992). *Practice makes practice: A critical study of learning to teach*. Albany, NY: SUNY Press.

Clandinin, D. J., & Connelly, F. M. (1995). *Teachers' professional knowledge landscapes.* New York: Teachers College Press.

Dyer, R. (1993). Entertainment and utopia. In S. During (Ed.), *The Cultural studies reader.* London: Routledge.

Ewen, S. (1988). *All consuming images: The politics of style in contemporary culture.* New York: Basic Books.

Farber, P., Provenzo, E., & Holm, G. (1994). *Schooling in the light of popular culture.* Albany: SUNY Press.

Fish, S. (1980). *Is there a text in this class? The authority of interpretive communities.* Cambridge: Harvard University Press.

Fish, S. (1989). *Doing what comes naturally: Change, rhetoric, and the practice of theory in literary and legal studies.* Durham, NC: Duke University Press.

Fiske, J. (1989). *Understanding popular culture.* Boston: Unwin Hyman.

Fiske, J. (1990). *Introduction to communication studies* (2nd ed.). London: Routledge.

Fiske, J. (1992). Cultural studies and the culture of everyday life. In L. Grossberg, C. Nelson, & P. Treichler (Eds.), *Cultural studies.* New York: Routledge.

Fullan, M. (1995). *Getting instructional research in our schools: A loveless marriage, temporary misunderstanding, or promising partnership?* A Symposium Presented at the Annual Meeting of the American Educational Research Association, San Francisco, CA.

Fullan, M. (1992). Teachers as critical consumers of research. Paper Commissioned by OECD for the CERI/OECD US Department of Education Seminar on Producers and Consumers of Research, Washington, D.C.

Giroux, H. (1983). *Theory and resistance in education: A pedagogy for the opposition.* Hadley: Bergin and Garvey.

Giroux, H. (1992). *Border crossings: Cultural workers and the politics of education.* New York: Routledge.

Giroux, H. (1994). *Disturbing pleasures: Learning popular culture.* New York: Routledge.

Giroux, H., & Simon, R. (1989). *Popular culture, schooling and everyday life.* New York: Bergin & Garvey.

Greenfield, B. (1992). The problem of the discoverer's authority in Lewis and Clark's history. In J. Arac & H. Rivo (Eds.), *Macropolitics of nineteenth century literature.* Philadelphia: University of Pennsylvania.

Hargreaves, A. (1996). Transforming knowledge: Blurring the boundaries between research, policy and practice, *Educational Evaluation and Policy Analysis*, 18, 105-122.

Hebdige, D. (1979). *Subculture: The meaning of style*. London: Methuen.

Hobson, D. (1982). *'Crossroads': The drama of a soap opera*. London: Methuen.

Hutchinson, J., & Huberman, M. (1993). *Knowledge dissemination and use in science and mathematics education: A literature review*. ERIC Document

Kellner, D. (1995). *Media culture: Cultural studies, identity, and politics between the modern and the postmodern*. London: Routledge.

Leming, J. (1991). Teacher characteristics and teacher education. In J. P. Shaver. (Ed.) *Handbook of research on social studies teaching and learning*. New York: Macmillan.

Leming, J. (1992). Ideological perspectives within the social studies profession: An empirical examination of the "two cultures" theses. *Theory and Research in Social Education*, 20, 293-312.

Louis, K.S. (1992). Comparative perspectives on dissemination and knowledge use policies. *Knowledge: Creation, Diffusion, Utilization*, 13, 287-304.

McGuigan, J. (1992). *Cultural populism*. London: Routledge.

Moores, S. (1993). *Interpreting audiences: The ethnography of media consumption*. London: Sage Publications.

Morely, D. (1980). *The nationwide audience: Structure and decoding*. London: BFI.

Mosse, G. (1991). *The nationalization of the masses*. New York: H. Fertig.

Nelson, R. (1990). *Aesthetic frontiers*. Jackson: University Press of Mississippi.

Noble, D. (1996). Revocation of the Anglo-Protestant Monopoly: Aesthetic Authority and the American Landscape. *Soundings*, 79, 149-168.

Parsons, T. (1951). *The social system*. Glencoe, IL: Free Press.

Poster, M. (1995). *The second media age*. Oxford: Polity.

Radway, J. (1991). *Reading the romance: Women, patriarchy, and popular literature*. Chapel Hill: The University of North Carolina Press.

Rothkopf, E. (1995). *Getting instructional research in our schools: A loveless marriage, temporary misunderstanding, or promising partnership?* A Symposium Presented at the Annual Meeting of the American Educational Research Association, San Francisco, CA.

Schwoch, J., White, M., & Reilly, S. (1992). *Media knowledge: readings in popular culture, pedagogy, and critical citizenship*. Albany: State University of New York Press.

Simon, R. (1992). *Against the grain: Texts for a pedagogy of possibility.* Westport, Connecticut: Bergin & Garvey.

Stacey, J. (1994). *Star gazing: Hollywood and female spectatorship.* London: Routledge.

Storey, J. (1993). *Cultural theory and popular culture.* Athens: University of Georgia Press.

Storey, J. (1996). *Cultural studies and the study of popular culture.* Athens: University of Georgia Press.

Weber, S., & Mitchell, C. (1995). *"That's funny, you don't look like a teacher'."* London: The Falmer Press.

Welker, R. (1992). *The teacher as expert: A theoretical and historical examination.* Albany, NY: SUNY Press.

Willis, P. (1990). *Common culture.* Boulder: Westview Press.

CHAPTER SIX

When Theory Bumps into Reality: The Form and Function of the Popular Culture of Teaching[1]

Aimee Howley and Linda Spatig

> Inevitably teachers find themselves influenced by existing social discourses and power relations; but they persist in seeking a kind of autonomy, a way of leaving a thumbprint they know is theirs. (Greene, 1995)

INTRODUCTION

Construing knowledge about teaching as contested discourse, this chapter examines the substance and strategic import of teachers' popular, taken-for-granted ideas about teaching. The "popular culture" of teaching is dominated by common sense, goes-without-saying nostrums drawn from teachers' personal school experiences (both as students and as educators) and from images of teaching presented in the popular and "professional" media (e.g., Clift, Houston, & Pugach, 1990; Raymond, Butt, & Townsend, 1991).[2] This knowledge functions in a contradictory way, with empowering as well as reproductive consequences. It contrasts with and, we will argue, often serves to neutralize a "high culture" knowledge about teaching, which is generated by university researchers and championed by both teacher education faculty and, perhaps more directly, by functionaries in state departments of education and other providers of staff development.

The chapter is particularly concerned with the interpretation of "popular" and "high-culture" knowledge about teaching and resultant shifts in meaning in both forms of discourse. For example, both "popular" and "high-culture" discourse about teaching make use of a "what works" motif, yet the motif's meaning shifts in both substantive and strategic ways in response to circumstances—local as well as more universal. The content of "what works" and the invocation of the "what-works" mantra are responsive to contextual factors, which shape and specify particular episodes of a broader contest.

Based on theoretical discussion and suggestive empirical evidence drawn from transcripts of interviews with elementary-school teachers, we argue that the numerous episodes in the contest are part of an on-going struggle for control of teaching practice that has ultimately contributed to an ideological stand-off. Teaching has failed to change, at least in part, because both forms of discourse have been resilient, with neither form able to prevail (cf. Sarason, 1971). Moreover, neither the "popular" nor the "high-culture" discourse tells the whole truth or points the way.

THEORETICAL GROUNDING

We use the term "popular culture of teaching" to refer to the constellation of beliefs that teachers hold about children, learning, and the teaching process. Whatever their source, these beliefs form the basis for teachers' daily practice.[3] Supporting teachers' specific pedagogical beliefs are also implicit theories about how knowledge about children, learning, and teaching is properly generated. As we will show later on, these meta-beliefs construe knowledge about teaching as "local knowledge," rooted in particular contexts and dependent upon teachers' personal and collective sense-making.

Elaborating upon the "popular culture" or "folk pedagogy" that animates teachers' professional talk and practice, Jerome Bruner (1996) notes:

> In theorizing about the practice of education in the classroom . . . you had better take into account the folk theories that those engaged in teaching and learning already have. For any innovations that you, as a "proper" pedagogical theorist, may wish to introduce will have to compete with, replace, or otherwise modify the folk theories that already guide both teachers and pupils. (p. 46)

Bruner speaks from the vantage of the researcher and, therefore, tends to construe "folk" pedagogies as an impediment to improvement in instructional technique. And he also identifies relevant "folk" theories rather narrowly as those pertaining to assumptions about the learner's mind. Nevertheless, his insight about the existence and resilience of such tacit theories is crucial to an understanding of the meaning teachers make of their experiences in classrooms. We suggest, however, that popular or folk pedagogies apply more broadly to a range of issues related to educational practice, and we argue that these tacit assumptions are not simply ignorant and dysfunctional but constitute, in some instances, a reasonable response to uncertainty and externally imposed pressures (cf. Brown & Rose, 1995).

We prefer to consider the popular culture of teaching as a disqualified discourse about teaching (Foucault, 1980b), not necessarily wise but *potentially* liberating simply by virtue of its disqualification. At the same time, and principally because of the way that it is situated within the disciplinary culture of schooling (Foucault, 1979), this popular pedagogy affirms technologies of power and knowledge that are both individuating and socially reproductive (Bourdieu & Passeron, 1977). Our sense of the matter is that this particular discourse serves to liberate teachers, on the one hand, but to exert control over students, on the other. That the issue of control contributes so much to the substance of teachers' professional talk seems fitting considering the rather complicated positioning of this discourse within the nexus of disciplinary power.

"High culture" pedagogy—the discourse of researchers, teacher educators, and staff developers—also has a contradictory effect. Invoking concern for the betterment of students and, often, society, this discourse typically dictates, with rather authoritarian conviction, the practices that teachers ought to adopt. The specific practices that are recommended, of course, differ depending upon the commitments of particular researchers and proselytizers. But the stated intention of these practices, with respect to teachers and students alike, is to give power, not to exert it. In many cases, "high culture" discourse claims to empower teachers by giving them techniques that "work" (e.g., Bennett, 1986). And it claims to empower students through the effective workings of "what works"—giving them knowledge-as-power so that they might become productive adults, defined in whatever terms.

An interesting and recent complexity is the variant of "high culture" pedagogy that especially privileges the voices of practicing teachers. Acknowledging that teachers place much more stock in knowledge derived from their lived experiences than from theoretical knowledge presented in classes, published works, and professional workshops (e.g., Anyon, 1995; Holt, 1992; Hsieh & Spodek, 1995), this line of thinking approaches the empowerment of teachers directly. Teachers, on this view, have been wise all along and so have researchers, but each group construes educational problems differently. There can, of course, be dialog between the groups, wherein lies the true path to the liberation of both.

Cohn and Kottkamp (1993) exemplify this approach in their account of the wisdom of practitioners. They note that teachers in contrast to researchers and reformers tend to imbue terms like "educational success" with meanings related to the process of instruction. These meanings take shape and then acquire power as craft knowledge—common sense explanations of the conditions relevant to the processes of teaching and learning. Such craft knowledge encompasses a variety of beliefs including tacit theories about the nature of the learner's mind (Bruner, 1996), the relationship between learners and content (Prawat, 1992), and the priority of classroom control (Cohn & Kottkamp, 1993; Hatch, 1993).

Validating the wisdom of practice may, of course, represent the best one can *do* as an educational researcher, teacher educator, or staff developer. But its inadequacies are evident. It is no more liberating in its own right than either the "popular" or conventional "high-culture" discourse, and its concern for recuperation through mutual understanding may obscure conflicts whose liberatory possibilities depend on dynamics that accentuate difference rather than terminate prematurely in consensus.

Our approach is somewhat different. Rather than imagining a dialog between researchers and teachers, we listen critically to the discourse of teachers, paying particular attention, first, to the ways that popular pedagogies shield teachers from being dominated by those with power over them, and second, to the ways that these same pedagogies protect teachers from being overwhelmed by the students over whom they have power. Throughout this analysis we examine points at which teachers' professional discourse co-opts, neutralizes, and reinscribes the language of educational researchers and reformers. By engaging in a critique of this nature, we are not discounting the importance of similar critiques of the "high-culture" discourse on pedagogy. Indeed, studying the culture of elites (i.e., "studying up") may reveal a great deal about the mechanisms of power that is obscured and compounded by "studying down." In some senses, of course, teachers themselves represent an elite (e.g., Gouldner, 1979), and this underscores our main point: Teachers' uncertain position with respect to power opens up to their practice an enormous realm of possible action, encompassing every possible effect from the most fully liberating to the most destructively domineering.

TEACHER TALK

The teacher talk we sampled came from interviews, in the spring of 1996, with thirteen second and third grade teachers. The teachers, who worked in some of the poorest neighborhoods in two adjacent counties in West Virginia, were participants in a federally sponsored Head Start extension program.[4]

For these teachers, the central focus of teaching was children— figuring out and doing what works to ensure that children behave and learn. The teachers believed that each must determine for herself what works with each child. They construed neither educational experts, such as university professors, nor educational research as useful in this endeavor. Teachers' efforts to ascertain and implement what works with the "needy" children in their classes were frustrated by their lack of control in many arenas. For example, they were unable to control the outside-of-school lives of these young children, they had little voice in determining curriculum, and they were removed from decision-making about the ways children's progress would be measured. In an effort to retain control in some arena, these teachers were protective of their right to control instructional methods. In short, they claimed exclusive ownership of knowledge about "what works."

WHAT WORKS

Based on our impression that an ethos of "what works" was central to these teachers' construction of teaching practice (see, for example, Spatig, 1995), we asked the teachers what it meant when they said that something "works" in the classroom. How did they know if something worked? Some teachers had difficulty discussing this. They wondered why we would ask such a silly question, taking it for granted that teachers, like everyone else, try to do what works and know how to tell the difference between what works and what doesn't. It went without saying; it did not need justification or elaboration.

Others explained that something worked if it resulted in good student behavior or learning. For example, Virginia Roberts talked about what worked in relation to the unusually good behavior in her class from the previous year.

> Some things really work with one group of children and they don't with another. Like the group I had last year—they were so in control and behaved so well . . . that we did not need rule one last year. . . . But if I would like to try to carry that over to this year's group it would not work at all because . . . you just [have to] change every year with the group you have. Sometimes being really strict works well and sometimes being really relaxed works well. . . . Sometimes you have to give rewards and have a pie fest and things like that. I find that's real helpful at the beginning of the year and as we go on we just forget about it and don't need it anymore. That really works.

Virginia also spoke about children's learning, explaining how she determines whether a certain lesson or activity has worked.

> [If it works] it will come up in a different subject area. Like in social studies we study needs, things that we absolutely need . . . like food, clothing, shelter, love . . . and then to have that three months later pop up in an answer to something in a reading story, you know. Then I know that they have really understood that. . . . Something that we studied and you know that they remembered it and they really did learn it.

Teachers believed that what works, whether to control student behavior or ensure student learning, is not static: it varies across teachers, children and circumstances. Jean Saunders addressed this issue explicitly.

> It works for me. It may not work next year. That teacher may have a holy terror time with him and she'll find out for herself what to do with that kid . . . in her classroom. It's kind of trial and error.

According to these teachers, each teacher must discover for herself what works, and must accomplish that primarily through trial and error, a process often requiring a great deal of patience and persistence.

> I have read a lot of materials that say this is what you should do and
> . . . you try them and they don't work. They don't work. You have to
> keep trying and trying [because] every child is different. You have to
> keep trying until you find something that works. And I've tried a lot
> of theories and a lot of things written up in textbooks and it sounds
> fantastic on paper, but it doesn't work in reality. (Jean Saunders)

Along the same lines, Kristi Elliott explained that teachers "need to keep changing or adapting to make something work. If it doesn't work, you drop back and punt. . . . The biggest word is persistency—in making something work."

Whereas teachers maintained that what works with one child or one group of children will not necessarily work with other children, they did draw on previous teaching experiences in making decisions about which strategies to use.

> I've been in the classroom 18 years and I feel like I've discovered
> things, you know, about choice, . . . and what works with one group
> and what works a little better [than something else]. I think I have the
> experience to pull from and make my own judgment about . . . what
> is more appropriate for that time and what's not so appropriate.

Teachers did not value university professors or educational consultants as sources of information about what works. Caroline Dunlap, for example, was more satisfied with her trial and error approach than with consultants and staff developers who offered teaching ideas.

> If it doesn't work this way, let's try another way and let's keep on
> going. I tried different ways of [integrating] different lessons, like
> math in with the reading. . . . [But] it burns me up whenever you get
> these people who come through and tell you, "This is going to work",
> and you disagree with them. I've put my foot in my mouth a million
> times! You don't tell somebody that is getting paid $3000 that their
> theory is a crock of you know what . . . [I feel like saying], "Yeah,
> right. Come into the room. You try that with my group of kids. That

may have worked with your group of kids, but I doubt it. . . . What
works in Timbucktu is not necessarily going to work here."

For the teachers we studied, expert advice, based on educational
research and theory, was not helpful because it lacked relevance to their
students and their particular classroom circumstances. Jodie Clarke
recalled a difficult situation when a child had not taken his medication
as an occasion where "reality bumped into the theory", arguing that
"you just have to adjust it [theory] to whatever the needs of your
children are." Also, research was not to be trusted because so much of it
"has been proven wrong", making it an unreliable guide for classroom
practice.

> Everything seems to follow a trend. And it depends on who they
> work with—who's being worked with and who does the research. . . .
> It just seems like nothing is true or factual, or will stick. You know,
> things change so often. . . . I guess I feel like it's so fragile or weak,
> one or the other, and it just doesn't stick a lot of the times. (Penny
> Lewis)

Most of the teachers viewed research as pretty slippery, not something
sturdy one could hold onto; as Rita Adkins said, "not to live and die
by." They preferred something "proven", something "beneficial," some
"meat"—something "you can really use with your children."

> I don't think that those theories have anything to do with what it is
> really like in a classroom. It may explain why the behavior occurs but
> it doesn't tell you how to handle it, what to do, how to do it. It
> doesn't tell you that. (Kristi Elliott)

Teachers argued that research findings do not necessarily "fit" or
"work" with their children, stressing the importance of focusing on the
children and their life circumstances rather than the theories.

> I may be wrong and people may disagree with me, but I think you
> need to consider the area you are in and the children that you have,
> because not . . . all children fit in [with] . . . Piaget or Erikson or . . .
> Bruner. I think the social place you live, the emotional place these

kids are coming from—I think those things have to be first in your mind. (Rita Adkins)

Overall, teachers saw the notion of "what works" in individualistic terms: each teacher must figure it out on her own—for herself and her children—and then recreate new knowledge about what works with each new child or class. From this perspective, it would be unwise for a teacher to depend on educational research to guide teaching practice. On this view, researchers and staff developers are distant from the particular children whose needs determine effective teaching practice, and this distance destroys their legitimacy in teachers' eyes. Teachers' expert knowledge, then, depends upon investigations to discover each child's needs, from which arises, almost as a self-evident by-product, knowledge about what to do—"what works"—to meet those needs.

NEEDY CHILDREN

The word teachers used most often to describe their children was "needy." They emphasized emotional neediness—the children's need to feel secure, to be loved, understood, valued and given attention—and their own efforts to meet these needs. Jackie Marcum's description of the children in her school was typical.

These kids are children [who] need our love. They need our support; they need our guidance; and they need all the encouragement that we can give them. And I think you have to be that kind of a teacher to probably teach here. . . . I think we have just a wide variety of problems, but I don't want to use the word problems. . . . I guess maybe what I'm trying to say is that they have so many different needs. That's where I'm trying to come from. And sometimes it's just very very hard to meet all those needs. . . . By the end of the day sometimes you just feel wiped out. And I don't think it's entirely from teaching. I think it's because I want to try to meet the needs that each child has.

Along the same lines, Penny Lewis recalled a particularly sad poem written by a "very needy" girl in her class.

One day she [the child] said, "I have a poem" that she made up. [The poem] said "I'm not needed at home." . . . It was very well written. I don't know if she had copied it or what, but it made me feel bad for her because it was a sad poem! She said her family loved her but they didn't need her. And it was, it was not a nice thing to hear, you know.

At times teachers found it difficult to respond to children's needs. In some cases, they simply felt discouraged and tired as a result of trying to satisfy the demand for hugs, attention, and comfort. In other cases, they were highly frustrated and emotionally burdened as a result of their limitations in assisting children with very serious problems. Rita Adkins, for example, related her experiences with a child who was sexually abused.

> How do you get over the fact that a child is coming in sexually abused? I had a child come in who was sexually abused. . . . How do you handle that? How do you go home? How do you deal with that? Welfare and I had a major war that evening. . . . They had to [respond] because the man actually went out and killed people. But it kills you. How do you personally deal with that knowledge? . . . That was the hardest thing for me, to get . . . to the point that there is only so much that you can do. Do all that you can do but there comes a point where it kind of goes out of your hands. . . . You're just so frustrated because you think child welfare ought to do this and ought to do that but then you realize their hands are tied, too. But then you have to save that child.

Expressing similar concerns, Jackie Marcum discussed her response to a third grader's disturbing journal entry.

> I said, "Lisa, I was really concerned when I read this." I said, "Do you really feel sadness in your heart?" And she said, "Yes." And I said, "Why?" And she said, "Well, because I'm always afraid that somebody in my family is going to be killed or my pets are going to be killed." And . . . that bothers me. . . . Lisa has often told me, and in several things she has written, she has implied that people in her neighborhood can be mean to her. And it's sad. But it's like she's constantly—she wants love. She needs a lot of hugs. And she just constantly seeks that.

Whereas the teachers were deeply concerned about the children in their care and struggled to find effective ways of identifying and addressing their needs, they did not seek assistance or guidance from educational experts. They believed such experts were too far removed from actual classroom life and too unfamiliar with children—specifically, their children—to be helpful. Pam Simpkins, for example, described university professors as people who "don't know kids."

> [They] sit in this little room with all these neat little theories and [do] not know a thing about reality and . . . [what] would work with a child . . . You've got to be with kids to know kids. You can't sit behind a desk in some office somewhere and know kids because kids are changing all the time. Kids are . . . as different today as—well, it's like night and day from when I started.

Along the same lines, Penny Lewis described university course work as providing little of value in terms of practical advice on how to identify and respond to her children's needs.

> [They] don't give you anything to work with as far as identifying needs or any of that. And I have taken classes on children with learning disabilities. . . . They give you some research. . . . To be honest, I don't even remember any characteristics given to identify a child who has a learning disability. They just mainly told you the legal aspects and maybe the steps you'd have to take in order to refer this child. But it had nothing to do with finding out that a kid has certain needs and that you might need to go further at looking at the kid's needs and doing something about it.

The general feeling seemed to be that in order to know about real classroom life and children, one had to be there. According to Virginia Roberts, a second grade teacher, the reason university professors lack important knowledge—that is, knowledge about children's needs—is their lack of classroom experience: "They know nothing! They know absolutely nothing about what it's like to be in the classroom. They don't know children. . . . And I didn't know children until I got in the classroom."

Most teachers attributed children's "neediness" to their home and community circumstances. Whereas a few teachers seemed to blame the parents, wondering why they didn't care more about their children, most described the parents as people who had grown up as needy children themselves, without much love and support, who were doing the best they could do for their children.

For these teachers, then, teaching involves single-handed efforts in a classroom, using trial and error to determine what strategies will develop good behavior and academic achievement in each emotionally needy child in the class. Considering the magnitude of these children's needs, the task seemed immense to most of the teachers. Moreover, they felt that they must accomplish it in the context of diminishing professional control.

THE PROFESSIONAL CONTEXT: LITTLE CONTROL

The teachers distinguished between parts of the teaching circumstance over which they exercised some control and parts over which they had little influence. In addition to feeling relatively powerless to affect children's outside-of-school lives, teachers talked about their lack of control over clerical work, room temperature, room design, time schedules, school-wide student behavior policies, the ways children responded to them and their classroom practices, assessment procedures and identification of at-risk children, and their own professional development. Whereas they did not control learner outcomes, textbooks or curriculum, they did have some authority over how they "cover the material." Kristi Elliott described it this way: "I feel that . . . what to teach is pretty much dictated to you—what has to be taught and by when. But I feel I have control over how I go about teaching that."

Others, not content with implementing an imposed curriculum, engaged in covert attempts to influence curriculum. Pam Simpkins described her quiet resistance to the county-dictated curriculum.

> Ok. I am required to use a certain curriculum within my classroom. I am required to do certain things with that classroom, but I also can do my own things with that curriculum and keep my mouth shut. . . . I've learned over the years [that] you do what you think is best and don't ask any questions and keep your mouth shut.

Many teachers emphasized the role of state-mandated standardized testing in determining curricula. Rita Adkins' comments about how the Comprehensive Test of Basic Skills (CTBS) is experienced by teachers in her school show her acceptance of teachers' lack of control over curriculum.

> I feel like our curriculum is really ours to take what we want from it until it comes close to CTBS time and then nothing is ours. . . . I think it really shocked some teachers because they feel like the control is taken from them. You know, they are no longer in charge, but once you get used to it, it's okay.

Most of the teachers we interviewed were more antagonistic towards the standardized testing program and its influence on their teaching.

> I feel like they are imposing the CTBS garbage on us. We are told not to even worry about the reading theories, to totally teach CTBS skills. I think that is a total waste. All it does is show how well they did on that test and to focus so much on that test is a waste of time. (Kristi Elliott)

Teachers opposed standardized testing on the grounds that it is not necessarily appropriate as an assessment tool for their particular children. In their view, these children, who often had behavior problems and academic problems in school, had the ability to learn, but were not achieving because of difficulties staying focused or lack of effort.

> I think the county administration needs to understand that every school is a different situation and understand that some of the things that we have to deal with here are unique to this area. . . . We were told that there were no differences, that the children were the same regardless of where they lived. And I'm sorry, but that's not true. I think if that could honestly be taken into consideration that would help. (Kristi Elliott)

From a similar vantage, Rita Adkins questioned the validity of the CTBS as an assessment of her children, arguing that the scores misrepresent their mental abilities.

> Our kids . . . did not know what a curb was [or] an escalator. . . . I want to make it very clear that I'm not putting down those [children]

... I think they're extremely intelligent, but they have an intelligence
that suits their situation and has helped them survive their situation,
[but] it is different from what we call important. . . . They're judged
by test scores and it makes them look stupid or not intelligent or
illiterate whereas really [it's] because they're measured [by this test].

Some teachers claimed they were able to assess children's potential
and achievement at least as well as the standardized tests. Jean
Saunders, for example, argued that teachers know their students well
and lamented the fact that this knowledge was not a valued part of the
assessment process.

I really believe that teachers [know their] students. I believe I could
take this group of 24 students in my room and put them in order
before I ever see what they did on their achievement test. I believe I
could put my children in order from top, to the middle to the bottom
. . . and be fairly correct [about] what they'll do on their achievement
tests or any other tests for that matter. . . . But that doesn't count. It
doesn't seem to me that teachers' opinions of what . . . a child can do
count.

Hearing these teachers describe their lack of control over so much
of the teaching process, we better understand why they may resist
attempts by outsiders to change or influence how they teach.
Instructional delivery is one of the few remaining ways they can use
their knowledge and skills as teachers. Most of the time they are room
managers, deliverers of state and county-mandated curriculum,
producers of acceptable test scores: in short, they are pawns in a never-
ending game of school improvement.

RESISTANCE AND REPRODUCTION

As the teachers' commentary suggests, teachers neither determine the
goals of instruction nor the methods of judging whether or not the goals
have been met. Although they do not necessarily agree with the goals
or the means of assessment, they admit defeat in the contest over these
educational questions. The contest over instructional method is,
however, unresolved and centers around the question of "what works."
Teachers claim that knowledge about "what works" comes from their

daily interaction with specific children in particular settings. It is local knowledge, generated and applied locally.

Educational researchers and various purveyors of educational research purport to deliver more universal knowledge, offered also under the banner, "what works." This knowledge comes from empirical study (i.e., science)—typically conducted locally—but supposedly applicable everywhere. As a suggestive indication of the prevalence of such "high culture" discourse about "what works," we searched the ERIC database using "what works" as our search term. We found, during the period January, 1992-March, 1996, 47 cases in which "high culture" educators (i.e., researchers, teacher educators, R & D specialists, staff developers, and functionaries of state education agencies) used research findings about "what works" to exhort teachers to change their instructional practice.[5] Notably, the most frequent targets of the "what works" research were children at risk of failure, the same group whose needs constituted the main concern of the teachers we interviewed.

Considering this circumstance, we think it plausible to conclude that the contest over instructional method, especially that which addresses the needs of "needy" children, constitutes a strategic point in the exercise of power (Foucault, 1980a). At this strategic point, the popular culture of teaching functions as a form of resistance against the domination of the "high culture," whose power is applied most directly in the form of edicts from state and local education agencies and whose legitimacy rests on the status of scientific research.

Teachers' insistence that knowledge about teaching must be generated locally serves as a defensive strategy in a contest about whose outcomes they may have substantial doubt. Having lost control over other parts of the teaching process, they are not likely to feel secure about retaining control over instructional decisions. Apart from its strategic function, however, their insight bears thoughtful examination. Are there, indeed, instructional methods that are applicable universally? Is it even possible to divorce questions of instructional method from questions of educational purpose? An unconventional interpretation holds that education depends upon local practice both to define its aims and to inspire its methods (McLaren & Giroux, 1990; Snauwaert, 1990; Webb, Shumway, & Shute, 1996). On this view, community members along with teachers—not individual teachers functioning alone—would make decisions democratically about the ends and means of instruction (cf. Covaleskie & Howley, 1994).

When teachers make such decisions alone, they may, in fact, be setting themselves apart from the community—from children, parents, and other citizens. Doing so makes it easier for teachers to view themselves as disinterested experts, supporting their role in situating and hence limiting students through knowledge of their particular abilities, inadequacies, and needs (Foucault, 1979). That this type of knowledge is most potent for the teachers we studied seems clear in their contrast between useless generalities that come from educational research and the valuable knowledge that inheres in the child. In their view, the primary task of the teacher is to decipher knowledge about each child and from that knowledge to develop ways to meet that child's needs.

Similar to teachers in other studies (e.g., Dirks & Spurgin, 1992), the teachers we studied saw their students as deficient—suffering from limitations either internal to themselves or situated in their immediate environment. In many cases, this perspective kept the teachers from focusing as much as they might on the children's capabilities. Furthermore, since they identified emotional needs as most important, these teachers centered instructional practice around the provision of love, support, encouragement, and comfort. To the extent that this approach overlooks academic concerns, it may, in fact, contribute to keeping these children "needy."

Interestingly, much of the "high culture" knowledge about "what works" with so-called at-risk students emphasizes cognitive development, not affective need. Nevertheless, the exhortatory literature is contradictory, recommending strategies ranging from academic acceleration to developmentally appropriate practice. In fact, the teachers in this study had recently been required to participate in staff development activities promoting this latter practice. Although the requirement to attend the staff development sessions provided a focus for some of the teachers' resistance (Spatig, Bickel, & Parrott, 1996), the content of the sessions tended to support their implicit theories about teaching. Unfortunately, what goes by the name "developmentally appropriate practice" often subordinates academic aims to affective ones, reinforcing negative stereotypes about impoverished children and contributing to socially reproductive ends (Katz, 1994; Levin, 1991; Stone, 1996).

SOME TENTATIVE CONCLUSIONS

As our analysis suggests, both the "popular" and "high culture" knowledges about teaching embed a contradictory set of theoretical assumptions and strategic opportunities. In addition, both discourses share vocabulary, attaching meanings differently within and across discourses in consideration primarily of the strategic value of the assertions.

This circumstance reveals a process by which dominant signifiers are continually inscribed and reinscribed to accomplish first hegemonic, then liberating, then again reactionary aims. Hebdige (1979) details this same type of process with regard to the use by adolescent subcultures of signifiers co-opted from the dominant culture. In particular, he explores the relationship between the *position* of the speaking subject (i.e., the subcultural group that is attaching meaning) and the form and content of the constructed meaning. In Hebdige's analysis, the subject's position plays a decisive role in establishing the meanings—socially reproductive, subversive, or liberating—that a particular signifier conveys. In the activity of meaning-making (i.e., signification) the subject engages in a practice, which has as its effect "a particular *transformation* of reality, a version of reality, an account of reality" (Hebdige, 1979, p. 118).

Interpretation, on this view, depends on analysis of (a) the subject's original position and (b) the substantive and strategic effects (i.e., the repositioning) resulting from the subject's practice of signification. In Hebdige's examples the adolescent members of subcultural groups were originally in a marginalized position—disqualified from mainstream culture. When their practice of signification, which at first had subversive effects, eventually turned out to accomplish reproductive aims, the adolescents' complicity was unwitting (see also Willis, 1977).

Teachers' original position, by contrast, is more ambiguous, both in relation to structural and ideological determinations. Many teachers, for instance, belong to or align themselves with local elites; they tend to support as well as to serve the interests of the upper classes (see e.g., Gardner, 1982; Strike, 1993). Consequently, their attempts to secure power over their own practice may have little to do with general strategies of liberation. Other teachers clearly do construe their commitments in terms of transformative practice (Giroux, 1988), but, at best, these teachers have limited, localized influence.

We do not mean to imply that educational researchers or purveyors of educational research are any more likely than teachers to sponsor transformative practice. Indeed, the points of greatest accord between the "popular" and "high culture" of teaching—for example, the attribution of deficiency to "at risk" children—may be the most suspect, obscuring rather than illuminating important struggles. With McLaren and Giroux (1990), we maintain that democratic practice in education rests on a conception of school culture that construes it "not . . . as a site of harmony and control but rather . . . as a site of disjuncture, rupture, and contradiction" (p. 164).

NOTES

1. Kate Conrad, Amy Dillon, and Laurel Parrott conducted and transcribed the teacher interviews discussed in this chapter. They also provided valuable critiques of our initial data analysis and first draft of the manuscript. We are indebted to them for their diligent and insightful work.

2. For a careful account of what's common about common sense, see Geertz, 1983.

3. Bruner (1996) uses the term "folk pedagogies" to refer to such beliefs, but to us that term seems condescending.

4. The Head Start Public School Transition Demonstration Project (TDP) is a federally funded social reform effort designed to extend Head Start benefits (social, health, parental and academic) into the early elementary grades. The goal is for low income children to maintain gains, academic and otherwise, that they made in the Head Start Program. Teachers in the West Virginia TDP attended monthly staff development sessions focused on reflective, child-centered teaching. In addition, an ethnographer observed (four or five times per semester for two semesters) in each teacher's classroom, recording detailed field notes describing a "focus child" in the class. Teacher interviews referred to in this chapter were conducted by three full-time ethnographers employed by the TDP.

5. The 47 citations represent just a fraction of the documents in the literature that prescribe "research-based" practices for teachers to follow. But the 47 we identified specifically invoked the phrase "what works" within the title or ERIC abstract. This finding is, of course, merely illustrative.

REFERENCES

Anyon, J. (1995). Race, social class, and educational reform in an inner-city school. *Teachers College Record, 97*(1), 69-94.

Bennett, W. J. (1986). *What works: Research about teaching and learning.* Pueblo, CO: Office of Educational Research and Improvement.

Bourdieu, P., & Passeron, J. (1977). *Reproduction in education, society, and culture.* Beverly Hills: Sage.

Brown, D. F., & Rose, T. D. (1995). Self-reported classroom impact of teachers' theories about learning and obstacles to implementation. *Action in Teacher Education, 17*(1), 20-29.

Bruner, J. (1996). *The culture of education.* Cambridge, MA: Harvard University Press.

Clift. R., Houston, R., & Pugach, M. (Eds.). (1990). *Encouraging reflective practice in education: An analysis of issues and programs.* New York: Teachers College Press.

Cohn, M. M., & Kottkamp, R. B. (1993). *Teachers: The missing voice in education.* Albany, NY: SUNY Press.

Covaleskie, J. F., & Howley, A. (1994). Education and the commons: Issues of "professionalization," *Educational Foundations, 8*(4), 59-73.

Dirks, J. M., & Spurgin, M. E. (1992). Implicit theories of adult basic education teachers: How their beliefs shape classroom practice. *Adult Basic Education, 2*(1), 20-41.

Foucault, M. (1979). *Discipline and punish: The birth of the prison.* New York: Vintage Books.

Foucault, M. (1980a). Power and strategies. In C. Gordon (Ed.), *Power/knowledge: Selected interviews and other writings 1972-1977* (pp. 134-145). New York: Pantheon Books.

Foucault, M. (1980b). Two lectures. In C. Gordon (Ed.), *Power/knowledge: Selected interviews and other writings 1972-1977* (pp. 78-108). New York: Pantheon Books.

Gardner, S. (1982). *Status of the American public school teacher, 1980-81.* Washington, DC: National Education Association.

Geertz, C. (1983). *Local knowledge: Further essays in interpretive anthropology.* New York: Basic Books.

Giroux, H. (1988). *Teachers as intellectuals: Toward a critical pedagogy of learning.* Granby, MA: Bergin & Garvey.

Gouldner, A. (1979). *The future of intellectuals and the rise of the new class.* New York: Oxford University Press.

158   *Popular Culture and Critical Pedagogy*

Greene, M. (1995). Forward. In S. K. Biklen, *School work: Gender and the cultural construction of teaching.* New York: Teachers College Press.

Hatch, J. A. (1993). Passing along teacher beliefs: A good day is. . . *Educational Horizons, 71*(2), 109-112.

Hebdige, D. (1979). *Subculture: The meaning of style.* London: Routledge.

Holt, R. D. (1992, April). *Preservice teachers and coursework: When is getting it right wrong?* Paper presented at the annual meeting of the American Educational Research Association, San Francisco, CA. (ERIC Document Reproduction Service No. ED 345 217)

Hsieh, Y., & Spodek, B. (1995, April). *Educational principles underlying the classroom decision-making of two kindergarten teachers.* Paper presented at the annual meeting of the American Educational Research Association, San Francisco, CA. (ERIC Document Reproduction Service No. ED 383 663)

Katz, L. (1994, April). *Child development knowledge and teacher preparation: Confronting assumptions.* Paper presented at the annual conference of the Midwest Association for the Education of Young Children, Peoria, IL. (ERIC Document Reproduction Service No. ED 385 374)

Levin, H. (1991). *Accelerating the progress of all students* (Rockefeller Institute Special Rep., No. 31). Albany, NY: Nelson A. Rockefeller Institute of Government. (ERIC Document Reproduction No. ED 344 313)

McLaren, P., & Giroux, H. (1990). Critical pedagogy and rural education: A challenge from Poland. *Peabody Journal of Education, 67*(4), 154-165.

Prawat, R. S. (1992). Teachers' beliefs about teaching and learning: A constructivist perspective. *American Journal of Education, 100*(3), 354-395.

Raymond, D., Butt, R., & Townsend, D. (1991). Contexts for teacher development: Insights from teachers' stories. In A. Hargreaves & M. Fullen (Eds.), *Understanding teacher development* (pp. 196-221). London: Cassells.

Sarason, S. (1971). *The culture of school and the problems of change.* Boston: Allyn & Bacon.

Snauwaert, D. T. (1990). Wendell Berry, liberalism, and democratic theory: Implications for the rural school. *Peabody Journal of Education, 67*(4), 118-130.

Spatig, L. (1995). Student teaching as social reproduction: An ethnography in Appalachia in the United States. In Ginsburg, M. & Lindsay, B. (Ed.) *The political dimension in teacher education: Comparative perspectives on policy formation, socialization and society*. Washington DC: The Falmer Press.

Spatig, L., Bickel, R., & Parrott, L. (1996, November). *Low income children lose: A case study of school reform in Appalachia*. Paper presented at the annual conference of the American Educational Studies Association, Montreal, Canada.

Stone, J. E. (1996). Developmentalism: An obscure but pervasive restriction on educational improvement. *Educational Policy Analysis Archives, 4*(8), http://olam.ed.asu.edu/epaa/page2.html.

Strike, K. (1993). Professionalism, democracy, and discursive communities: Normative reflections on restructuring. *American Educational Research Journal, 30*(2), 255-275.

Webb, C. D., Shumway, L. K., & Shute, R. W. (1996). *Local schools of thought*. Charleston, WV: ERIC Clearinghouse on Rural Education and Small Schools.

Willis, P. (1977). *Learning to labour*. London: Saxon House.

Popular Culture as Critical Pedagogy

CHAPTER SEVEN

Rap Pedagogies: "Bring(ing) the Noise" of "Knowledge Born on the Microphone" to Radical Education[1]

Toby Daspit

"The Great Books won't save us . . . but rap may because it might finally allow us to recognize that the world is no longer white and one might say no longer bookish." (Houston Baker, in Castenell & Pinar, 1993)

INTRODUCTION: SCENES FROM THE SCHOOLHOUSE (AND BEYOND)

One

The week before I begin my first high school teaching assignment I hold a conference with each student I teach and her/his parent(s) or guardian(s). While meeting with the mother of one young African American, she warns me, "I don't know what you're going to do with Scott. All he's interested in is his rap."

Two

My friend's younger sister, a thirteen-year-old, white, rural, Louisianan, makes a tape that she plays whenever she rides in my car (so that she won't have to listen to "my" music). She labels it, "Here's some cool gangsta' shit." Song titles include, "Death Around the

Corner," "I Don't Give a Fuck," "Born Gangsta," "Diary of a Mad Bitch," and "Fuck the World."

Three

Even though Scott transfers out of class after a couple of months, he periodically visits. Typically, he loans me another rap tape, saying, "You've got to hear this."

Four

I think I knew something was happening, to paraphrase Bob Dylan (1965), but I know that I didn't know what.

POPULAR CULTURE, RAP MUSIC, AND THE SEARCH FOR RADICAL PEDAGOGIES

Dominant modes of schooling in the United States have traditionally attempted to be impositional, relying on positivistic conceptions of objectivity and truth to justify their mission of transmitting supposedly relevant, value neutral, and universal knowledge. What has all too frequently been silenced, however, is knowledge emanating from the experiences of participants in schools, especially the experiences of students. Furthermore, a fundamental component of students' experiences, the terrain of popular culture, has generally been given only cursory attention by educators.

Rap music minimally offers the "lessons of lived experiences" (Kelley, cited in Lusane, 1993, p. 49). I believe it offers much more. Rap is big business, generating more than $700 million a year (Lusane, 1993, p. 44) with nearly 60 percent of Americans under the age of 20 responding that they "strongly like rap music" (SounData, 1996). And although rap is an important articulation of African American culture (KRS-ONE of Boogie Down Productions (1990) says it is the "last voice of black people in America"), nearly three-quarters of rap music is purchased by white consumers (Lusane, 1993).

Rap is thus a "hybrid" (Baker, 1993, p. 89) in more than simply aesthetic terms. It moves from urban landscapes where it typically originates as part of the "larger context of what is termed Hip-Hop culture" (Ransby and Matthews, 1993, p. 57) into white suburban culture, producing a hybrid culture that blends urban realities, myths, and narratives with suburban ones. bell hooks (1994) contends that rap music is "one of the spaces where black vernacular speech is used in a manner that invites dominant mainstream culture to listen—to hear—and, to some extent, be transformed" (p. 171).

I wish to use rap music in a similar fashion to Miklitsch's (1994) appropriation of punk music as a transformative pedagogy. Rap is representative of a distinct "subculture," albeit a hybrid one, and such cultures by definition "ostensibly 'contain' an element of resistance to the dominant hegemony" (p. 67). The dynamics of a hybrid culture that mixes Hip-Hop's actions under the shadow of dominance with the suburban culture that casts a large part of that shadow offers intriguing possibilities in the development of a "critical multiculturalism" which "need(s) multiple languages of resistance" (McLaren, quoted in Estrada and McLaren, 1993, p. 29).

Although my focus is on rap music, I find it necessary to initially speak about popular culture in general as it intersects (or has typically failed to effectively intersect) with radical pedagogies. Gore (1993) notes the importance of using the plural form of pedagogy, writing that "(pedagogies) use is important to signify the multiple approaches and practices that fall under the pedagogy umbrella" whereas "rely(ing) on the singular form is to imply greater unity and coherence than is warranted" (p. 7). Radical pedagogies, whether informed by critical neo-Marxism, feminism, post-modernism, or some combination/ extension thereof, must forge an intimate relationship with popular culture, especially those emerging hybrid forms which rap epitomizes. We must actively seek, to update Roger Simon's phrase, "pedagog(ies) of possibility" that "create images of that which is not yet" (cited in Ellsworth, 1987, p. 33).

Curricular appropriation of popular culture may assist in reorganizing the prevailing narratives that schooling has perpetuated. As Simon notes, "(e)very time we organize narratives in our classrooms we are implicated in the organization of a particular way of understanding the world and the concomitant vision of one's place in that world and in the future" (p. 33). But heeding Giroux's (1994) call to use "popular cultural texts as serious objects of study" (p. 297) can serve to continue to disempower students if the dialogical nature of emancipatory classrooms continue to favor a narrative of authority which privileges the "teacher."

Students have particular expectations when they interact with various cultural phenomena and they correspondingly engage these phenomena with various levels of investment. Thus, they typically approach texts offered as "schoolwork" differently from texts they engage outside of school. This can be problematical when popular culture intersects with schooling. Although the realm of popular culture manifests itself in a variety of overt and covert ways in schools, popular culture incorporated as academic subject matter may be viewed by students as an invasion of personal space.[2] Since it is through investment in and expression of the popular that potentially emancipatory points of resistance and agency are located, the appropriation by schools of such possibly empowering cultural forms may ultimately disempower students. Forcing everyday student experiences into institutional frameworks where they are not "logically" associated must be approached cautiously lest we dismantle the very forces that offer liberatory experiences.

By attempting to encompass a broader range of student experiences, including non-school, popular "pleasures," which hooks (1994) notes is a term generally absent from academic discourse, we can begin to envision pedagogies where the struggles over knowledge, power, and pleasure are radically reorganized.[3] Although theorists like Weiler (1988) and Willis (1981) contend that the dominant ideology is not uniformly reproduced and is met at varying sites with different levels of resistance, the manner in which we view schooling practices is relatively hermetic—in the sense that we still think in terms of "teachers," "students," and even "classrooms." Therefore, the most significant challenge confronting radical pedagogies is not simply the reconceptualization of the relations of knowledge and power, but also the transformation of their "institutional" frameworks. How might a "classroom," a "school," an "education" infused with popular culture manifest itself?[4]

In trying to tentatively articulate some salient features of radical pedagogies, I consciously wish to minimize the tendency to focus on teachers, not because they play no role but because I believe that their role has been inflated in radical pedagogical discourses. An emancipatory praxis must be informed by the experiences and voices of the disempowered. We must begin to not only speak of, as Freire (1968, 1970) does, pedagogies *"with*, not *for*, the oppressed" (p. 33, emphases in original)—but we must make a further prepositional shift and consider pedagogies *from* the "oppressed."

It is my position, therefore, that student experiences are of tantamount importance. Students, by traditional definitions, have been systematically placed in positions of little power. I acknowledge that speaking of students in this fashion inverts the traditional teacher/student binary, but I do not think it is sufficient to argue, as Kreisberg (1992) does, for "power with" (p. 195) students to empower both teachers and students. While Kreisberg does not simplify the issue and explores the contradictions of trying to transform "power over" into "power with" without reproducing "power over," it is useful to keep in mind that without students schools would be rendered meaningless. I think, though, that schools can exist without teachers.

McLaren (1989) persuasively argues for the consideration of "student voice" (which like pedagogies is best considered in its plural form), "that constitutive force that both mediates and shapes reality within historically constructed practices and relationships of power" (p. 230). Furthermore, Weiler (1988) contends that "empowerment of students means encouraging them to explore and analyze the forces acting upon their lives" (p. 152). If, as Aronowitz (1989) argues, identity is the result of the intersection of three factors—1) biologically determined characteristics whose meanings may be socially constructed, but which are nevertheless genetically determined (i.e., race and sex); 2) interaction with "conventional institutions" like the family, school, and religion; and 3) "the technological sensorium that we call mass or popular culture" (p. 197)—then consideration of popular culture is essential to understanding student voices. Yet, as Giroux and Simon (1989) note, "radical educational theorists have nonetheless almost completely ignored the importance of popular culture both for developing a more critical understanding of student experience and for examining pedagogy in a critical and theoretically expanded fashion" (p. 2).

I propose that the convergence of the institutional dynamics of schooling and the terrain of the popular is crucial to the rearticulation and development of radical pedagogies. As Grossberg (1989) writes, "(u)nless one begins where people live their lives, one will be unable to engage with the struggles over larger and more explicit ideological positions" (p. 92). Rather than contest the fact, as teachers are apt to, that student experiences are profoundly influenced by music, television, films, comic books, video games, etc., educators must "discover" relevant points of appropriation that facilitate empowerment.[5] The task, Grossberg argues, "is to identify the strategic sites of empowerment

made available in forms of contemporary culture" (p. 114). One such
site, I believe, is rap music.

SCENES FROM THE SCHOOLHOUSE (AND BEYOND)— PART II

Five

Each student in African American Studies chooses a topic and has one
class period to conduct a "seminar" in any fashion she/he decides.
Charles selects the genres of rap music and opens his seminar with a
"pop quiz." Questions that I am forced to guess at include, "Who titled
his album, *Compton's Most Wanted?*," "How many albums has Too
Short made?," and "In your own opinion who was the 'realest' brother
of N.W.A. (Niggers with Attitude)?"

Six

A good friend from high school that I haven't seen in years stops by for
a visit. During late night discussions he reveals his "conversion" to hip
hop music. I respond apathetically, smiling and nodding a lot but not
understanding his enthusiasm. Before heading back home he leaves me
with my first sampler tape of rap music. I politely accept but don't
listen to it for several months.

RAP'S HISTORICAL AND CULTURAL CONTEXT: THE "NOISE" OF LIBERATION?

> Listen for lessons I'm saying inside music that the critics are blasting
> me for . . .

> Turn it up! Bring the noise (Public Enemy, "Bring the Noise," 1988)

> (T)he power of pop lies not in its meaning but its noise, not in its
> import but its force. (Simon Reynolds, cited in Jarrett, 1991, p. 816)

> The rhythm is the rebel. (Public Enemy, "Louder Than a Bomb,"
> 1988)

On the cover of Sir Mix-a-Lot's (1989) album *Seminar* he sits at a table
with three members of his "posse"—all are wearing togas. This

"classical" scene is disrupted by more than just African American males in togas. They are also adorned with gold chains, one is using a cellular phone, and their reflections in the clearly contemporary table reveal them in modern garb. In accordance with rap's aesthetics this scene "mixes" and recombines seemingly disparate elements. Sir Mix-a-Lot is poised, mallet and chisel in his hands, over a stone tablet in which he has already inscribed the word "seminar." With a fierce look on his face, one wonders what he is writing next (he has already chiseled the letters "n" and "a"), or if he is prepared to shatter the tablet. Inscription, reinscription, disruption, invitation, intertextuality, self-referential—*Seminar's* cover models the aesthetic power of rap music.

As one of the more intriguing critiques of the "pre-millennium tension" (Tricky, 1996) we exist in, rap is sometimes seen as simply an extension of a traditional "African American/African diasporic aesthetic" (Bartlett, 1994, p. 639). Others see it in distinctly post-modern terms (Baker, 1993; Miller, 1996; Roberts, 1991; 1996), emphasizing the medium's "nonauthoritative collaging or archiving of sound and styles that bespeaks a deconstructive hybridity (where) (l)inearity and progress yield to a dizzying synchronicity" (Baker, 1993, p. 89). Rose (1994) contends that both "postmodern and premodern interpretive frames fail to do justice to (rap's) complexities," and that it must instead be understood within the "context of deindustrialization . . . (which) simultaneously reflect(s) and contest(s) the social roles open to urban inner-city youths at the end of the twentieth century" (p. 22). However one defines the medium, it seems to occupy a significant position in our cultural milieu, one worthy of more serious attention than it has heretofore received (Brennan, 1994).

Before progressing to the cultural and historical contexts of rap music, I would like to draw attention to another aspect of the art form. While I agree with Ross (1991) that words are inadequate in analyzing song lyrics, they seem especially deficient in dealing with the other "half" of the equation—the music, the beat, the sonic barrage, the rhythm, the "noise." Rose (1994) summarizes the power and force of this fundamental component of rap:

> Rap's rhythms . . . are its most powerful effect. Rap's primary focus is sonic . . . Rap music centers on the quality and nature of rhythm and sound, the lowest, "fattest beats" being the most significant and emotionally charged . . . The arrangement and selection of sounds rap

musicians have invented via samples, turntables, tape machines, and sound systems are at once deconstructive (in that they actually take apart recorded musical compositions) and recuperative (because they recontextualize these elements creating new meanings for cultural sounds that have been relegated to commercial wastebins). . . . "Noise" on the one hand and communal countermemory on the other, rap music conjures and razes in one stroke. (pp. 64-65)

So, what is rap music? And how can the written word approximate the dynamism of its history, form, and content?

The genesis and evolution of rap has been the subject of lengthy narratives (Fernando, 1994; Toop, 1992, 1984) as well as more compact analyses (Keyes, 1984; Lusane, 1993; Zook, 1992). Zook (1992) observes that rap music emerged in the late 1970s in the black and Puerto Rican male communities of the South Bronx in New York City. Zook identifies rap as "an extension of African expressive forms such as 'signifying,' 'playing the dozens,' and creating praisesongs in the tradition of the griot, or African storyteller (p. 257).

Several have defined rap by distilling dominant trends. Baker (1993) comments on the technological nature of rap which involves:

scratching: rapidly moving the 'wheels of steel' (i.e., turntables) back and forth with the disc cued, creating a deconstructed sound . . . (and) sampling: taking a portion (phrase, riff, percussive vamp, etc.) of a known or unknown record (or a video game squawk, a touch-tone telephone medley, verbal tag from Malcolm X or Martin Luther King) and combining it in the overall mix . . . (p. 90)

And Rose (1994), who gives credit for identifying the following elements to film maker and critic Arthur Jafa, elaborates on the "stylistic continuities" between rap and other aspects of hip hop culture:

(B)reaking, graffiti style, rapping, and musical construction seem to center around three concepts: flow, layering, and ruptures in line. In hip hop, visual, physical, musical, and lyrical lines are set in motion, broken abruptly with sharp angular breaks, yet they sustain motion and energy through fluidity and flow. . . . (O)ne can argue that they create and sustain rhythmic motion, continuity, and circularity via flow; accumulate, reinforce, and embellish this continuity through

layering; and manage threats to these narratives by building in
ruptures that highlight the continuity as it momentarily challenges it.
These effects at the level of style and aesthetics suggest affirmative
ways in which profound social dislocation and rupture can be
managed and perhaps contested in the cultural arena. (pp. 38-39)

Lusane (1993) believes that rap music is shaped by "material
conditions of black life" (p. 42). He argues that the economic blight that
plagued black urban life in the Reagan and Bush eras fueled this
incipient art form. Lusane notes that it was

perfectly logical that Hip Hop culture should initially emerge most
strongly in those cities hardest hit by Reagonomics with large
minority youth populations—New York, Los Angeles, Houston, and
Oakland. . . . In a period when black labor was in low demand, if one
could not shoot a basketball like Michael Jordan, then the
entertainment industry was one of the few legal avenues available for
the get-rich consciousness that dominated the social ethos of the
1980s. (p. 43)

Lusane contends that rap paradoxically thrived in the very market
economy that was destroying African American communities.

The rage resulting from such urban realities was expressed in songs
like "The Message" by Grandmaster Flash and the Furious Five where
they rap about an environment with "Broken glass everywhere/People
pissing on the stairs" and "Rats in the front room, roaches in the back"
(1982, quoted in Fernando, 1994). Hence is evidenced one of rap's
contradictory dimensions. Such social commentary is responsible in
some measure for the medium's success, but it is also commentary
contingent upon oppressive economic realities. Without the social crisis
engulfing African American urban communities, one must question
whether rap would have succeeded at all.

The issue of commodification is frequently addressed in rap songs.
The question is whether "a dominant community (is) repeatedly co-
opting the cultural forms of oppressed communities, stripping them of
their vitality and form . . ." (Van Der Meer, cited in Blair, p. 21). As
mentioned previously rap is a lucrative industry, and one which has
tremendous cross-over appeal into white suburban culture.[6] But in spite
of success stories of black rap stars and record producers highlighted by
the media, the situation is probably more closely akin to Chuck D's

(1996) observation that ". . . between ownership and creativity in the entertainment and music industry blacks are not presented the options of how they can participate in it besides singing, rapping, dancing, telling jokes, or acting." The magnitude of white economic, social, and political profiteering at the expense of black cultural forms is expressed when Chuck D raps in "Free Big Willie" that "entertaining is today's way of pickin cotton" (1996).

Gangsta rap, illuminating the "strength of street knowledge," arrived on the national scene most notably with N.W.A.'s *Straight Outta Compton* (1988). Gangsta rappers confront "material misery with a battery of blunts and forty ounces, guns and gangs, 'bitches' and hood-rats (and) rudely depart from the aesthetics and ideology of their more politically conscious kin" (Dyson, 1996, p. 168). Gangsta rap also illustrates the tension between negotiation with and co-option by capitalism.

The success of N.W.A. and other gangsta rappers led to a flood of imitators, and in turn, intriguing internal rap discourse policing by artists like Paris (1994) and Public Enemy (1994). Paris simultaneously levels criticism at "Bandwagon niggas (who) want to be the new gangsta of the week" and record companies who "put everything they got to that shit (gangsta rap)" but "never push anything real for the good of the community" in "One Time Fo' Ya Mind" (1994). And Public Enemy, in "So Whatcha Gone Do Now?," attack the "moral bankruptcy and racial betrayal of gangsta rap" (Dyson, 1996, p. 168-69), criticizing the genre's glorification of black on black violence which profits others.

Rap has also been criticized for its phallo-centrism (Lusane, 1993; Ransby and Matthews, 1993). As Ransby and Matthews observe, in spite of "an oppositional edge which offers respite from the oppressive realities of daily life in a hostile dominant culture," rap music also "represents a very male-centered definition of the problems confronting the Black community and proposes pseudo-solutions which further marginalize and denigrate Black women" (p. 57). A graphic example is the song "Hoes" by Too Short which reinforces stereotypical categories of "pimp," "hoe (whore)," and "bitch," and where he brags that he'll "hit small towns and sell pussy everywhere" (cited in Fernando, 1994, p. 113). Thus, in spite of the seemingly dissident nature of some rap music, it is tempered by a political vision which uncritically accepts and internalizes the dominant society's narrow and patriarchal definitions of manhood, and then defines liberation as the extent to which Black men meet those criteria: the acquisition of money, violent military conquest and the successful subjugation of women as domestic and sexual servants. (Ransby and Matthews, p. 66)

But one shouldn't conclude that rap music is monolithically misogynistic. Such stereotyping is openly challenged by rappers like Queen Latifah, Monie Love, Salt 'N' Pepa, and MC Lyte who espouse feminist ideals in their music and videos (Roberts, 1994; 1996; Rose, 1994). Queen Latifah (1989) even challenges the belief that rap is a male domain in her song "Ladies First" where she proclaims that "Some think that we can't flow/Stereotypes they got to go" and declares that she's going to "flip the scene into reverse." And female rappers like Boss (1993) invert gender norms and appropriate the violence of gangsta rap to direct it toward questioning the genre's rampant sexual braggadocio.

Davis (1995) sees the entire issue of misogyny in rap in more complex terms, explaining her choice to buy gangsta rapper Snoop Doggy Dogg's *Doggystyle* instead of Queen Latifah's *Black Reign* with her last $15:

... I don't fit into a puritanical, dualistic feminism that recognizes only indignant innocence (buying *Black Reign*) or unenlightened guilt (buying into *Doggystyle*). I don't have to choose. ... the actual dilemma I was experiencing was how to explain that I don't feel oppressed by Snoop or defined by his conception of women—without denying that in Snoop's world, he is defining me and all women. ... There are no excuses for lyrical sexism. ... Yet I still feel virtually untouched by this verbal and visual violence toward women, and I believe this feeling springs from an increased sense of freedom rather than from apathetic resignation. (pp. 131-33)

She continues by identifying the ironic position black male rappers are in:

Male hip-hop artists recognize that they are hunted; they flesh out all of white America's fears by carrying out, lyrically, unthinkable acts of sociopathic destruction. The fantastical crime setting of gangsta and horrorcore rap, starring protagonists who drip with testosterone, features a masculinity that defines itself by an ability to annihilate any challenger, female or male. When this protagonist commits sexual and violent crimes, he satisfies a specifically black male yet generic desire for total power. . . . Misogyny here becomes a reactionary act with a subversive gloss. (p. 134)

Rap music thus oscillates in a form of limbo, somewhere between (or beyond) tradition and post-modernity, replete with the contradictions and paradoxes that accompany any cultural form trying to negotiate its place in the world. The dynamic nature of this negotiation is what we need to consider as we consider rap's implications for radical teaching, for finding "strategies to make the process of learning a democratic act—an act which refuses to be satisfied with dominant definitions of knowledge, intelligence, and school success" (Kincheloe, 1992, p. 3).

SCENES FROM THE SCHOOLHOUSE (AND BEYOND)— PART III

Seven

Several of the artists on the sampler tape catch my attention—Kool Moe Dee, Queen Latifah, Boogie Down Productions, Jungle Brothers, Sir Mix-a-Lot, Paris. I even incorporate some of the songs into my final project for a graduate seminar in educational foundations.

Eight

I decide to incorporate my newfound interest into the classroom. On the first day of African American Studies I hand out lyrics that I have transcribed to Jungle Brothers' "Acknowledge Your Own History" and play the song. Several of the students look at each other quizzically. One student asks, "Mr. D., where did you find this? This sounds like 'Old School' stuff."

INFUSING RADICAL EDUCATION WITH HIP HOP AESTHETICS

> Rap is teaching white kids what it means to be black, and that causes
> a problem for the infrastructure. (Chuck D., 1996a)

> Rap is rhythm and poetry I thought you knew it
> But who would have ever thought that we would use it the way we be
> using it? (Paris, "Check It Out Ch'All," 1992)

> You know the rhythm, the rhyme plus the beat is designed
> So I can enter your mind (Public Enemy, "Rebel Without a Pause,"
> 1988)

Charles, the high school student who stumped me with his quiz on rap
music, wrote the following to accompany his presentation:

> Rap is a form of music that has been around for generations, or as
> long as I can remember. You can't find this topic in books or the real
> meaning of the word "rap" in the dictionary . . . today rap has
> emerged into categories or forms that have different deliveries and
> different messages. . . . Take for instance Public Enemy. They want
> us to fight the powers that be. We could fight or we could speak but
> the point is we will be heard. . . (M)y personal favorite is the gansta
> rap. . . . Yes it has been in the media and everywhere else . . . If you
> can't relate to this music don't try to listen to it. If you say you don't
> like some of the lyrics no one if forcing you to listen to it. Nobody
> tells you it is mandatory to get Scarface's album, Snoop's CD, Ice
> Cube's cassette, etc. Yes, they talk about guns, they rap on
> violence. . . . if you can't relate to it you will have something to say.
> This music is not influential, but it will be only if you let. . . . So
> don't open your mouth and say negative thoughts about this black,
> legal business. . . .

Charles, rather forcefully I feel, reveals the high levels of affective
intensity that students frequently invest in rap music. It is, in every
sense of the word, his music, and it produces a sense of shared meaning
and a common ground for discourse. In other words, students like the
music and because it speaks to them in terms they understand it offers

some degree of empowerment, some of the "everyday conversation" that bell hooks (1994) believes is essential for theories that can "educate the public" (p. 64). Theories of liberation already exist in rap music. It's just a matter of how much we, in Charles' word, can "relate" to it and allow it to transform our classrooms.

One of the most transformative possibilities of rap, or more accurately of hip hop aesthetic sensibilities, is the model it offers as a mixing, sampling, recombinant text. Paul Miller (1996), A.K.A. DJ Spooky, Spatial Engineer of the Invisible City, explains the dynamic nature of the art of DJing (disc jockeying), one of the fundamental components of rap music:

> It is in this singularly improvisational role of "recombiner" that the DJ creates what I like to call a "post symbolic mood sculpture," or the mix; a disembodied and transient text . . . The implications of this style of creating art are three fold: 1) by its very nature it critiques the entire idea of intellectual property and copyright law, 2) it reifies a communal art value structure in contrast to most forms of art in late capitalist social contexts, 3) it interfaces communications technology in a manner that anthropomorphizes it. (pp. 12-13)

If we were to begin thinking of our classrooms as a "mix," as recombinant, fluid entities where the "copyrighting" privilege of authority in the guise of "teacher" is challenged, where the entire process of learning becomes more communal, and where technology and popular culture become "human" forces, we can see how hip hop aesthetics is transformative pedagogically. The classroom might become, in my favorite image of post-modern curriculum which Doll (1993) borrows from Milan Kundera and Richard Rorty, a "fascinating imaginative realm where no one owns the truth and everyone has the right to be understood" (p. 151).

After several shaky starts attempting to introduce rap music into high school classrooms, I realized that part of the problem was that I was trying to be the "copyrighter," trying to control the situation, trying to force my tastes (or lack thereof) on students. Once I allowed students to help decide the tenor of the classroom mix, to decide which songs we would use as texts, their interest seemed to increase, and the classroom dynamics changed. Highly charged discussions emerged about sexism and violence in gangsta rap; intertextual comparisons were made between Henry David Thoreau and Rage Against the Machine, a group who fuses "rap, rock, and funk" (Lewis, p. 706); Paris (1989/1990; 1992; 1994), the self-proclaimed "black panther of hip hop," provided the texts for comparing revolutionary ideologies. Rap thus became both text and pedagogy—a way of organizing, or better yet a way of understanding how the transient nature of the classroom might emerge as recombinant teaching and learning.

Knowledge itself is even loosened from the stasis of modernity into flux, process, and re-birth through rap's aesthetics. As Paris (1989/1990) suggests, it becomes "knowledge born on the microphone." Dynamic, intertextual, and availing itself of technology, it is the "noise" of knowledge-in-process as Serres (1995) envisions it in *Genesis.*

I am convinced that something, however ineffable that something is, about rap provides insights and attitudes that can inform radical pedagogies. In seeking such pedagogies which can provide counterdiscourses to prevailing ones, however, we must also acknowledge how these counterdiscourses might function in contradictory, disempowering ways. "Revolution," as Paris (1989/1990) says, "ain't never been simple." But there is, I believe, revolutionary power in rap, and in allowing its aesthetics to reorient our ways of being in the classroom and the world.

Fernando (1994) perhaps best sums up the situation with the graphical dictum (p. xv):

WoRdSoUnD
is
PoWeR

Or as Laquan (1990) exhorts us in the opening of "Notes of a Native Son," it might be as simple as to:

Listen!

POSTSCRIPT: SCENES FROM THE SCHOOLYARD (AND BEYOND) REVISITED

Nine

I never travel anywhere without a Paris or Public Enemy tape. I rarely write without the "noise" of rap somewhere in the background, or foreground.

Ten

I am still exploring the medium, wondering what is considered "Old School," wondering how loud I should play *Straight Outta Compton.*
   Very loud I think.
   Very loud indeed.[7]

NOTES

   1. Culled from the title of Public Enemy's (1988) "Bring the Noise" and a line in Paris' (1989/1990) "Break the Grip of Shame" where he invites listeners to "enter into a new realm" and "witness knowledge born on the microphone."
   2. There are the more visible elements of popular culture evident in such things as modes of fashion. But even when officially "banned," technology offered students that I taught a variety of opportunities to "smuggle" popular culture into the classroom, primarily through small headphones and portable compact disc players hidden in book bags or purses.
   3. "Pleasure" is a deceptive term because it is often used to dismiss popular culture as a site of serious inquiry. But understanding the affective dimensions of student investment in popular culture does not trivialize its significance. In fact, it broadens attempts to conceptualize how resistance and agency might emerge from students' interaction with the terrain of the popular.
   4. I am talking about more than simply "teaching" popular culture. The dialogical nature of radical pedagogies requires that they constantly be in process, informed by the dynamic experiences of students and teachers, and not simply packaged as transformative "lesson plans" with pre-ordained objectives. It means striving toward "knowledge-in-action" instead of "knowledge of" (Applebee, 1996, pp. 101-18).
   5. "Discovery" is used to imply the process by which popular culture can transform teaching. Discovery involves a receptive orientation on the part of the educator and classroom dynamics that allow ever evolving student cultural forms to be heard and seen on their own terms.
   6. Rose (1994) notes that such appropriation of black music by whites is nothing new. The history of blues, jazz, and rock 'n' roll evidence this. Rose writes, "(W)hite America has always had an intense interest in black culture. . . . Black culture in the United States has always had elements that have been at least bifocal—speaking to both a black audience and a larger predominantly white context" (p. 4-5). She continues that the attraction is because whites are "listening in on black culture, fascinated by its differences,

drawn in by mainstream constructions of black culture as a forbidden narrative, as a symbol of rebellion" (p. 5).

7. I would like to thank Scott Fontenot, Pableaux Johnson, and Clarence Cormier for helping me "turn on" and "tune in" to rap music, and Petra Munro and William Pinar for commenting on early drafts. This essay is dedicated to the memory of Helen Fontenot, who first clued me in to the revolutionary, transformative potential of rap.

REFERENCES

Applebee, A. (1996). *Curriculum as conversation: Transforming traditions of teaching and learning. Chicago*: The University of Chicago Press.

Aronowitz, S. (1989). Working-class identity and celluloid fantasy. In H. Giroux & R. Simon (Eds.), *Popular culture, schooling and everyday life* (197-218). New York: Bergin & Garvey.

Baker, H. (1993). *Black studies, rap, and the academy.* Chicago: University of Chicago Press.

Bartlett, A. (1994). Airshafts, loudspeakers, and the hip hop sample: Contexts and African American musical aesthetics. *African American Review*, 28 (4), 639-52.

Blair, M. E. (1993). Commercialization of the rap music youth subculture. *Journal of Popular Culture,* 27 (3), 21-33.

Boogie Down Productions. (1990). *Exhibit A. Recorded on Edutainment.* New York: Zomba Recording Corporation.

Boss. (1993). *Born gangstaz.* New York: Sony Music Entertainment.

Brennan, T. (1994). Off the gangsta tip: A rap appreciation, or forgetting about Los Angeles. *Critical Inquiry 20,* 663-93.

Castenell, L., & Pinar, W. (Eds.). (1993). *Understanding curriculum as racial text: Representations of identity and difference in education.* Albany, NY: SUNY Press.

Chuck D. (1996). *Autobiography of mistachuck.* New York: Mercury Records.

Chuck D. (1996a). In J. Buckley & M. Ellingham (Eds.), *The rough guide to rock* (p. 694). London: Rough Guides.

Davis, E. (1995). Sexism and the art of feminist hip-hop maintenance. In R. Walker (Ed.), *To be real: Telling the truth and changing the face of feminism* (pp. 127-141). New York: Anchor Books.

Doll, W. (1993). *A post-modern perspective on curriculum.* New York: Teachers College Press.

Dylan, B. (1965). *Ballad of a thin man. Recorded on Highway 61 revisited.* New York: Columbia Records.

Dyson, M. (1996). *Between God and gangsta rap: Bearing witness to black culture.* New York: Oxford University Press.

Ellsworth, E. (1987). Educational films against critical pedagogy. *Journal of Education,* 169(3), 32-47.

Estrada, K. & McLaren, P. (1993). A dialogue on multiculturalism and democratic culture. *Educational Researcher,* 22 (3), 27-33.

Fernando, S.J., Jr. (1994). *The new beats: Exploring the music, culture, and attitudes of hip-hop.* New York: Anchor Books.

Freire, P. (1968,1970). *Pedagogy of the oppressed.* New York: Seabury.

Giroux, H. (1994). Doing cultural studies: Youth and the challenge of pedagogy. *Harvard Education Review,* 64(3), 278-308.

Giroux, H. & Simon, R. (1989). Schooling, popular culture, and a pedagogy of possibility. In H. Giroux & R. Simon (Eds.), *Popular culture, schooling and everyday life* (pp. 219-235). New York: Bergin & Garvey.

Gore, J. (1993). *The struggle for pedagogies: Critical and feminist discourses as regimes of truth.* New York: Routledge.

Grossberg, L. (1989). Pedagogy in the present: Politics, postmodernity, and the popular. In H. Giroux & R. Simon (Eds.), *Popular culture, schooling and everyday life* (pp. 91-115). New York: Bergin & Garvey.

hooks, b. (1994). *Teaching to transgress: Education as the practice of freedom.* New York: Routledge.

Jarrett, M. (1991). Concerning the progress of rock & roll. *South Atlantic Quarterly,* 90(4), 803-18.

Keyes, C. (1984). Verbal art performance in rap music: The conversation of the 80s. *Folklore Forum,* 2(17), 143-152.

Kincheloe, J. (1992). Introduction: The questions we ask, the stories we tell about education. In J. Kincheloe & S. Steinberg (Eds.), *Thirteen questions: Reframing education's conversation* (pp. 1-19). New York: Peter Lang.

Kreisberg, S. (1992). *Transforming power: Domination, empowerment, and education.* Albany, NY: SUNY Press.

Laquan. (1990). *Notes of a native son.* New York: Island Records.

Lewis, A. (1996). In J. Buckley & M. Ellingham (Eds.), *The rough guide to rock.* London: Rough Guides.

Lusane, C. (1993). *Rap, race and politics.* Race & Class, 35(1), 41-56.

McLaren, P. (1989). *Life in schools: An introduction to critical pedagogy in the foundations of education.* New York: Longman.

Miklitsch, R. (1994). Punk pedagogy or performing contradiction: The risks and rewards of anti-transference. *The Review of Education/Pedagogy/ Cultural Studies,* 16 (1), pp. 57-67.

Miller, P. (1996). An excerpt from a recombinant text entitled: "Flow my blood the DJ said." In the notes for the album *Songs of a Dead Dreamer by DJ Spooky*. New York: Asphodel.

N.W.A. (1988). *Straight outta Compton*. Hollywood, CA: Priority Records.

Paris. (1989/1990). *The devil made me do it*. New York: Tommy Boy Music.

Paris. (1992). *Sleeping with the enemy*. Oakland, CA: Scarface Records.

Paris. (1994). *Guerilla funk*. Los Angeles, CA: Priority Records.

Public Enemy. (1988). *It takes a nation of millions to hold us back*. New York: Def Jam Recordings.

Public Enemy. (1994). *Muse sick-n-hour mess age*. New York: Def Jam Recordings.

Queen Latifah. (1989). *All hail the queen*. New York: Tommy Boy Music.

Ransby, B. & Matthews, T. (1993). *Black popular culture and the transcendence of patriarchal illusions*. Race & Class, 35(1), 57-68.

Roberts, R. (1996). *Ladies first: Women in music videos*. Jackson: University Press of Mississippi

Roberts, R. (1994). "Ladies first": Queen Latifah's Afrocentric feminist music video. *African American Review*, 28(2), 245-57.

Roberts, R. (1991). Music videos, performance, and resistance: Feminist rappers. *Journal of Popular Culture*, 25(2), 141-52.

Rose, T. (1994). *Black noise: Rap music and black culture in contemporary America*. Hanover, NH: University Press of New England.

Ross, A. (1991). Poetry and motion: Madonna and Public Enemy. In A. Easthope & J. Thompson (Eds.), *Contemporary poetry meets modern theory*. Toronto: University of Toronto Press.

Serres, M. (1995). *Genesis*. Translated by G. James & J. Nielson. Originally published in 1982.

Sir Mix-a-Lot. (1989). Seminar. Burbank, CA: Def American Recordings.

SounData. (1996, November 11). Rap's audience. Graphic in The Advertiser (Lafayette, LA), p. 5B.

Toop, D. (1992). *Rap attack 2*. Boston: Consortium Press.

Toop, D. (1984). *The rap attack: African jive to New York hip hop*. London: Pluto Press.

Tricky. (1996). *Pre-millennium tension*. New York: Island Records.

Weiler, K. (1988). *Women teaching for change: Gender, class and power*. New York: Bergin & Garvey.

Willis, P. (1981). *Learning to labour: How working class kids get working class jobs*. New York: Columbia.

Zook, K. (1992). Reconstructions of nationalist thought in black music and
    culture. In R. Garofalo (Ed.), *Rockin' the boat: Mass music and mass
    movements*. Boston, MA: South End Press.

CHAPTER EIGHT

Outlaw Women Writers, (Un)Popular Popular Culture, and Critical Pedagogy

Dianne Smith

Marilyn Zuckerman (1994) writes a passage in her poem, "After Sixty,"

> Now there is time to tell the story, time to invent the new one- to
> chain myself to a fence outside the missile base, to throw my body
> before a truck loaded with phallic images, to write Thou Shalt Not
> Kill on the hull of a Trident submarine, to pour my own blood on the
> walls of the Pentagon, to walk a thousand miles with a begging bowl
> in my hand. (p. 185)

And Clarissa Pinkola Estes (1992) surmises that "to further our kinship relationship with the instinctual nature, it assists greatly if we understand stories as though we are inside them, rather than as though they are outside of us" (p. 25). She continues by stating that "Bone by bone, hair by hair, Wild Woman comes back. Through night dreams, through events half understood and half remembered, Wild Woman comes back. She comes back through story" (p. 26).

I begin this narrative essay with these two women writers because their theories remind me of a recent conversation that I had with my niece, Mache, who lives in North Carolina. Mache is the oldest of the nieces and nephews in my family. I had called her mother, Vera, my sister, to give her some good news about a book contract. Vera was not home and Mache answered the telephone. She married in August 1996 and so I proceeded to tease her about having two addresses. Somehow our conversation became one of storytelling about family events and family members, dead and alive. I realize that Mache is quite thirsty for information regarding her grandfather and grandmother, my parents (Pete and Elizabeth Smith). I begin an engagement in recalling some "dangerous memories" (Foucault, 1977) relevant to my childhood; memories that Mache had not been told.

These memories move Mache to ask more questions. And then she asks me if I remember when she was about four years old how she would see a strange man standing at the edge of the driveway each night. She said, "Dianne, you remember! He would just stand there with a cane in his hand. I would tell mama to go look at him." I said to her, "I think that I do. Did it scare you?" She said, "Yes, because I didn't have anyone to talk to about it. Mama said that I was probably born with a veil over my face. What does that mean?" I tell her that many black folks believe that a baby born with a veil has powers to see spirits and make predictions about the future. I said to Mache, "You should accept it as a gift. I believe that human beings have powers that we don't know about and understand." She says to me, "If I had someone to talk to then I wouldn't be afraid." I respond with, "Remember, I'm your weird aunt. You can talk to me about anything."

After I hang up from an hour-long conversation with Mache, I wonder why I did not tell her about my childhood sexual abuse experience. For she wants information about her family; she desires stories. Why is it that her mom and I will share childhood memories about family violence, alcohol abuse, extramarital affairs, and other "stuff" but we never tell these stories while we are in the presence of our sisters, brothers, nieces and nephews? This question leads me to confess that we consciously and unconsciously ban these stories from our lips. Therefore, I better understand why Dorothy Allison's book, *Bastard out of Carolina* (1992), has been banned from a high school's English classes. The *Newsletter on Intellectual Freedom* (1996) documents that Dorothy Allison's book is "Removed from the Mt. Abram High School English classes in Salem, Maine (1995) because the language and subject matter were inappropriate for fifteen-year-olds" (p. 49).

It is banned because Dorothy Allison's main protagonist, Bone Boatwright, is sexually and physically abused by her step-father, Daddy Glen. Bone Boatwright is called a bastard because her mother, Ruth

Boatwright, had her "out of wedlock"; she is labeled "white trash" by the community folks; and her aunt Raylene speaks of loving a woman. It is my summation that high school adolescents, with proper guidance, can engage in meaningful dialogue regarding Bone Boatwright's experiences. I believe that most female and male adolescents will understand Bone Boatwright's story. For example, she tells her reader that

> Everything hurt me: my arm in its cotton sling; the memory of the nurse's careful fingers; the light that glinted into my eyes from the flawed glass of Raylene's window; my hip where it pressed against the mattress. Most of all my heart hurt me, a huge swollen obstruction in my chest. Every time I closed my eyes there was a flash of Glen's face as he had looked above me. (p. 302)

Our young people are constantly bombarded with visual images of violence through various forms of popular culture and mass media. And these various forms of popular culture become absorbed, unquestioned pedagogy. For example, I recall sitting in a local movie theatre watching "Sugar Hill." The character, Romello, shoots a gangster who had shot and beaten his father. A group of young black males began to yell in agreement with this act of violent revenge: "Blow the muthafucker away. That's right man, kill the son-of-a-bitch." Additionally, another bothersome scene, for me, is a violent date rape. Romello's "girlfriend," Melissa, accepts an invitation to a guy's house for drinks. He, "a famous athlete," calls her a "skeezer" (a whore, a slut). Again, a group of young black males yell in agreement as this character slaps, kicks, and tries to force Melissa to suck his penis. However, I know many young black males who view violence as senseless acts.

Thus, it becomes imperative that we insert cultural texts in schools that disrupt boundaries and embrace critical questioning. At this juncture I will use a rather lengthy bell hooks (1994) quote to illuminate my point:

> And indeed I tell the girls, 'I'm into red cause it's so revolutionary,' a comment that sparks intense giggles. We begin our talk about cultural studies with the color red, with its meaning in black life. Already they know that red is a color for seduction and desire. We talk about the Lawrence painting, what they see when they really look at it--hard--

hard. . . .We talk about the jet black color of their bodies and the bright red of the table next to them. Already they know about color caste, about the way dark black color makes one less desirable. Connecting all these pieces, we find a way to understand Jacob Lawrence, desire and passion in black life. We practice culture criticism and feel the fun and excitement of learning in relation to living regular life, of using everything we already know to know more. (p. 2)

What bell hooks is doing is tapping into the lived experiences of the black girls involved in this journey learning about the artist Jacob Lawrence, the color red, revolution, desire and passion, and oppression. She starts with what they already know in order to know more. This is what Dorothy Allison does with her novel: she starts with what we already know so that we will know more about poor white Appalachian culture through the eyes of Bone Boatwright, her family members, and those around her. So, bell hooks and Dorothy Allison are busy doing what Henry Giroux (1994) posits: ". . . to address how representations are constructed and taken up through social memories that are taught, learned, mediated, and appropriated within particular institutional and discursive formations of power" (p. 45).

Consequently, in this essay I will argue for the insertion of cultural texts in public schools that "transgress boundaries" (hooks, 1994) and add "intellectual resources in order to understand what keeps making the lives we live, and the societies we live in, profoundly and deeply inhumane" (Hall, 1992b, pp. 17-18). In so doing, I will present some black women writers who have written against the grain of struggle, toward a terrain of healing and self-actualization. I will conclude with a discussion about some ways in which I have used cultural texts at an urban university to teach educators the importance of disrupting our home spaces to know more in order to work in "borderlands." I will not provide a recipe for I do not believe that critical education is a step-by-step process. Rather, critical education is experiential, experimental, and changes to meet the needs of the learners involved at a given moment. Included in this section is, I hope, a recognition that cultural texts are mechanisms that can move us beyond rediscovering what we already know to understanding the complexities embedded within struggle (Grossberg, 1994).

WILD BLACK WOMEN WRITE UNPOPULAR CULTURAL TEXTS

In 1993 I completed a book chapter entitled "Black Women Teachers Speak About Child Abuse" (Smith, 1993) and I asked four of my male friends to read it and to give me some feedback (one is black and three are white). I would wait patiently for their responses and each one asked, "Why are you so angry? It's real fiery." Concurrently, I asked some of my sister friends to read this chapter, white and black, and they had a completely different response. "This is fire and passion. All teachers, and women, need to read this." I recall this story because it appears that when wild women uncover dangerous tales we are labeled as bashers, angry, and confused. And yes, the potential for such emotions are part of the healing process. However, I now choose to accept Maya Angelou's perspective: "Without willing it, I had gone from being ignorant of being ignorant to being aware of being aware" (1970, p. 230).

What I mean by this is that women of all races have used the literary canon to move from silence to speech: in order to become speaking, thinking, knowing subjects. Maria Lugones and Elizabeth Spelman suggest that

> . . . the demand that the woman's voice be heard and attended to has been made for a variety of reasons: not just so as to greatly increase the chances that true accounts of women's lives will be given, but also because the articulation of experience (in myriad ways) is among the hallmarks of a self-determining individual or community. There are just not epistemological, but moral and political, reasons for demanding that the woman's voice be heard after centuries of androcentric din. (1983, p. 574)

Maria Lugones and Elizabeth Spelman resonate the black woman's need to claim her voice to subjectify herself as a positive force to be reckoned with: to redefine herself as one who exemplifies intelligence, brilliance and a survivor of a Eurocentric, patriarchic system that is oppressive.

For example, the enslaved black woman's autobiography is an artery for naming the ownership of their bodies; to speak about the disintegration of their families; and to reveal the mutilations and lynchings that were so much a part the system as the tyrannical rapes of their bodies and souls. Angela Davis (1981) writes that

> since women were viewed as profitable labor-units, they might as well have been genderless. Slave women were classified as 'breeders' as opposed to 'mothers,' their infant children could be sold away from them like calves from cows. As females, slave women were inherently vulnerable to all forms of sexual coercion. (pp. 5-7)

That is, as Linda Brent (1861) documents in her autobiography, *Incidents in the Life of a Slave Girl: Written by Herself*:

> When they told me my new-born was a girl, my heart was heavier than it had ever been before. Slavery is terrible for men; but it is far more terrible for women. Superadded to the burden common to all, *they* have wrongs, and sufferings, and mortifications peculiarly their own. (p. 43)

Linda Brent knew that her daughter, Ellen, would become a victim of sexual abuse known to plantation life.

Harriet E. Wilson explicates the theme of black female oppression in the form of white woman hatred and abuse of the black female in her book, *Our Nig* (1859). Alfrado, the enslaved girl, was blamed for pushing the white girl, Mary (of the big house), into a stream of water (although this was not true; in fact the little white girl tried to push Alfrado in the stream but fell in herself). The author discloses the following:

> 'How do we know but she has told the truth? I shall not punish her,' he replied (the white father), and left the house, as he usually did when a tempest threatened to envelop him. No sooner was he out of sight than Mrs. B. and Mary commenced beating her inhumanely; then propping her mouth open with a piece of food, shut her up in a dark room, without supper. For employment, while the tempest raged within, Mr. Bellmont went for the cows, a task belonging to Frado, and thus unintentionally prolonged her pain. (p. 93)

In *Incidents*, Linda Brent has devoted an entire chapter on "The Jealous Mistress" to expose the rage and anger lavished upon the slave woman by the white woman.

Amanda Smith (1893, as excerpted in Ann Allen Shockley, 1988) takes her reader to another dimension in that she names the oppression--sexual, economic, and class—"we" black women commonly experience, but do not name, by our black men. She writes about her experience with a group of black male preachers as they (she included) prepared to attend an annual general conference:

> He looked at me in surprise, mingled with half disgust; the very idea of one looking like me to want to go to General Conference; they cut their eye at my poke Quaker bonnet, with not a flower, not a feather. He said, 'I tell you Sister, it will cost money to go down there; and if you ain't got plenty of it, it's no use to go'; and turned away and smiled; another said: 'What does she want to go for? Woman preacher'; 'they want to be ordained,' was the reply. 'I mean to fight that thing,' said the other. 'Yes, indeed, so will I,' said another. (p. 229)

Amanda Smith opened the door for other black women to speak about the abuses that we experience in our communities with our black men; this is a definite "no-no" among black women, so I am treading on dangerous ground. However, Abbey Lincoln (1970) follows Amanda Smith's path by stating, and I agree, that

> But strange as it is, I've heard it echoed by too many Black full-grown males that Black womanhood is the downfall of the Black man in that she is 'evil,' 'hard to get along with,' 'domineering,' 'suspicious,' and 'narrow-minded.' In short, a black, ugly, evil you-know-what.

> Her head is more regularly beatened than any other woman's, and by her own man; she's the scapegoat for Mr. Charlie; she is forced to stark realism and chided if caught dreaming; her aspirations for her and hers are, for sanity's sake, stunted; her physical image has been criminally maligned, assaulted, and negated; she's the first to be called ugly and never beautiful, and as a consequence is forced to see her man (an exact copy of her, emotionally and physically), brainwashed and wallowing in self-loathing, pick for his own the

physical antithesis of her (the white woman and incubator of his heretofore arch enemy the white man). Then, to add guilt to insult and injury, she (the Black woman) stands accused as the emasculator of the only [*sic*] thing she has ever cared for, her Black man. (p. 82)

Furthermore, Kay Lindsey (1970) makes connections with the aforementioned outlaw women in that she suggests that "when we are defined by those other than ourselves, the qualities ascribed to us are not in our interests, but rather reflect the nature of the roles which we are intended to play" (p. 89). Thus, as Amanda Smith, Abbey Lincoln, and Kay Lindsey "speak out" against female oppression and racism by many of our men, many white men and white women, Alice Walker (1982) joins the ranks of naming black female oppression in the outrageous novel, *The Color Purple*. One reason I think that the novel is deemed outrageous and dangerous is that she creates a group of female protagonists, particularly Celie Johnson, who approach this theme, e. g., sexual exploitation, incest, black lesbianism, and violence with fiery energy.

For instance, Celie Johnson writes a letter to God, one of many, concerning the rape of her self by her "assumed" father. She tells God about a conversation that she has with Shug Avery:

> But one time when mama not at home, he come. Told me he want me to trim his hair. He bring the scissors and comb and brush and a stool. While I trim his hair he look at me funny. He a little nervous too, but I don't know why, till he grab hold of me and cram me up tween his legs. It hurt me you know. I was just going on fourteen. How it hurt and how much I was surprise. How it stung while I finish trimming his hair. How the blood drip down my leg and mess up my stocking. How he don't never look at me straight after that. (pp. 108-109)

Not only does Alice Walker break the forbidden rule of naming rape in the black family by many black men, but she broaches the mistreatment of "us" by our men through Celie Johnson and her relationship with Mister, her husband: "Mr. come git me to take care his rotten children. He never ast me nothing bout myself. He clam on top of me and fuck and fuck, even when my head bandaged. Nobody ever love me" (p. 109).

Additionally, while most black feminists did not challenge sexism which imbues homophobia, Alice Walker unveils the love that many black women share with each other. For her, in *Purple*, it appears important "to name the reality that black women do engage in lovemaking and comfort each other" (p. 109). That is, Alice Walker's protagonists, Celie Johnson and Shug Avery, care for each other in a sexual as well as nonsexual manner. In a letter to God, Celie Johnson talks about their first sexual encounter:

> Oh, Miss Celie, she say. And put her arms round me. They black and smooth and kind of glowy from the lamplight. I start to cry too. I cry and cry and cry. Don't cry, Celie, Shug say. Don't cry. She start kissing the water as it come down side my face. . . . Nobody ever love me, I say. She say, I love you, Miss Celie. And then she haul off and kiss me on the mouth. *Um*, she say, like she surprise. I kiss her back, say, *um*, too. Us kiss and kiss till us can't hardly kiss no more. Then us touch each other. I don't know nothing bout it, I say to Shug. I don't know much, she say. Then I feels something real soft and wet on my breast, feel like one of my little lost babies' mouth. Way after while, I act like a little lost baby too. (p. 165)

Alice Walker continues to be criticized for her revelations in *Purple*. She writes (1996): "I thought of how, when *The Color Purple* was published, and later filmed, it was a rare critic who showed any compassion for, or even noted, the suffering of the women and children explored in that book, while I was called a liar for showing that black men sometimes perpetuate domestic violence" (p. 38-39). Alice Walker continues by writing that "Of all the accusations, it was hardest to tolerate the charge that I hated black men. Out of respect, I worked hard to reassure my nephews, uncles, brothers, friends, and former lovers that the monster they saw being projected was not the aunt, niece, sister, woman who loved them" (p. 23).

These black women writers that I have presented in this essay, among others not mentioned, have chosen the process of identifying their selves and the selves of other black women as "inherently valuable, and it is perceived by the dominant white/male culture as most threatening because it challenges the culture's foundations" (Bethel, 1982, p.184). Or, as Maxine Greene (1988) writes in reference to black women's struggle for change. The stories of resistance by black women "shed many kinds of light on the meanings of freedom and the search for freedom ... in such writings we find a dialectical relation to what surrounds us, a conscious pursuit of freedom as an existential project, a central life task" (p. 66-67).

That is, as Marilyn Zuckerman (1994) suggests, "Now there is time to tell the story, time to invent the new one ..." (p. 185). In our writings we choose to tell the story and invent new ones. We choose to tell stories that are oppositional to accepted regimes of truth (Foucault, 1977) about who we are as black women. For example, a popular story about enslaved black women is that they tended not to resist their condition on the plantation and that those held in bondage exhibited a sense of satisfaction (Phillips, 1918). However, as I illuminate, Linda Brent and others are prime examples of enslaved women fighting and resisting their given "place" in their worlds.

As I conclude this section, I want to make it known that I was thirty- three years old when I realized that there were so many books and essays written by and about black women. It is during my graduate studies at Miami University (Ohio) that my teachers, Richard Quantz, Henry Giroux, and Laurie McDade, "turned" me on to unpopular popular texts; crossing into the borderlands (Giroux, 1994). I recall the hunger for more, the excitement of "knowing" the experiences revealed, and the anger for feeling "duped" because of the lies and untold "other" truths. Subsequently, it is my mission as a critical teacher to change the ways in which we continue to hide and misuse information. I want my niece, Mache (and others), to have access to stories such as Bone Boatwright's; those unpopular stories in order to understand "why." I want "our" youths to be able to read Bone Boatwright's Aunt Raylene's story,

> Bone, no woman can stand to choose between her baby and her lover, between her child and her husband. I made the woman I loved choose. She stayed with her baby, and I came back here alone. It should never have come to that. It never should. It just about killed her. It just about killed me (Allison, 1992, p. 300).

What I mean by this is that I want "our" youths to understand, as Clarissa Pinkola Estes (1992) suggests, "stories as though we are inside them, rather than as though they are outside us" (p. 26); embrace difference; to make connections with others' love, joy, pain, and struggle; and to desire a just world. Therefore, in conclusion, I constantly tell my dear friend, Ralph Parish, that there are two kinds of rage: one that is violent and oppressive and one that is compassionate and loving. I prefer the latter for change, for revolution. The latter is what I dream for our young people. Thus, what follows next is a discussion regarding some of my pedagogical practices that include some unpopular cultural texts and borderland crossing.

CRITICAL PEDAGOGY AND DISTURBING THE PLEASURES OF SILENCE

I want to begin this section with a disclaimer and a claimer: I do not romanticize the use of oppositional cultural texts, for there are contradictions and complexities embedded within such texts. For example, bell hooks (1994) writes about the contradictions in Paulo Freire's liberatory theory:

> I came to Freire thirsty, dying of thirst (in that way that the colonized, the marginalized subject who is still unsure of how to break the hold of the status quo, who longs for change, is needy, is thirsty), and I found in his work (and the work of Malcolm X, Fanon, etc.) a way to quench that thirst. To have work that promotes one's liberation is such a powerful gift that it does not matter so much if the gift is flawed. Think of the work as water that contains some dirt. Because you are thirsty you are not too proud to extract the dirt and be nourished by the water. (p. 50)

I agree with bell hooks, it is important for us to know and name the contradictions in our work. For I name some of my contradictions: "I dance in and out of fear and courage; I dance in and out of subservience and subversiveness; I dance in and out of talking back and silence; and I dance in and out of being ignorant and being aware" (Smith, 1996, p. 181). However, my claim is that I do have a passion for a pedagogy that seeks to bring forth the complexities and freedom embedded within struggle. I argue for a pedagogy that helps us to understand how we participate in hegemony within classrooms. As Peter McLaren (1994) writes, "Hegemony was at work in my own practices as an elementary school teacher. Because I did not teach my students to question the prevailing values, attitudes, and social practices of the dominant culture in a sustained critical manner, my classroom preserved the hegemony of the dominant culture" (p. 182).

Further, I advocate a pedagogy that nurtures diverse voices and breaks the silencing of experience that is crucial to understanding who we are as individuals; individuals who comprise a community. I stand for a pedagogy that is "radical but not doctrinaire" (Giroux, 1994, p. 133). One that, as Giroux defines,

> . . . self-consciously operates from a perspective in which teaching and learning are committed to expanding rather than restricting the opportunities for students and others to be social, political, and economic agents. As agents, students and others need to learn how to take risks, to understand how power works differently as both productive and a dominating force, to be able to 'read' the world from a variety of perspectives, and to be willing to think beyond the commonsense assumptions that govern everyday existence. (p. 133)

This leads me back to Dorothy Allison's *Bastard out of Carolina*. I use her book in an advanced curriculum theory course and her unpopular cultural text becomes pedagogy that creates opportunity for us to "study" our own autobiography as we travel down the dusty Appalachian hills with Bone Boatwright. In addition, black students can experience poor, white Appalachian culture from Bone Boatwright's perspective. This is important for these students to "see" that not "all" white people are economically and socially privileged. The Boatwrights make visible the need for social relations that inform a number of considerations that cut across our society's diverse terrain (Giroux, 1994).

I specifically identify black students because I listen to many of their stories regarding white racism and there seems to be consensus, among them, that "all" whites have access to certain forms of materialism that blacks do not. I certainly do not trivialize their lived experiences relevant to racism and colonization; and I do know that race is a powerful divider of human beings. However, my commitment to justice moves me in practice to be morally and ethically correct: to "gently" push black students to understand how power works and read the world through a variety of lens. I think that it is imperative for blacks to move from home space and embrace others' experiences around difference. I want them to be able to read Dorothy Allison's proceeding testimony and place her language and experience inside, rather than outside:

> What I know for sure is that class, gender, sexual preference, and racial prejudice form an intricate lattice that both restricts and shapes our lives, and that resistance to that hatred is not a simple act. Claiming your identity in the cauldron of hatred and resistance to hatred is more than complicated; it is almost unexplainable. (1993, p. 143)

Furthermore, I want black women and men in my classes to be able to engage in meaningful dialogue regarding black male patriarchy and violence in order to lead to healthy relationships and healthy communities. For example, one semester Maya Angelou's *I Know Why the Caged Bird Sings* (1970) was a required text: it also is an unpopular cultural text on some schools' banned list. The class was fairly mixed with a predominant representation of white students. My goal in all of my classes is to think of ways to create dialogue that address social, political, and economic agendas in schools. The white students tended to be silent and uncomfortable in talking about Maya's experiences with racism. However, the black students were "knowingly" engaging the text, specifically around racism. This resonates with bell hooks' assertion that "All students, not just those from marginalized groups, seem more eager to enter energetically into classroom discussion when they perceive it as pertaining directly to them (when non-white students talk in class only when they feel connected via experience it is not aberrant behavior)" (1994, p. 87).

What became clear for me was that there was no naming of Maya's childhood rape experience, by her mother's boyfriend. As I indicate in this essay, I seek to practice pedagogy that is risky and powerful; therefore, I raised the issue of black male violence perpetuated against the young Maya. The black women students became angry that I would raise such an issue in "mixed company." They "slapped me on my wrist" for hanging "our" dirty clothes out for the "enemy" to see. Their belief was that black women should be fighting against racism not sexism in order to protect "our" men. I vehemently disagree that there should be silencing relevant to this issue. However, I agree with Dorothy Allison's position that ". . . racial prejudice forms an intricate lattice that both restricts and shapes our lives, and that resistance to that hatred is not a simple act" (p. 143).

This leads me to reveal that the black southern part of me admits that I want to protect my father, my brothers, my nephews, my lovers and friends; however, the critically conscious "me" knows and understands that it is not as simple. And I named this in class at that moment for I was vulnerable. I wanted these black women and men to know that I know the experiences, too well. I wanted them to know that my critical examination was done with care and love, not malice. But when education is for the practice of freedom both teacher and students are at risk. We are at risk for pain, unwanted dangerous memories, and a form of nakedness that seems uncoverable. However, there is a dialectical relationship at work whereby we stand to gain justice, freedom, and healthy, nurturing relationships and communities.

The danger, for me, is that if we are not risky in our pedagogy then we continue self-normalizing practice; that is, "our willingness to accept and internalize questionable limits on what we can know about ourselves and how we might act" (Pignatelli, 1993, p. 412). For when we engage in knowing and naming we bring private lives out onto the public stages; by keeping personal matters private we not only allow immoral practices to continue but we also legitimate authority by covering it with the cloak of our confidentiality (Farganis, 1987). There is room for a disturbance of silencing which is a self-normalizing practice.

In conclusion, a pedagogy of possibility (or critical pedagogy) empowers us to practice dreams and to understand why things are the way they are; to critically appropriate forms of knowledge that exist outside our immediate experience; to take risks and struggle with ongoing relations of power from within life-affirming moral culture; and to envisage versions of a world which is not yet in order to be able to alter the grounds upon which life is lived (Simon, 1988). For me this means that I must continue to go deep inside in order to understand why some storytelling is "good" and some is "bad." I must remember to tell my niece, Mache, stories that she is yearning to hear and know.

Furthermore, I must continue to use unpopular popular texts to critically appropriate forms of knowledge that exist outside our immediate experiences; to open gates of experience that are risky; and to understand that it is not always so simple, and almost unexplainable. "So, while I do the contradictory dance called the 'two step' I understand that it is more dangerous to be silent" (Smith, 1996, p. 181). As Audre Lorde (1984) testifies:

> And of course I am afraid, because the transformation of silence into language and action is an act of self-revelation, and that always seems

fraught with danger. But my daughter, when I told her of our topic and my difficulty with it, said, 'Tell them about how you're never really a whole person if you remain silent, because there's always that one little piece inside you that wants to be spoken out, and if you keep ignoring it, it gets madder and madder and hotter and hotter, and if you don't speak it out one day it will just up and punch you in the mouth from the inside.' (p. 42)

And I add Leslie Marmon Silko's (1996, pp. 125-126) story to Audre Lorde's story for closure.

Tse'itsi'nako, Thought Woman, is sitting in her room and whatever she thinks about appears. She thought of her sisters, Nau'ts'ity'i and I'tcts'ity'i, and together they created the Universe this world and the four worlds below. Thought Woman, the spider, named things and as she named them they appeared. She is sitting in her room thinking of a story now I'm telling you the story she is thinking.

REFERENCES

Allison, D. (1993). A question of class. In A. Stein (Ed.), *Sisters, sexperts, queers: Beyond the lesbian nation* (pp. 133-155). New York: Plume.

Allison, D. (1992). *Bastard out of Carolina*. New York: Dutton Press.

Angelou, M. (1970). *I know why the caged bird sings*. New York: Bantam.

Bethel, L. (1982). This infinity of conscious pain: Zora Neale Hurston and the black female literary tradition. In G. T. Hull, P. Bell, & B. Smith (Eds.), *All the women are white, all the blacks are men, but some of us are brave* (pp. 176-188). New York: The Feminist Press.

Brent, L. (1861). *Incidents in the life of a slave girl: Written by herself*. Boston: Thayer and Eldridge.

Davis, A. Y. (1981). Rape, racism and the capitalist setting. *The Black Scholar 12*, 39-45.

Estes, C. P. (1992). *Women who run with the wolves*. New York: Ballantine.

Farganis, S. (1987). *Social reconstruction of the feminine character*. Totowa, NJ: Rowan and Littlefield.

Foucault, M. (1977). *Power and knowledge*. (C. Gordon, L. Marshall, J. Mepham, & K. Soper, Trans.). New York: Pantheon.

Giroux, H. A. (1994). *Disturbing pleasures: Learning popular culture*. New York: Routledge.

Greene, M. (1988). *The dialectic of freedom*. New York: Teachers College Press.

Grossberg, L. (1994). Introduction: Bringin' it all back home—Pedagogy and cultural studies. In H. A. Giroux & P. McLaren (Eds.), *Between borders: Pedagogy and the politics of cultural studies* (pp. 1-25). New York: Routledge.

Hall, S. (1992b). Race, culture, and communication: Looking backward and forward at cultural studies. *Rethinking Marxism, 5*, 10-18.

hooks, b. (1994). *Outlaw culture: Resisting representations*. New York: Routledge.

hooks, b. (1994). *Teaching to transgress: Education for the practice of freedom*. New York: Routledge.

Kritzman, L. D. (Ed.). (1988). *Michel Foucault: Politics, philosophy, culture*. New York: Routledge.

Lincoln, A. (1970). Who will revere the black woman? In T. Cade (Ed.), *The black woman: An anthology* (pp. 80-84). New York: Mentor Books.

Lindsey, K. (1970). The black woman as a woman. In T. Cade (Ed.), *The black woman: An anthology* (pp. 85-89). New York: Mentor Books.

Lorde, A. (1984). *Sister outsider: Freedom*. CA: Crossing Press.

Lugones, M. & Spelman, E. (1983). Have we got a theory for you! Feminist theory, cultural imperialism and the demand for the woman's voice. *Women's International Studies Forum 6*, 573-581.

McLaren, P. (1994). *Life in schools* (2nd ed.). New York: Longman.

Newsletter on intellectual freedom. (1993, March). Chicago: American Library Association Office for Intellectual Freedom.

Phillips, U. B. (1918). *American Negro slavery: A survey of the supply, employment and control of Negro labor as determined by the plantation regimen*. New York: D. Appleton.

Pignatelli, F. (1993). What can I do! Foucault on freedom and the question of teacher agency. *Educational Theory, 43* (4), 411-432.

Schockly, A. A. (1988). *Afro-American women writers 1745-1933: An anthology and critical guide*. New York: Meridan.

Silko, L. M. (1996). *Yellow woman and a beauty of the spirit: Essays on Native American life*. New York: Simon & Schuster.

Simon, R. (1988). For a pedagogy of possibility. *Critical Pedagogy Networker, 1*, 1-4.

Smith, A. B. (1893). *An autobiography: The story of the Lord's dealings with Mrs. Amanda Smith, the colored evangelist*. Chicago: Mayer and Brother.

Smith, D. (1996). Womanism and me: An (un)caged black bird sings for freedom. *The High School Journal, 79* (3), 176-182.

Smith, D. (1993). Black women teachers speak about child abuse. In J. James & R. Farmer (Eds.), *Spirit, space, and survival:African American women in (white) academe* (pp. 158-178). New York: Routledge.

Walker, A. (1996). *The same river twice: Honoring the difficult.* New York: Scribner.

Walker, A. (1982). *The color purple.* New York: Washington Square.

Wilson, H. E. (1859). *Our nig: Or, sketches from the life a free black, in a two-story white house north, showing that slavery's shadows fall even there.* Reprinted 1983. New York: Random House.

Zuckerman, M. (1994). After sixty. In S. H. Martz (Ed.), *I am becoming the woman I've wanted* (p. 185). Watsonville, CA: Papier-Mache Press.

CHAPTER NINE

Popular Culture and Higher Education: Using Aesthetics and Seminars to Reconceptualize Curriculum

Patrick Slattery

In this chapter I will propose that reconceptualized understandings of curriculum in higher education, particularly in a freshman level orientation course and a graduate education seminar, can provide an opportunity for challenging dominant interpretations of the teaching and learning process in the university and redirect the way that students are enculturated into an educational environment that is too often controlling, manipulative, depersonalized, and devoid of popular culture. I will present a theory of aesthetics to guide seminar classes for undergraduate and graduate students. I will report on an experimental freshman seminar that utilized popular culture and autobiography to provide an avenue for empowerment, a critical language for resistance to dominant pedagogical methodologies, and a source of legitimation for reconnecting students to the learning process in the university.

The freshman seminar is a mandatory course for all first semester freshmen at Ashland University. Historically, this three semester hour course has been used as an orientation to campus facilities and activities, an introduction to the liberal arts tradition of the university, a laboratory for improving retention rates, and a method to introduce students to campus life. The literature associated with freshman orientation programs offers conflicting perspectives on the success of orientation programs nationwide. Ashland, like most universities, has received mixed reviews from students who have participated in freshmen orientation in the past twenty years on the course evaluation instruments. Some universities have eliminated freshman orientation programs, others have revised the program endlessly in a desperate attempt to create a meaningful and successful program. During the 1995-1996 school year, Ashland University implemented an experimental freshman seminar in which I participated. I will report on one section of this seminar which incorporated popular culture and autobiography in a course entitled "Get a Life: Autobiography and the Education of the Whole Person."

In my pedagogy in the freshman seminar course I am creating a space for students to speak autobiographically and recognize their ability to create alternative and empowering meanings that power-blocs (especially traditional university teaching methodologies) avoid, silence, and deny. I encourage students to create alternative emancipatory interpretations independent from the dominant interpretations of art, literature, texts, music, the self, learning, and, ultimately, liberal arts curriculum.

In a second example, I will report on an experimental graduate seminar for MEd students at Ashland university. In 1995 the university allowed a few professors to offer a five credit hour inquiry seminar on a topic of the professor's choice. This seminar replaced the traditional five chapter practicum research project that had been a requirement of the university for twenty years. The theme of my seminar was "Contemporary Art and Postmodern Education." The students created an art installation for their culminating project that reflects an autobiographical reflection on popular culture.

These two experimental courses provide concrete examples of ways that curriculum can be reconceptualized in higher education by incorporating autobiography and popular culture. My discussion of these two courses is not intended to be a model for the construction of undergraduate seminars nor masters degree culminating projects. I report on these two seminars as examples of the process of incorporating reconceptualized curriculum theories into the curriculum by using popular culture and autobiography as the organizing theme.

INTRODUCTION

John Dewey (1897), writing exactly one hundred years ago in an essay entitled "My Pedagogic Creed," outlines his philosophy of education:

> I believe that all education proceeds by the participation of the individual in the social consciousness of the race. . . . I believe that the only true education comes through the stimulation of the child's powers by the demands of the social situations in which he [*sic*] finds himself. . . . I believe that knowledge of social conditions, of the present state of civilization, is necessary in order properly to interpret the child's powers. . . . In sum, I believe that the individual who is to be educated is a social individual and that society is an organic union of individuals. . . I believe that education, therefore, is a process of living and not a preparation for future living. [Thus,] schools must represent life—life as real and vital to the child as that which he carries on in the home, in the neighborhood, or on the playground. (pp. 77-80)

In his pedagogic creed John Dewey insists that society is the function of education and that schooling must not simply reproduce the status quo social arrangements, prepare students for a future living, or slot students into predetermined or decontextualized tracks or vocations.

Our work as educators on all levels of schooling must challenge the structures that prevent individuals and communities from participating fully in democracy and investigating meaningfully the cultural context of their lives. Along with Dewey, I believe that education must enhance the lives of those who are marginalized and create social consequences of value. With Dewey, I also believe that society is a function of education and that my job as an educator is to be a prophetic voice in the wilderness of modernity that ignores the autobiographical and cultural context of human persons.

In this chapter I report on two experimental curriculum seminars that I facilitated in 1995 at Ashland University in Ohio. The first is a three credit hour freshman orientation seminar entitled "Get a Life: Autobiography and the Education of the Whole Person." The second is a five credit hour graduate education seminar entitled "Contemporary Art and Postmodern Education" which was provisionally approved as an alternative to the traditional practicum research project at the end of the master degree program. I had the opportunity to teach both of these experimental seminars in 1995. The juxtaposition of teaching an experimental seminar to first semester freshmen and to graduating masters degree students was in itself instructive. I discovered that the issues of autobiography and popular culture must permeate the educational enterprise regardless of the age or level of schooling of the students.

I begin with the assumption that popular culture must be understood from multiple perspectives. In the postmodern era it is meaningless to separate high culture from low culture. There is an eclectic and fluid movement within diverse sites of cultural experiences, and delineation of absolute parameters is not only problematic but also perpetuates modern bifurcations. The contemporary dancer Mark Morris illustrates this point. Part Isadora Duncan, part Charlie Chaplin, Morris has been called "the bad boy of modern dance" because he has "combined high art and low in a remarkable *pas de deux*" (Friedman, 1996, p. 28). In *The Hard Nut* Morris created a mod version of *The Nutcracker* where he turned toy soldiers into G.I. Joes and mice into rats. He collaborated with Baryshnikov on the White Oak Dance Project and choreographed for American Ballet Theater and the Paris Opera Ballet. When asked about his inclusive and eclectic style, Morris commented, "I don't differentiate between high and low brow. Art is entertaining" (cited in Friedman, 1996, p. 28). In the same sense, in my seminars I do not make a distinction between high art and low art. The aesthetic experience is more than a voyeuristic tour of canonical cultural artifacts, it becomes an autobiographical journey into so called high art, low art, and postmodern art that is educational because it is eclectic and evocative. With Morris, it is also entertaining. The aesthetic seminars create what Maxine Greene calls "wide-awakeness" (1978) and "release of the imagination" (1995). In a postmodern sense, the aesthetic evokes-dramatically elicits--responses to cultural and social issues.

AESTHETICS

In my seminars I have an interest in exploring ways of knowing and learning that create what William Pinar and Madeleine Grumet (1976) call "synthetical moments." In the synthesizing moment there is a reconstruction of the self and an experience of solidarity of the intellect, the body, the spirit, and the cosmos, as well as an intrinsic coherence of time, place, and meaning. Michel Serres (1982) writes about a sense of contemporaneousness. Serres uses provoking metaphors and analogies to explain that there is convergence in particular events where many things come together and similar forms provide a passage for making connections on the journey of life. While Serres insists on keeping things separate, his analogies help to make connections through which we experience contemporaneousness. Pinar, Grumet, and Serres provide options for rethinking modern obsessions with establishing causal links in space over time. Linear explanations are replaced by concepts of contemporaneousness, convergence, and synthesis. Such meaning-full and awe-full moments are integral to the seminar experience--indeed all curriculum--and not peripheral. It is here that all cultural artifacts--whether the traditional high culture of opera or orchestra, or the noncanonical popular representations of rap or reggae--become legitimate and progressive sites for educational investigation. The aesthetic philosophy that I propose, combined with the synthetical autobiography and contemporaneousness proposed by Pinar, Grumet, and Serres, offers an opportunity for multiple cultural art forms to inform the thinking process, evoke understanding, arouse passion, and "inspire social consequences of value" (Dewey, 1934a)

The goal of the aesthetic seminar is the integration of eclectic cultural experiences that affirm the uniqueness of individual creativity, contemporaneousness of time and place, as well as global solidarity. Modern emphasis on rational discourse, high culture, the western canon, and objective knowledge, discourages these aesthetic experiences and promotes external information, standardized interpretation, and uniformity in the core of the curriculum and in the teaching and learning process. In my seminars I attempt to use a wide range of aesthetic forms to evoke synthetical moments. In this space, students are empowered and free to explore ideas, challenge sedimented preceptors, experiment with multiple forms of representation, reconceptualize their positionality in the web of life, and create autobiographical artifacts. It is here that the curriculum becomes a process of active participation in the construction of knowledge and meaning rather than the certification of modern interpretations.

Perhaps John Dewey provides the most cogent analysis of aesthetics in education in *Art as Experience*. Dewey (1934b) writes about the significance of the arts, and concludes, "In the end, works of art are the only media of complete and unhindered communication between man and man [*sic*] that can occur in a world full of gulfs and walls that limit community of experience" (p. 105). Richard Rorty (1982) provides philosophical support for this position:

> The burden of my argument so far has been that if we get rid of notions of "objectivity" and "scientific method" we shall be able to see the social sciences as continuous with literature--as interpreting other people to us, and thus enlarging and deepening our sense of community. . . . One can emphasize, as Dewey did, the moral importance of the social sciences--their role in widening and deepening our sense of community. Or one can emphasize, as Michel Foucault does, the way in which the social sciences have served as instruments of the "disciplinary society," the connection between knowledge and power rather than between knowledge and human solidarity. (pp. 203-204)

In either case, Dewey, Rorty, and Foucault point the way to a consideration of human solidarity in the aesthetic process. High art and low art lose their distinction; popular culture becomes expansive and inclusive. The autobiographical experience expands the nature of the aesthetic process.

The experience of curriculum introduced above is orchestrated in such a way that improvisation and spontaneity enhance the educational experience. Like improvisational jazz, zydeco, or Cajun music, one sound or beat leads to another, forming an eclectic mixture of instruments and rhythms. Success in improvisational music and curriculum has one fundamental requirement, according to David Smith (1991), ". . . the group members must be committed to staying 'with' each other, constantly listening to subtle nuances of tempo and melody, with one person never stealing the show for the entire session" (p. 198). In education, this community solidarity requires giving of one's self over to conversation with students and building a common shared reality in a spirit of self-forgetfulness in order to discover oneself in relation to the entire community experience. This is the experience that I attempt to create in my experimental seminars for college freshmen and graduate education students.

Attention to the alternatives that provide hope is called "wide-awakeness" by Maxine Greene. She argues for a strong emphasis on arts and humanities in education to promote this wide-awakeness and self-understanding that emerges from synthetical moments. Greene turns to the writer Henry David Thoreau for inspiration. Greene (1978) writes, "Thoreau writes passionately about throwing off sleep. He talks about how few people are awake enough for a poetic or divine life. He asserts that to be awake is to be alive"(p. 162). David Orr (1992) also turns to Thoreau for understanding, "Thoreau did not research Walden Pond, rather, he went to live 'deliberately'" (p. 125). Thus, *Walden* becomes a mosaic of philosophy, poetry, natural history, geology, folklore, archeology, economics, politics, and education for Thoreau, and in this sense aesthetics leads to wholeness. Orr (1992) explains, "Thoreau's subject matter was Thoreau; his goal, wholeness; his tool, Walden Pond; and his methodology, simplification" (p. 125). This is the antithesis of the modern curriculum that artificially separates subject matter, isolates and analyzes discrete parts, and obfuscates simple beauty. Orr (1992) concludes:

> Aside from its merits as literature or philosophy, *Walden* is an antidote to the idea that education is a passive, indoor activity occurring between the ages of six and twenty-one. In contrast to the tendencies to segregate disciplines, and to segregate intellect from its surroundings, *Walden* is a model of the possible unity between personhood, pedagogy, and place. For Thoreau, Walden was more than his location. It was a laboratory for observation and experimentation; a library of data about geology, history, flora, fauna; a source of inspiration and renewal; and a testing ground for the man. *Walden* is no monologue, it is a dialogue between a man and a place. In a sense, *Walden* wrote Thoreau. His genius, I think, was to allow himself to be shaped by his place, to allow it to speak with his voice. (pp. 125-126)

This, too, is the purpose of the curriculum in my seminars: the inspiration of nature and poetry; the unity of self, pedagogy, and place; becoming through encounters with place; and uncovering the silenced and repressed voices.

In the teaching and learning process I assume that we cannot define with precision the nature of being or the meaning of knowledge; ontology and epistemology are elusive and evolving. The emphasis in the teaching and learning process should be placed on *possibility* and *becoming,* for human consciousness can never be static. Jean-Paul

Sartre argues that human consciousness (being-for-itself) can never become a substance or an objective thing (being-in-itself), and this is why possibility must be the focus of educational inquiry. Hence, each new experience adds to the accumulated meaning of experience for each individual and sets the stage for present and future possibilities. While the present is conditioned by the past, every moment is also pregnant with future possibilities for change and new directions. The aesthetic experience can inspire new personal realizations, as John Dewey (1934b) in *Art as Experience* explains:

> A work of art, no matter how old or classic, is actually, not just potentially, a work of art only when it lives in some individual experience. A piece of parchment, of marble, of canvas, it remains self-identical throughout the ages. But as a work of art it is re-created every time it is aesthetically experienced. . . . The Parthenon, or whatever, is universal because it can continue to inspire new personal realizations in experience. (pp. 108-109)

Pablo Picasso (1971) has also described artistic creation in a similar way:

> A picture is not thought out and settled beforehand. While it is being done it changes as one's thoughts change. And when it is finished it still goes on changing according to the state of mind of whoever is looking at it. A picture lives a life like a living creature, undergoing the changes imposed on us by our life from day, to day. This is natural enough, as the picture lives only through the man [*sic*] who is looking at it. (p. 268)

Picasso and Dewey reflect one of the important dimensions of aesthetics as related to my seminars: events find their meaning in subjective encounters where knowledge is constructed and reconstructed in every new situation. In this sense, a work of art truly exists only in the encounter; a lesson or classroom discussion cannot be predetermined with goals or outcomes. Understanding emerges in the process of becoming. If locked in a darkened vault, a painting is simply an aggregate of materials. Art, like the curriculum, is the process of becoming and recreating in each new situation. In my seminars I seek descriptions and insights into how the world is experienced by students.

Martin Heidegger calls this a method or science of the phenomenon of consciousness. The purpose here, though, is not just description of phenomena, but the understanding of what lies behind them, their *being* or ontology. Our seminar conversations and experiences take us on an aesthetic journey through our autobiographical context to a sense of solidarity with the seminar group to broader ecological and sociological connections.

This phenomenological understanding of curriculum replaces the modern obsession with standardized interpretation of high art in literature and painting, predetermined methodologies and styles for writing, painting, and researching, and universal master narratives that can be applied to knowledge acquisition. For Maurice Merleau-Ponty (1962) perception is primary, as in the actual feelings of amputated limbs perceived by amputees--called the phantom limb. Understanding, empathy, eclectic interpretations, kaleidoscopic insights, and heightened perception replaces certainty, outcomes, memorization, codification, categorization, and standardization as reflected in the modern linear educational paradigm.

Maxine Greene applies an understanding of form and content to education and contends that involvement with the arts and humanities has the potential for provoking reflectiveness. She challenges educators to devise ways of integrating arts into what is taught at all levels of the educational enterprise. This has direct implications for social and moral issues in postmodern curriculum and in art education. Greene (1978) explains the implications as follows, "I would like to believe that the concerns of art educators are akin to those I have described: to enhance qualitative awareness, to release imagination, and to free people to see, shape, and transform. I would hope for the kinds of curricula that permit an easy and articulated transaction between making and attending" (p. 74).

Ronald Padgham contends that there is no right or wrong way to teach, just as there is no right or wrong way to paint. There is only one's natural way. Padgham (1988) writes, "To discover one's natural way necessitates self-discovery or consciousness of self" (p. 367). Jackson Pollock (1971) explains how this process evolves:

> When I am in my painting, I am not aware of what I am doing. It is only after a short get acquainted period that I see what I have been about. I have no fears about making changes, destroying the image, etc. Because the painting has a life of its own, I try to let it come

through. It is only when I lose contact with the painting that the result is a mess. Otherwise there is pure harmony, an easy give and take, and the painting comes out well. (p. 548)

This experience, in turn, leads to new expressive qualities in the observer's world. Because postmodern curriculum understands the future as that which brings to completion what has already been set in motion, the alternative possibilities offer a vision of hope for schools and society. This vision would remain idealized and romanticized were it not for the dimension of aesthetic understanding and hope called "wide-awakeness" by Maxine Greene, "fusion of horizons" by Hans-Georg Gadamer, "becoming" by Ronald Padgham, "experience" by John Dewey, "rich inner lives" by Max van Manen, "synthetical moments" by William Pinar and Madeleine Grumet, and "contemporaneousness" by Michel Serres.

Although characterized in many unique, ironic, and even contradictory ways, the aesthetic dimensions of learning in postmodern curriculum emphasize the primacy of experience, the merging of form and content, the recursion and convergence of time, the celebration of the self-conscious individual and the understanding of phenomenological experience. This perspective on curriculum offers the individual a process for growing and becoming. It also offers schools an opportunity for critical reflection which is open to what has not yet been but what is also absolutely possible. In fact, aesthetic phenomenon may ultimately be the only justification for our curriculum theorizing, even for our very existence, according to Friedrich Nietzsche (1968) when he writes in *The Birth of Tragedy,* "We have our highest dignity in our significance as works of art--for it is only as an aesthetic phenomenon that existence and the world are eternally justified" (p. 52).

THE SEMINAR EXPERIENCE

The most important element of the freshman seminar experience at Ashland University is that each professor is allowed and encouraged to select her or his own reading assignments and student experiences. The syllabus only demands that each section of the seminar experience include reading and writing assignments. Some of the activities that are prominent in my seminar are visits with artists, museum tours, and readings on art theory. Following from my aesthetic philosophy, I incorporate popular art, contemporary art, museum art, and autobiographical aesthetic creations into the teaching and learning process.

For example, on a visit to the Cleveland Museum of Art we sat on the floor and discussed the painting *Lot's Wife* by Anselm Kiefer. Kiefer is a contemporary Jewish painter who came to maturity in post World War II Germany. He incorporates themes of the aftermath of the war and the Holocaust into his art. I use this painting of a desolate and ecologically destroyed landscape as a part of a phenomenological exercise that I orchestrate for my students. Kiefer offers the opportunity not only to deconstruct memories of violence and destruction but especially to elicit fresh understandings of the positionality of the self in relation to memories. I will take a circuitous route to the Kiefer exercise through bell hooks, Jean-Michel Basquiat, Friedrich Nietzsche, and Michel Foucault.

bell hooks has written about the 1992 retrospective of the work of Jean-Michel Basquiat at the Whitney Museum in New York City. With the recent release of the Julian Schnabel (1996) film *Basquiat,* there is a renewed interest in the life of this widely misunderstood artist. hooks (1993) writes:

> It is much too simplistic a reading to see works like *Jack Johnson* (1982), *Untitled (Sugar Ray Robinson)* (1982), and the like, as solely celebrating black culture. Appearing always in these paintings as half-formed or somewhat mutilated, the black male body becomes, iconographically, a sign of lack and absence. . . . In Basquiat's work, flesh on the black body is almost always falling away. Like skeletal figures in the Australian aboriginal bark painting, . . . these figures have been worked down to the bone. To do justice to this work, then, our gaze must do more than reflect on surface appearances. Daring us to probe the heart of darkness, to move our eyes beyond the colonizing gaze, the paintings ask that we hold in our memory the bones of the dead while we consider the world of the black immediate, the familiar. To see and understand these paintings, one must be willing to accept the tragic dimension of black life . . . Basquiat's work gives that private anguish artistic expression. (pp. 71-72)

This anguish described by hooks also permeates Kiefer's paintings. As Basquiat confronts us with the naked black image, Kiefer confronts us with the naked ravages of post-war terrain. The body is diminished in Basquiat; the landscape is barren in Kiefer. In *Lot's Wife,* Kiefer paints two abandoned and bombed out railroad tracks vanishing into a desolate plateau on the horizon at the center of the canvas. Above the horizon explode huge white puffs of smoke or clouds or human ashes. Kiefer mixes salt and his semen in the paint. As we gaze back to the Holocaust, we are like Lot's wife who looked back on Sodom and Gomorrah. We may assume at first that she was turned into a pillar of salt for her disobedience to a God who had commanded that Lot and his family move away without turning around. Yes, Lot's wife ignored the patriarchy to look back to the friends and family members she had left behind. In the agony of her exodus, she would not erase the memory of her loved ones. In the looking back she is transformed and becomes the salt of the Earth, not as a punishment as traditional theology has assumed but rather as a model of the prophetic vision. Salt is the substance of wisdom in alchemy and in Biblical literature.

The backward glance transforms our lives. With Nietzsche, this takes us to the point of becoming more of what we are not so as to free ourselves from the limits of what we live. We do this violence that results when the culture and traditions of a people are erased. Sodom and Gomorrah have been the scapegoats for colonization and hegemonic domination for too long. We must look back with the real heroine of the Biblical story, Lot's wife, and become the pillar of life giving salt for an Earth where global communities have repeatedly burned and bombed their cities and obliterated their peoples for centuries. hooks (1993) concludes, "The erasure is rendered all the more problematic when artifacts of that vanishing culture are commodified to enhance the aesthetics of those perpetuating the erasure" (p. 72). Thus, the memory of Lot's wife is commodified for a conservative religious hermeneutic, and Sodom and Gomorrah remain fixed in the collective memory as evil and decadent. Kiefer, Basquiat, and hooks refute the vanquishing.

It is in this spirit that I take my students to visit *Lot's Wife* at the Cleveland Museum of Art. Typical of the reaction of my students who are willing to deconstruct linear notions of time and space and look back, look within, and look forward in a single glance, is "Daniel's" response to the painting. After over an hour of discussion and quiet meditation on this painting, Daniel, an eighteen-year-old freshman, insisted that for the first time in his life he understood the Holocaust; he was haunted by the intensity of the presence of the desolate landscape. Why, he asked, was the memory so haunting?

Early in the next semester Daniel contacted me to say that over the break he had discussed his experience at the museum with his devoutly Christian parents. Daniel's glance had uncovered a purposeful erasure of a family memory, the death of Jewish family members in the Holocaust. Daniel, like *Lot's wife*, found himself in the imagery of smoke, clouds, salt, ashes, and semen on Kiefer's canvas. Daniel is not unlike many of us who can discover ourselves in the phenomenological lived experience. This is my postmodern vision of a curriculum for museums and classrooms that will evoke such memories. We must re-member our bodies and re-connect our lives if the colonization and erasure is to be resisted and overcome. High art, cultural events, and autobiography merge in the process; objective distinctions between self, place, voice and cultural artifacts become meaningless.

Like Foucault's notion of "simulated surveillance" that engenders the kind of blind obedience that regulated Lot and persuaded him not to look back, the refusal of museums and classrooms to challenge sedimented preceptors and explode colonizing structures of power also regulates our bodies and imprisons our minds. The work of Anselm Kiefer is a good example of using contemporary art to challenge structures that have been created by such surveillance.

GRADUATE SEMINAR

The second example of reconceptualized curriculum practices that creates synthetical moments and contemporaneousness is a graduate seminar for masters degree students. For twenty years Ashland University has required a five chapter quantitative research practicum based on a site based project in order to complete the master of education degree. In 1995 the university allowed a few professors to offer a five credit hour inquiry seminar on a topic of the professor's choice as an alternative choice to the practicum. Students in each seminar were required to read books and journal articles on the selected topic, produce a written artifact, and present a public presentation as a group. The seminars were purposely designed to allow for maximum flexibility in reading, writing, and the public event. The theme of my seminar was "Contemporary Art and Postmodern Education." This seminar group explored postmodern philosophy through the lens of contemporary art, and for the public presentation the graduate students created an art installation that reflected their autobiographical understandings of education and popular culture. The art installation was first presented in a middle school gymnasium in Mentor, Ohio. Two months later the students presented their art installation at the JCT curriculum conference in Monteagle, Tennessee. Future installations continue to be planned.

What is most important about this graduate seminar for our current discussion is that the art installation included diverse elements of both "high" and "low" art all incorporated into an installation project. The space itself was arranged like a religious place of worship. Instead of pews, primary school desks were arranged in rows in the center of the space. Around the walls of the space were 14 original creations--one by each of the students in the seminar--arranged like the stations of the cross in a Catholic church. In place of an altar were 13 large red, white, and blue stars with passages from the postmodern texts pasted on the front and back. The stars hung from the ceiling and were attached to the back wall. This entire arrangement was designed to create a sense of worship. However, the juxtaposition of contemporary art and postmodern texts in the place of traditional religious symbols initially jolts the viewer. This is especially true as viewers enter the room from behind a teacher's podium and are invited to put on earphones and listen to Rage Against the Machine sing "Take the Power Back." The song is a polemic against traditional teaching methods and colonializing and racist curriculums. Listeners are jolted as they appear to view a traditional educational setting in a religious shrine format while being urged to take the power back. The message from popular culture is clear: traditional approaches to education have disenfranchised and disempowered people for too long. The viewer is then invited to walk through the installation and experience the discomfort of further contradictions. Each of the art pieces challenges modern notions of curriculum and instruction.

The postmodern literature that the students read in this seminar provided the validation for their autobiographical and artistic expressions. Lyotard's (1984) rejection of metanarratives as essential to the postmodern condition and Foucault's (1982) insightful analysis of deconstruction in *This Is Not a Pipe* forced students to deconstruct their own educational metanarratives. David Ray Griffin's (1990) constructive postmodernism challenged students to develop sacred interconnections in place of the metanarratives. Thus, a deconstruction in a simulated sacred space emerged. This art installation reflected the eclectic nature of not only postmodernism but also the emerging curriculum proposed by the reconceptualization (Pinar et al., 1995). Their public presentation forced viewers to reflect on the negative impact of curricular practices that disempower students, erase dangerous memories, ignore ethnic, racial, gendered, and religious minority voices in favor of the established western, European, male, heterosexual, and Christian canons.

CONCLUSION

What we have seen in the two examples of alternative approaches to curriculum in higher education seminars is the emergence of postmodern alternatives to linear, quantitative, and uniform requirements. There are several practices in operation in both of these examples that can inform and enrich our understanding of pedagogy. First, the curriculum must foreground the autobiographical experiences of the students. It is no longer acceptable to assume that students must be passive receptors of information. Second, professors must be free to orchestrate learning from his or her strengths. While professors initiate readings and assignments, the practice of allowing student interests to emerge is essential. In both seminars I selected initial readings, but I also allowed the students to supplement the readings and then express their understandings of the seminar materials from their own autobiographical perspective. Third, curriculum is a process of becoming and not a benchmark for certification or credentialing. Thus, the curriculum process must focus on emergent understandings. Knowledge is constructed, not predetermined. Finally, popular culture must permeate the teaching and leaning experience. A curriculum that does not make connections to the art, music, literature, sciences, and other artifacts of the human community is devoid of meaning and purpose. In the postmodern era it is no longer acceptable to marginalize voices. The nature of education is changing, and the curriculum must reflect the emerging values of the postmodern era. Eclectic inclusiveness, interconnectedness, incredulity toward metanarratives, synthetical moments, popular culture, autobiography, among other things, must be foregrounded. These alternative seminars provide examples of how such a postmodern curriculum with a focus on popular culture is emerging. Empowered students and professors will no longer tolerate a return to the disenfranchisement of traditional methodologies that excluded the voice of popular culture. May the process of reconceptualizing curriculum in higher education continue in earnest.

REFERENCES

Dewey, J. (1897). My pedagogic creed. *The School Journal, 54* (3), pp. 77-80.

Dewey, J. (1934a). *A common faith.* New Haven, CT: Yale University Press.

Dewey, J. (1934b). *Art as experience.* New York: Minton, Balch, & Company.

Foucault, M. (1982). *This is not a pipe.* Berkeley: University of California Press.

Friedman, R. (1996, July 15). The 50 most influential boomers. *Life Magazine,* pp. 14-28.

Greene, M. (1978). *Landscapes of learning.* New York: Teachers College Press.

Greene, M. (1995). *Releasing the imagination: Essays on education, the arts, and social change.* San Francisco: Jossey-Bass Publishers.

Griffin, D. R. (1990). *Sacred interconnections: Postmodern spirituality, political economy, and art.* Albany, NY: SUNY Press.

hooks, bell. (1993, June). *Altars of sacrifice: Re-membering Basquiat. Art in America,* pp. 67-75.

Lyotard, J-F. (1984). *The postmodern condition: A report on knowledge.* Minneapolis: The University of Minnesota Press.

Merleau-Ponty, M. (1962). *Phenomenology of perception.* London: Routledge and Kegan Paul.

Nietzsche, F. (1879, 1977). *A Nietzsche reader.* New York: Penguin.

Nietzsche, F. (1968). The birth of tragedy. In W. Kaufmann (Trans. and Ed.), *Basic writings of Nietzsche* (3rd ed.). New York: Modern Library.

Orr, D. W. (1992). *Ecological literacy: Education and the transition to a postmodern world.* Albany, NY: SUNY Press.

Padgham, R. (1988). Correspondence: Contemporary curriculum theory and contemporary art. In W. F. Pinar (Ed.) *Contemporary curriculum discourses* (pp. 359-379). Scottsdale, AZ: Gorsuch, Scarisbrick.

Picasso, P. (1971). Conversations. In H. B. Chipps (Ed.), *Theories of modern art: A source book of artists and critics* (p. 268). Berkeley, CA: University of California Press.

Pinar, W. F., & Grumet, N. R. (1976). *Toward a poor curriculum.* Dubuque, IA: Kendall/Hunt.

Pinar, W. F., Reynolds, W., Slattery, P., & Taubman, P. (1995). *Understanding curriculum: An introduction to the study of historical and contemporary curriculum discourses.* New York: Peter Lang.

Pollock, J. (1971). My painting. In H. B. Chipps (Ed.), *Theories of modern art: A sourcebook of artists and critics* (pp. 540-556). Berkeley: University of California Press.

Rorty, R. (1982). *Consequences of pragmatism.* Minneapolis: University of Minnesota Press.

Serres, H. (1982). *Hermes: Literature, science, philosophy.* Baltimore: Johns Hopkins University Press.

Smith, D. G. (1991). Hermeneutic inquiry: The hermeneutic imagination and the pedagogic text. In E. C. Short (Ed.), *Forms of curriculum inquiry* (pp. 187-210). Albany, NY: SUNY Press.

About the Contributors

PETER APPELBAUM teaches mathematics and science education at William Paterson University of New Jersey. The author of *Popular Culture, Educational Discourse, and Mathematics* (SUNY Press) his research interests include curriculum and mass culture technology, and nomadic epistemology.

TOBY DASPIT (still!) plays air guitar when he thinks no one is watching, and is honing his air DJing skills as well. When not practicing, Toby teaches in the College of Education at Western Michigan University.

DAVID DEES is a part-time faculty member in the School of Theater and Dance at Kent State University. His dissertation and research interests, both having been delayed from too much television (see Chapter 2), center around the development and exploration of teaching artistry. Drawing from the traditions of Principal Skinner and Mrs. Krabapple. Mr. Dees hopes to contribute to the development of teaching artists that are even more gifted than the ones we find at Springfield Elementary.

JASON EARLE apprenticed with James Bond for much of his life. For a short period he also studied under James Coburn of *In Like Flint*. His current cover identity is that of an assistant professor teaching foundations courses at John Carroll University. More recently he sought to bolster this cover identity by co-authoring (with Sharon Kruse) a book, *Organizational Literacy for Educators* forthcoming from Lawrence Erlbaum. On the weekends Jason still performs deep cover work in various movie houses and in front of television screens in the Northeast Ohio area.

DON GUENTHER has been a cultural foundations instructor in Kent State University's college of education while completing his doctoral work. His doctoral research efforts have focused on popular culture representations of teachers and school settings. These studies are in no small way enriched by his prized collection of feature films and television shows which now numbers in the several thousands. When not engaged in the wonderful escape from reality provided by film and television viewing, Don enjoys other flights of fantasy including reading utopian literature and experiencing academic life. Don's "previous life" was as a social worker in private psychotherapeutic practice, which provides some clue as to his other research interests, the affective domain in teaching and learning.

AIMEE HOWLEY is a professor in the Educational Studies Department at Ohio University. Her research critiques dominant educational theories, policies and practices such as developmentalism, parent involvement, and gifted education. Concentrating on schooling in rural America, Dr. Howley is currently examining the tensions between local and universal knowledge.

MARY E. REEVES is currently an assistant professor in the college of education at Northwestern State University in Natchitoches, Louisiana. She relishes the study of popular culture, delighting in the irony of finding professional expression for an adult's interest in toys and television. She is currently working on an investigation of the television habits of elementary and middle school children and she has asked Santa for an "Electronic Mega Mall" this year, which she expects will be part of future papers on the popular culture of young women.

PATRICK SLATTERY is associate professor at Texas A & M University where he teaches curriculum theory and foundations of education. He conducts seminars for undergraduate and graduate students on the topics of autobiography, multiculturalism, critical theory, and aesthetics. He is the author of *Curriculum Development in the Postmodern Era* (Garland, 1995) and co-author of *Contextualizing Teaching* (Longman, 1998). Slattery enjoys volunteering as a museum docent, and he has a particular affection for Jackson Pollock, Georgia O'Keefe, Anselm Kiefer, and Edward and Nancy Keinholtz. He believes that education must be intimately tied to aesthetics in order to be meaningfully and passionately experienced.

DIANNE SMITH is a full-time consultant for Star Fleet Command. Her primary responsibility is to advise Captain James T. Kirk of issues pertaining to womanist/feminist politics, as related to his leadership of the *Enterprise*. During her vacations on Planet Earth, she is an associate professor of education at the University of Missouri-Kansas City. She teaches curriculum theory as a form of cultural politics. In addition, she is an admitted premier hootchie Mama.

PENNY SMITH has an undergraduate degree in English, a Ph.D. in History, and an Ed.D. in educational administration. She has worked as a parochial school teacher, a public school teacher, a principal, and an associate superintendent; she currently teaches at Western Carolina University. Obviously a major life theme is unfocused career development; in response to that indecision she watches movies.

LINDA SPATIG is an associate professor of Educational Foundations at Marshall University in Huntington, West Virginia. Her research has focused on the role of schooling in strengthening and/or challenging social inequalities. Currently, she is working on an ethnography of a five year Head Start to public school transition demonstration project in Appalachia.

JOHN A. WEAVER studied Philosophy with Roseanne, Urban Studies with Ice Cube, and Literature with Octavia Butler. In spite of these scholarly endeavors John was able to earn a Ph.D. from the University of Pittsburgh working with Mark Ginsburg and Noreen Garman. Teaching at the University of Akron, his writing focuses on popular culture, information technology, and science fiction. His hobbies include academic work.

Subject Index

Name Index